P9-AFA-738

Books in the **Contemporary World Issues** series address vital issues in today's society such as genetic engineering, pollution, and biodiversity. Written by professional writers, scholars, and nonacademic experts, these books are authoritative, clearly written, up-to-date, and objective. They provide a good starting point for research by high school and college students, scholars, and general readers as well as by legislators, businesspeople, activists, and others.

Each book, carefully organized and easy to use, contains an overview of the subject, a detailed chronology, biographical sketches, facts and data and/or documents and other primary source material, a forum of authoritative perspective essays, annotated lists of print and nonprint resources, and an index.

Readers of books in the Contemporary World Issues series will find the information they need in order to have a better understanding of the social, political, environmental, and economic issues facing the world today.

Marijuana

A REFERENCE HANDBOOK

Second Edition

David E. Newton

ABC-CLIO™

An Imprint of ABC-CLIO, LLC

Santa Barbara, California • Denver, Colorado

Library of Congress Cataloging-in-Publication Data

Names: Newton, David E., author.
Title: Marijuana : a reference handbook / David E. Newton.
Description: Second edition. | Santa Barbara, California :
    ABC-CLIO, [2017] | Series: Contemporary world issues |
    Includes bibliographical references and index.
Identifiers: LCCN 2016042067 (print) | LCCN 2016055665
    (ebook) | ISBN 9781440850516 (alk. paper) |
    ISBN 9781440850523 (ebook)
Subjects: LCSH: Marijuana—Therapeutic use—United States. |
    Marijuana—History. | Drug legalization—United States.
Classification: LCC RM666.C266 N48 2017 (print) |
    LCC RM666.C266 (ebook) | DDC 615.3/23648—dc23
LC record available at https://lccn.loc.gov/2016042067

ISBN: 978-1-4408-5051-6
EISBN: 978-1-4408-5052-3

21 20 19 18 17   1 2 3 4 5

This book is also available as an eBook.

ABC-CLIO
An Imprint of ABC-CLIO, LLC

ABC-CLIO, LLC
130 Cremona Drive, P.O. Box 1911
Santa Barbara, California 93116-1911
www.abc-clio.com

This book is printed on acid-free paper ∞

Manufactured in the United States of America

For Mary Agnes (Mickey)
With many very fond memories!

Cannabis sativa is one of the oldest crop plants known to humans. One form of the plant known as hemp has been used for the production of textiles, rope, canvas, paper, and other products for at least 6,000 years, and probably much longer. Another form of the plant, known by a variety of names such as marijuana and hashish, has been a part of religious and mystical ceremonies for just as long. It has an especially long cultural tradition in India, where the Hindu god Siva is said to have sought comfort after a family quarrel by resting under a cannabis plant and eating its leaves. The story explains Siva's alternate name of the Lord of Bhang (bhang being a special concoction containing marijuana).

Marijuana has also been used for centuries as a recreational drug, a mind-altering substance that allows users to experience a form of the world around them often very different from that experienced in daily life. Archaeological research has found evidence of vessels apparently used for smoking marijuana that date as far back as the first millennium CE in places as widespread as China, India, Assyria, and Africa. The use of marijuana as a recreational drug persists today, with the UN Office on Drugs and Crime reporting in 2011 that there were an estimated 125 to 203 million individuals worldwide who had used the drug for recreational purposes at least once in the previous year.

For most of human history, cannabis has been held in high regard for all of these applications. It has been praised as one of the most durable, attractive, and useful of all fabrics; it has been honored as a gateway to spiritual insights; and it has been cherished as a relaxing release from the troubles of everyday life. Which is not to say that questions have not been raised about possible harmful effects of the plant and its derivatives. Indeed, at the very times cannabis was most popular in some cultures as a source of clothing, a sacramental herb, or a healing medication, some individuals and groups have warned about the damage cannabis can cause to the human body and mind. At one time in ancient China, for example, laws were passed prohibiting the use of marijuana for certain purposes because in people who used it the most, it tended to bring out riotous aspects of their personalities, thus posing a possible threat to peace and order in the general society.

Such concerns have often led to conferences, conventions, and other meetings at which experts reassess the possible benefits and risks of using various forms of cannabis (usually, marijuana and hashish). Interestingly enough, these meetings have almost always concluded with a renewed statement of the many benefits provided by the cannabis plant and limited warnings about the risks of overexposure to the drug. Committee reports, like those of the Indian Hemp Drug Commission of 1895, almost always say that cannabis products do no physical, mental, or moral harm; may actually be good for you; and are safe, even "far safer than many foods we commonly consume," according to one official of the U.S. Drug Enforcement Administration (DEA) in 1988.

And yet, in the second decade of the 21st century, the use of cannabis and its derivatives is illegal in almost every nation in the world. Beginning in the early 20th century, a movement to change public views about the use of cannabis products began to develop, perhaps most strongly in the United States, but in other parts of the world also. International meetings, such as the International Opium Convention of 1912, were called to develop strategies for limiting or banning the production, transport, and consumption of cannabis products throughout the world. Penalties for the use of such products were severe, sometimes more severe than penalties for other major crimes, such as rape, assault, and armed robbery. Such penalties are still in existence in some parts of the world; drug trafficking can result in the death penalty in some countries, and prison sentences of up to 20 years for possession of cannabis are still in place in some states of the United States.

What happened to bring about this dramatic change in official attitudes about hemp, marijuana, and other cannabis products in the early twentieth 20th century? How did this revered plant go from being regarded as a blessing to human civilization to one of the most reviled products in the world? That question is one of the themes of this book because it helps to inform the current debate over cannabis in the world today. This debate focuses at its most fundamental level on the question of whether cannabis should be criminalized at all and, if so, under what circumstances. On a somewhat more limited, but equally important and controversial, level, the debate has to do with the use of marijuana and related substances for medical purposes.

The purpose of this book is to provide an introduction to the topic of marijuana. Chapter 1 provides a general background about the science of the plant and its history in human civilization. Chapter 2 focuses on the two major disputes over cannabis in today's world: should cannabis products be legally available and, if so, under what conditions, and should a special dispensation be allowed for the use of medical marijuana, regardless of general laws and regulations regarding the personal use of the substance? The remaining chapters of the book provide background information for readers who wish to continue their study of these issues in more detail. Chapter 3 provides some statements pro and con on the legality of marijuana in general and for medical purposes. Chapter 4 offers profiles of some important individuals and organizations who have been involved in the debates over cannabis both in recent years and in earlier history. Chapter 5 is a collection of some especially important documents—laws, policy statements, and court decisions—related to marijuana issues, as well as data on production and consumption of marijuana products. Chapter 6 provides an annotated list of books, articles, and reports, as well as electronic resources on marijuana. Chapter 7 is a timeline of important events in the history of marijuana, and the book ends with a glossary of basic terms used in discussions of cannabis and related products.

At the end of 2016, marijuana was still listed as a Schedule I drug in the United States. It was placed in that category because federal officials had decided that marijuana currently has no accepted medical use and a high potential for drug abuse. At the same time, eight states and the District of Columbia had approved marijuana for recreational use of small amounts of the drug and 28 states and the District of Columbia had approved the use of marijuana for medical purposes. In addition, between 2009 and 2013, the U.S. Department of Justice had issued three memoranda outlining federal policy on state marijuana laws, one seemingly indicating that the government would not interfere with marijuana use in those states where it had been approved, one apparently making a different case for federal intervention in all forms of marijuana use, and a third (the latest) saying that the federal government would become involved in the regulation of marijuana use in states where it had been approved only under special circumstances. So what's going on here?

Americans are clearly rethinking a century-long policy of treating marijuana as a highly dangerous drug, comparable to heroin, lysergic acid diethylamide (LSD), peyote, MDMA (ecstasy), and methaqualone (Quaalude). A substance that not so long ago drew multiyear prison sentences and fines ranging in the thousands of dollars was now being reclassified, in at least some states, as a safe and harmless form of recreation and, even more strikingly, as a medicine that could be used to treat pain and a variety of medical conditions.

This change seems almost like a revolution in thinking about a controversial psychoactive substance. Yet, it is one with a long and contentious history that dates back more than two millennia. The purpose of this second edition of *Marijuana: A Reference Handbook* is to bring readers up-to-date on the changes that have taken place in our understanding of the science, technology, sociology, psychology, politics, and economics of marijuana since the book's first appearance less than a decade ago. The current edition not only reviews the specific changes that have occurred, such as the adoption of marijuana laws in a number of states, but also updates references that readers can use in their own research on the topic, such as new books, articles, and Internet resource; an updated list of organization and important figures in the field; and an updated chronology of marijuana events. Perhaps the most important message to be derived from the current edition is that the status of marijuana in American society has undergone a rapid change in the past five years but, perhaps more importantly, current indications are that such changes are only in their earliest manifestations. Any future third edition of the book may only confirm that, as more data become available about the effects of legal marijuana, Americans' views on marijuana are likely to evolve even more over the next few years.

Marijuana

Introduction

The researchers were not quite sure what to make of their discovery. The pottery shards they had found in their excavations at Yangmingshan, close to modern Taipei, Taiwan, were obviously very old. And the decorations on the pottery had clearly been made by some type of rope. But what was the rope made of? It was certainly one of the oldest woven materials the archaeologists had ever seen. Could it be that the fiber used to decorate the pots was the oldest material of its kind in human history?

As it turned out, this discovery was as exciting as the researchers had hoped it would be. Further analysis proved that the rope used to decorate the pottery fragments was made of hemp, a material made from the plant now known as *Cannabis sativa*. Carbon dating of the fibers found that the hemp was about 12,000 years old, dating back to a Neolithic society known as the Tapenkeng culture (Booth 2005, 20). So, yes, the hemp found in this archaeological dig may well be the oldest fiber ever produced by humans.

A worker processes hemp in Kentucky. Hemp was first introduced to Kentucky in 1775, and it was an important part of the state's economy during the centuries that followed. (Public Records Division, Kentucky Department for Libraries and Archives)

What Is *Cannabis Sativa*?

This story from Neolithic Taiwan provides just a hint of the very long history of an amazing plant, *Cannabis sativa*. Before continuing that story, it is necessary to describe in more detail that plant, now commonly known simply as cannabis (sometimes correctly spelled with a capital "C," as Cannabis, but more commonly spelled with a lower case "c," as cannabis).

As its scientific name suggests, *Cannabis sativa* belongs to the genus Cannabis, in the family Cannabaceae (also known as the hemp family), the order Urticales, the class Magnoliopsida (the dicotyledons), and the division Magnoliophyta (the flowering plants). The species name is often given as *Cannabis sativa L.*, with the capital "L" representing the name of the person who originally named the plant, Linnaeus. There is some disagreement among experts as to the number of species in the genus Cannabis, with some authorities recognizing two other species in addition to *C. sativa*: *C. indica* and *C. ruderalis*. Many taxonomists argue that *C. indica* and *C. ruderalis* are subspecies of *C. sativa*, rather than true species themselves. Many taxonomic listings of the genus show both classifications for *C. indica* and *C. ruderalis*. *C. sativa* is thought to have originated in eastern Asia, although some authorities claim that it may also have developed in Africa or parts of the Americas.

C. sativa is an annual flowering dioecious herb with erect stems that may reach a height of five meters (about 16 feet). The term *dioecious* means that the plant may occur as male or female, in contrast to monecious plants, which have both male and female parts on the same plant. The dioecious character of the cannabis plant was recognized as early as the third century BCE by Chinese naturalists, who called the male plant *xi* and the female plant *fu*. (The Chinese name for cannabis itself is *ma*.) Reproduction of the cannabis plant, then, can occur only when male and female plants are in proximity to each other so that microspores from the male plant can be transferred to the megaspores of a second female plant. The plant typically flowers in the summer and produces its fruit in late summer to early fall. It grows year-around in the tropics but is a deciduous annual in temperate regions.

Cannabis belongs to a family of plants known as short-day plants, plants that require some given amount of darkness in order to flower. Flowering does not occur if nights are not long enough, that is, if there is too much daylight within a 24-hour period. Flowering of a short-day plant can be inhibited, for example, simply by shining a bright light on the plant in the middle of the night, thus interrupting the period of darkness it requires for flowering. This characteristic explains the tendency of cannabis plants to begin flowering later in the summer (after the summer solstice, on or about June 21).

The *C. sativa* plant is often described as "leggy" because it has long branches with large narrow-bladed leaves. The plant also has large internodal distances. The internodal distance on a plant is the space between two nodes on a stem (a node is the point at which an individual leaf grows off the stem). The plant has a large, sprawling root system.

The cannabis fruit is usually a shiny brown achene (a small, dry fruit with a single distinct interior seed) that may be either plain in color or marked in a variety of ways. At maturation, it detaches from the plant and is blown away, the mechanism by which the plant reproduces.

The subspecies *C. indica* differs from *C. sativa* in a number of ways. First, it tends to be shorter and bushier than the main species, with a more compact root system. Its leaves are broader, a darker green, and more densely arranged on the plant than in *C. sativa*. These traits tend to make it more popular among growers who have a limited amount of space in which to locate their plants, such as indoor growers. The subspecies also has distinctly different pharmacological effects than those experienced with the main species. *C. indica* is thought to have originated on the Indian subcontinent.

The subspecies *C. ruderalis* is even smaller and more compact than *C. indica*. It is a scrubby plant of little interest to marijuana growers because it has a very low concentration of THC, tending to produce headaches rather than the more pleasant effects obtained by ingesting *C. sativa* or *C. indica*. (THC is the abbreviation for Δ^9-tetrahydrocannabinol, a compound that produces the psychoactive effects associated with the ingestion of cannabis products.) *C. ruderalis* is thought to have originated in Russia, Central Europe, or Central Asia, and was first introduced to the modern world when seeds were brought to Amsterdam in the 1980s.

The three forms of cannabis discussed thus far have been variously called distinct species, species and subspecies, species and strains, or species and varieties. Strains and varieties are forms of a plant that differ from each other in important characteristics, but that do not differ sufficiently to be assigned distinct taxa. For example, cannabis growers typically attempt to produce new strains (or varieties) by pollinating one form of *C. sativa*, *C. indica*, or *C. ruderalis* with a second form of one of the three varietals. The purpose of such experiments is to produce new types of cannabis that have especially desirable qualities favored by users of the plant. Today, there are well over 100 different strains of the cannabis plant that have been produced by years of this cross-breeding technology (Oner 2013, xi). Some of those strains are called Afghani, Amsterdam Indica, Aussie Blues, Big Bud, Charas, Durban Poison, Haze Marijuana, Island Lady, Kush, Light of Jah, Mauwie Wauwie, New York Diesel, Purple Haze Marijuana, Super Skunk, Swiss Miss, and White Queen. Many strains are developed because they grow best in either indoor or outdoor settings.

Among individuals for whom the cannabis plant is a source of a recreational drug (marijuana), probably the most interesting and important part of the plant is the trichomes. A trichome is a small hair or other outgrowth from the epidermis of a plant, usually consisting of a single cell. Trichomes typically exude a sticky, resinous substance to which bits of dust, male sex spores, small insects, and other materials become stuck. Botanists have hypothesized that the primary evolutionary purpose of trichomes is, as part of the plants' defensive system, protecting them from attacking insects (Freeman and Beattie 2008). Research indicates that chemicals found in the exudate of trichomes are toxic to insects that prey on the plant.

A number of important organic compounds are found at the base of a trichome, including a number of phenols and terpenes. Phenols are organic compounds related to phenol (hydroxybenzene), a ring compound with one hydroxyl (-OH) group. The chemical formula for phenol is C_6H_5OH. Terpenes are organic compounds that are found commonly in plants. They constitute a large and diverse collection of compounds derived from the simply unsaturated hydrocarbon isoprene (2-methyl-1,3-butadiene; C_5H_8). As phenols and terpenes migrate upward from the base of a trichome to the bud at its tip, a series of chemical reactions occur that convert these simple basic compounds into a large variety of more complex compounds, the most important of which is THC. THC is a light yellow resinous oil that is sticky at room temperature and solidifies upon refrigeration. It is virtually insoluble in water, but soluble in most organic solvents. THC is of interest both to scientists and to users of marijuana because it is the most psychoactive of the many compounds found in the cannabis plant. It is also of interest to chemists because it is the only known psychoactive plant material that does not contain the element nitrogen. Overall, more than 400 distinct chemicals have been extracted from the cannabis plant, 66 of which are unique to that plant ("Definitions and Explanations" 2016). These 66 chemicals are collectively known as cannabinoids. Many cannabinoids are isomers of each other; that is, they have the same chemical formula (such as that of THC: $C_{21}H_{30}O_2$), but different arrangements of atoms. Table 1.1 gives the names and abbreviations of the classes of cannabinoids found in the cannabis plant.

One of the most interesting discoveries made by researchers in the past few decades is that animals produce compounds with properties similar to those of the cannabinoids that occur in plants (the *phytocannabinoids*). These animal-based

Table 1.1   Cannabinoids Present in the Cannabis Plant

Class of Cannaboid	Abbreviation
Δ^9-tetrahydrocannabinol	Δ^9-THC; THC
Δ^8-tetrahydrocannabinol	Δ^8-THC
Cannabichromene	CBC
Cannabicyclol	CBL
Cannabidiol	CBD
Cannabielsoin	CBE
Cannabigerol	CBG
Cannabinidiol	CBND
Cannabinol	CBN
Cannabitriol	CBT
Cannabichromanone	CBCN
Isocannabinoids	

compounds are called *endocannabinoids*. They appear to operate on almost every part of an animal's body and brain, producing effects similar to those caused by THC and other phytocannabinoids. Researchers believe that endocannabinoids may have a number of medical and pharmacological applications because they stimulate the same receptors in the nervous system as those affected by phytocannabinoids. One of the first products intended for the commercial market of this type was a drug called rimonabant (Acomplia), originally designed for the treatment of obesity. The drug worked by blocking the action of endocannabinoids produced by the brain that stimulate a person's appetite. Rimonabant was withdrawn from the market in 2009, and research discontinued on the drug because of possible dangerous side effects (Acomplia 2016).

In addition to the naturally occurring cannabinoids, a number of synthetic cannabinoids have been produced by researchers. These compounds do not necessarily exist naturally in plants, but they have many of the same physiological and pharmacological properties as do naturally occurring cannabinoids.

One reason for the preparation of synthetic cannabinoids is to study with more specificity their effects on body systems. The result of this research may be helpful in developing synthetic products that can be used to treat a variety of physical and mental conditions. Probably the best known synthetic cannabinoid is a compound called dronabinol, manufactured by AbbVie, Inc. Dronabinol is chemically identical to the active form of THC found in cannabis. It is sold under the trade name of Marinol and is recommended for the treatment of anorexia associated with weight loss in patients with HIV/AIDS and for the nausea and vomiting associated with cancer chemotherapy in patients who have not responded to other treatments (Marinol 2016). Dronabinol is listed as a Schedule III drug because it is regarded as a non-narcotic with low risk of physical or mental dependency. That listing has drawn some attention and comment since the synthetic compound dronabinol is chemically identical to the form of THC that is regarded as the most psychoactive component of natural marijuana (Backes 2014, 84).

A second synthetic cannabinoid is nabilone, marketed as Cesamet and listed as a Schedule II drug because of its high potential for abuse. Like dronabinol, nabilone is used almost exclusively for treating the nausea and vomiting associated with cancer chemotherapy ("Cesamet" 2016).

Another interesting analog of THC that research chemists developed has the chemical name 1-pentyl-3-(1-naphthoyl) indole, although it is more commonly known as AM-678 or JWH-018 or, commercially, as K2 or Spice. The compound was first synthesized by John W. Huffman, an organic chemist at Clemson University. It has essentially the same effect (except more powerfully) on cannabinoid receptors in the body as does THC, although its chemical structure is significantly different. An herbal incense ("not for human consumption") called "Spice" that contains JWH-018 first appeared in Europe in 2004 and rapidly became popular there. When authorities analyzed the product and found that it contained a powerful synthetic cannabinoid, they banned it. JWH-018 has since been classified as a Schedule I in the United States (Stafford 2009).

Hemp versus Marijuana

In today's world, two forms of cannabis are grown for quite different purposes. Both forms are classified botanically as *C. sativa*, but their physical appearances and other properties are different from each other. The form known as *hemp* usually occurs as a tall plant, ranging in height from one to more than five meters (3 to nearly 20 feet). Plant appearance depends on the conditions under which it is grown. In uncrowded conditions, the plant has many branches and a relatively thick stalk that can reach more than 50 millimeters (two inches) in diameter. In crowded conditions, the hemp plant has few branches, except at the very top. The stalk is much reduced in size, with a diameter of no more than about 20 millimeters (about 0.75 inch).

Hemp is grown for two purposes: fibers, which are made from the plant's stalk and stems, and oil, which is made from its seeds. The manufacture of fiber from the hemp plant begins with a process known as *retting*, in which stalks and stems are soaked in water that contains bacteria or special kinds of chemicals. These bacteria or chemicals attack the stems and stalks, breaking them down into their component parts. One of those parts is called *bast* or *bast fiber*, a material found between the woody core of the plant and its outer covering (the epidermis and cortex). Bast fibers are long stringy strands up to two meters (six feet) in length that provide the hemp plant with strength and that, when separated from the rest of the plant, produce strong, durable fibers. These fibers are yellowish, pale green, or gray in color and are not easily dyed, accounting for the pale color associated with most hemp fibers. The fibers are used for a host of purposes, including the manufacture of all styles of clothing, paper, ropes and other types of cordage, sail canvas, and netting. Hemp has long been a popular agricultural crop because it grows quickly, requires little fertilizer or pesticide application, produces large yields per acre compared to other plants, and has few deleterious environmental impacts.

A second use of the hemp plant is the production of oil, which is made from the plant's seeds. Growing hemp for oil production cannot be combined with growing hemp for fiber production because in the latter process, plants are harvested before they begin to flower; thus, no seeds are produced that can be used for oil production. Hemp plants destined for use in oil production must be allowed to grow a few weeks longer than those used for fiber production, permitting the growth of flowers and the development of seeds. When this point has been reached, the seeds are harvested and then pressed to produce an oil that is similar to safflower, linseed, tung, and perilla oils. Freshly prepared unrefined hempseed oil is light green to dark green in color with a pleasant nutty aroma. It is rich in unsaturated fatty acids and has significant nutritional value. But it is also a fragile material that must be stored in dark, cool, oxygen-free conditions to prevent breakdown. Because of its instability, hempseed oil cannot be used for cooking. Its nutritional value, however, has made it popular, especially among natural and organic food devotees, as a nutritional supplement that can be used as a condiment and in the preparation of sauces and specialized foods, such as pesto.

In some ways, the most important feature of the hemp plant is its concentration of THC. Over the centuries, the hemp plant has been cross-bred to have low concentrations of THC, presently about 0.3%. By contrast, cannabis plants raised for the production of marijuana have much higher concentrations of THC, ranging from about 2 to as much as 20%. Until recently, this difference in THC content in hemp and marijuana plants was irrelevant to federal laws in the United States, where plants containing any amount of THC greater than zero had long been illegal (DEA Clarifies Status of Hemp in the *Federal Register* 2001). That situation changed in 2014, when the federal farm bill included a provision allowing farmers to grow hemp in pilot programs in states where such a practice was permitted. In the first year, crops of hemp were planted in three states (Colorado, Kentucky, and Vermont), with plans for expanding the number of such states in following years (Johnson 2015).

One form of hemp that is still found in the United States is called *feral hemp* or *ditchweed* (or *ditch weed*). Feral hemp, as the name suggests, is hemp that has self-seeded from plants that were once grown legally in virtually every part of the United States. They are vigorous plants that have survived many decades of attempted eradication. At one point, up to 99% of all marijuana plants eradicated annually by the U.S. Drug Enforcement Administration (DEA) were not those cultivated intentionally for the production of marijuana; rather, they were feral plants (98 Percent of All Domestically Eradicated Marijuana Is "Ditchweed," DEA Admits 2006). Since 2006, DEA has changed that practice and no longer lists ditchweed as marijuana eradicated in the program (Green 2011).

The Cannabis Plant in History

Whatever the diverse forms in which it is currently found, *C. sativa* almost certainly existed as only a single type of plant when it was first used by humans. The date of that first use, as noted previously, was at least 10,000 BCE on the modern island of Taiwan. Its cultivation and use later radiated outward throughout most of the world.

Cannabis in China

Much of what we know about the early history of cannabis comes from China, where the plant became widely popular with the rise of Chinese civilization. Indeed, in some of the oldest documents available, ancient China was sometimes referred to as "the Land of Mulberry and Hemp" (Booth 2005, 20). An archaeological find in China of some interest that is similar to the Taiwanese discovery was reported in 1974. It consisted of a number of artifacts indicating the use of hemp in the culture of the time, including a design on pottery similar to that found in Taiwan and some imprints made from hemp clothing on the then-damp pottery (Merlin 2003, 304).

Like the Taiwan discovery, the earliest evidence for the use of hemp in China comes from archaeological digs in which remnants of cloth, seeds, rope imprints (like those from the Taiwan site), and other visual evidence of the plant and its use are available. For example, a fragment of cloth made from hemp was discovered in 1972 in a grave dating to the Zhou dynasty (1045–256 BCE). The find is sometimes described as the "oldest preserved specimen" of hemp cloth ever discovered (Hanuš and Mechoulam 2008, 50). Many other hemp products have also been recovered from ancient Chinese sites. Fragments of textiles made from hemp have been discovered at a site at Anyang in Henan Province dating to the Shan dynasty (1600–1046 BCE), and cemeteries at the same site dating to the Zhou dynasty contain thousands of funerary objects, some of which were made of hemp. Excavations in Gansu Province have discovered graves dating to the Han dynasty (206 BCE–220 CE) in which corpses were wrapped in cloth made of hemp (Fleming and Clarke 1998).

Written records of the role of hemp in Chinese culture began to appear as early as the 16th century BCE when it was listed as an important crop in what is regarded as the oldest Chinese agricultural manuscript, the *Xia Xiao Zheng* (*Summer Almanac*). The role of hemp in agriculture was also mentioned and described in a number of other early documents. These documents include the *Shi Ching* (*Book of Songs*) and the *Zhushu Jinian* (*Bamboo Annals*), both written between 476 and 221 BCE; *Shi Jing* (*Book of Odes*), dating to the 11th to 6th centuries BCE; *Si Min Yue Ling* (Eastern Han dynasty; 25 to 220 CE); and *Qi Min Yao Shu* (Northern Wei dynasty; 386 to 534 CE). All of these texts provided detailed information about the planting and cultivation of hemp plants, indicating their essential role in Chinese culture (Fleming and Clarke 1998, 87). An example of the kind of instruction found in these books is the following.

If we pull out the male hemp before it scatters pollen, the female plant cannot make seed. Otherwise, the female plant's seed production will be influenced by the male hemp plants scattering pollen and during this period of time, the fiber of the male hemp plant is the best. (Cited in Lu and Clarke, 1995. This article contains a number of other passages dealing with the cultivation of cannabis for the production of hemp.)

A considerable body of evidence indicates that hemp seed was also used as an essential part of the diet among the early Chinese. Early histories and other documents list hemp seed as one of the essential nine (in some references) or five (in other references) grains that constituted a typical diet. Although it was certainly part of the average Chinese diet for many centuries, it also seems to have been a specialty food among the royalty during certain months of the year (Li 1974a, 443). The seed was also crushed to obtain its oil, which was used both for frying foods and for industrial applications. Over time, the use of hemp seed as a food and a source of oil was gradually phased out as superior natural products became available. An interesting side note, however, is that a resurgence of the use of hemp seed occurred at one point in history, around 28 CE, when a great famine caused by war and natural disasters forced people to return to the ancient practice of eating hemp seeds as a major part of their diets (Li 1974a, 444). As late as the 9th century CE, writers were still describing a porridge made with cannabis seeds, but, before long, the product "was completely forgotten as a human food" (Li 1974a, 444).

Given the widespread use of cannabis as a food, it is hardly surprising that humans would rather quickly recognize the plant's medical and psychoactive effects. One could hardly consume cannabis seeds without experiencing at least some kinds of mind-altering events from time to time. The first mention of cannabis as a medical product is usually given as about 2000 BCE, when it is described in the earliest known pharmacopeia, the

Pĕn-ts'ao Ching, attributed to the legendary emperor Shen Nung. That attribution is almost certainly wrong since Shen Nung was probably not a real person, and the oldest known copy of the book actually dates to the first or second century CE. However, authorities believe that the text accurately reflects prehistoric practices, as its "earliest" mention of medical cannabis is usually taken as valid.

In any case, Chinese shamans used virtually every part of the cannabis plant to treat a variety of illnesses. A 1911 text on Chinese herbal medicine, for example, notes that "[e]very part of the hemp plant is used in medicine; the dried flowers, the ach'enia, the seeds, the oil, the leaves, the stalk, the root, and the juice" (Smith 1911, 91). These materials were put to a plethora of applications used to treat a long list of illness and disorders, including nausea, vomiting, malaria, beriberi, constipation, rheumatic pains, absent-mindedness, nervous disorders, female disorders (including post-partum depression), ulcers and other eruptions of the skin, scorpion stings, wounds, hair loss, sulfur poisoning, dryness of the throat, and worm infestations (an incomplete list at that!).

The cannabis plant was also used as an anesthetic for surgical procedures, perhaps as early as the second century CE. Although there is considerable dispute about the details of this history, it appears that the famous Chinese physician Hua Tuo used powdered cannabis in a concoction to produce numbness during surgery. Reputedly, the product used by Hua was made of a concoction of cannabis mixed with wine. It was called *mafeisan*, which means cannabis ("ma") + boil ("fei") + powder ("san") (Hua Tuo 2014)

The use of the cannabis plant for both medical and psychoactive purposes in ancient history is hardly surprising. A practitioner who purported to heal individuals of physical and mental disorders was commonly a shaman, a person who used minerals, herbs, and other natural products to treat the patient, but who was also in contact with the spirit world and could thus draw on supernatural resources to bring about cures. It has seemed clear to such practitioners perhaps since the beginning of human civilization that the cannabis plant produced both kinds of results: as an herb, it could directly cure a host of physical and mental ailments; as a psychoactive material, it could give a patient or the practitioner access to a world of spirits who could perhaps provide cures on an entirely different psychical plane.

References to the use of cannabis as both a medical substance and a psychoactive material date to the earliest of the Chinese pharmacopoeias, *Pen Ching*. There one can find the following admonition:

> To take too much makes people see demons and throw themselves about like maniacs. But if one takes it over a long period of time one can communicate with the spirits and one's own body becomes light. (Rudgley 1998, 47)

The fact that the Chinese knew about the hallucinatory effects of cannabis early in history comes, interestingly enough, from linguistic studies. In a 1974 article in *Economic Botany*, Hui-Lin Li of the Morris Arboretum at the University of Pennsylvania points out that the Chinese character for "ma" (the Chinese name for cannabis) is a combination of simpler characters that represent "numerous" or "chaotic," apparently from the nature of hemp fibers themselves, and "numbness" or "senselessness," apparently from the plant's physical effects. He concludes that these linguistic clues indicate "that the stupefying effect of the hemp plant was commonly known from extremely early times" (Li 1974b, 296).

In spite of a number of mentions such as these in early Chinese documents, use of cannabis for psychoactive purposes was probably relatively limited. Observers note that Chinese society was highly ordered, and activities that would disrupt that order were frowned upon and often restricted. As Martin Booth has written in his history of cannabis:

> The use of cannabis [for recreational purposes], however, never really became more than a passing phase. Chinese

culture, being based on social order, family values and the reverence of ancestors and the elderly, looked down upon drugs. (Booth 2005, 23)

Cannabis in India and Central Asia

The same cannot be said for other parts of Asia. In fact, the use of cannabis products for psychoactive experiences has a long history, dating back to at least 1400 BCE. Historians are uncertain as to the mechanism by which knowledge of the cannabis plant worked its way from China (or, perhaps, Central Asia), but there is no question of the central role that the plant had in Indian culture from its earliest days. The sacred Hindu texts, known as the Vedas, contain many references to the psychoactive effects of the cannabis plant, an effect that is universally praised and encouraged. In one segment of the *Artharvaveda*, for example, cannabis is referred to as one of the herbs that "release us from anxiety" (Rudgley 1998, 48).

According to one of the central stories told in the Vedas, the cannabis plant first appeared on Earth when a drop of heavenly nectar fell to Earth, took root, and grew as a cannabis plant. A drink prepared from the plant later became the favorite refreshment of Indra, the Hindu Lord of Kings. Another popular myth recounts the experience of Lord Shiva who, after an angry fight within his family, wandered off into the fields and fell asleep under the leaves of a cannabis plant. When he awoke, he decided to slake his hunger by eating a leaf off the plant, and found it to be delicious and refreshing. In later life, he came to be known as the Lord of Bhang because of his love of the plant (Gumbiner 2011).

Bhang is one of a number of forms in which cannabis was (and is) consumed in India. It is a mixture with a variable composition. One that has been described consists of cannabis, poppy seed, pepper, ginger, caraway seed, clove, cardamom, cinnamon, cucumber seed, almonds, nutmeg, and rosebud, all boiled together in milk (Abel 1980, Chapter 1). In this recipe, the cannabis is taken from the large green leaves and flowering shoots of either the male or female plant. Two other cannabis preparations that have been popular throughout history are *ganja* and *charas*. Ganja is made from the top leaves and the unfertilized flower of the young female plant, which are then dried and smoked or brewed as a tea. This preparation produces an effect similar to smoking a mild grade of marijuana that is available today. Charas is made from the resin obtained from the top leaves and unfertilized flower of the female plant, which are then dried and smoked. This is the strongest preparation of cannabis available and is comparable in its effects to hashish. Hashish preparations can have some of the highest concentrations of THC of any form of cannabis and have been popular in many parts of the world throughout much of human history (Hashish 2015).

Cannabis preparations have traditionally played a role in Indian culture similar to that played by alcohol in Western culture. They are commonly smoked by groups of people who are gathered for social occasions. For example, legend has it that evil spirits hover around wedding ceremonies waiting for an opportunity to cause misery in the lives of the bride and groom. A gift of bhang from the bride's father is considered a sufficient protection against these terrible events. Bhang was (and still is) offered to visitors to one's home, and anyone who ignores this tradition is usually regarded as "miserly and misanthropic" (Abel 1982).

Many scholars today believe that cannabis was first domesticated and used not in China or India, but in Central Asia. Martin Booth, author of *Cannabis: A History*, argues that the plant's original home may have been near the Irtysh River, which flows from Mongolia, along the southern edge of the Gobi Desert, into the lowlands of western Siberia or in the Takla Makan Desert north of Tibet. The plant still grows in abundance in these regions whenever the Earth is disturbed by floods or erosion (Booth 2005, 3). In such a case, the plant was probably then dispersed eastward into China and southward into India. One of the most solid pieces of evidence arguing for a long (if not the longest) history of cannabis in Central Asia comes from the writings of the Greek historian Herodotus, who lived from about 484 to about 425 BCE. In his work, *Histories*, Herodotus tells of a popular tradition among the Scythians in which cannabis was smoked for religious, ceremonial, and perhaps recreational purposes. The Scythians thrived from about 600 BCE to about 300 CE across an extensive region that covered most of the southern part of modern Russia. For their ceremonies, the Scythians first built a tent with three long wooden poles tied together at the top and covered with animal skin. They then placed dried cannabis seeds into a hot bowl in the center of the tent and took their places inside the tent around the bowl. In this position, they inhaled the vapors of the roasting cannabis seeds, experiencing such pleasure that, according to Herodotus, "they would howl with pleasure" (cited in Merlin 2003, 313).

Fortunately, it is not necessary to rely just on the words of Herodotus about this custom. In 1929, the Russian archaeologist S. I. Rudenko visited the region in which the Scythians once lived and found that the tradition reported by Herodotus continues today. He reported that these modern descendants of the Scythians follow the traditional practice not for religious or ceremonial reasons, but simply as a form of day-to-day relaxation. Even more recent information about this practice became available in 1993 when a group of Russian archaeologists discovered the body of a 2,000-year-old woman buried in the permafrost in Siberia near the location of Rudenko's research. The archaeologists found the woman buried in a tree trunk along with a small cask containing cannabis seeds, which they hypothesized were "smoked for pleasure and used in pagan rituals" (Spicer 2002; Stanley 1994).

A few authorities have argued for a very early appearance of cannabis in the Middle East. In a 1938 book on cannabis, *Marijuana, America's New Drug Problem*, for example, physician and reputed "authority on marijuana," Robert P. Walton, referred to mentions on Assyrian tablets of cannabis dating to about 650 BCE, and possibly much earlier (as cited in Brecher and the Editors of Consumer Reports 1972, 397). Since this early comment, there have been only a few significant discoveries pointing to an early history of cannabis in the Middle East. In the early 1960s, for example, archaeologists discovered pieces of hemp fabric in a grave mound at a dig in the region known as Gordion that dates to the 8th BCE. An even more recent and more fascinating discovery was made in the 1990s in the town of Beit Shemesh, near Jerusalem. The discovery consisted of the skeleton of a young woman who was about 14 years of age and had apparently died during childbirth. Interred with the body was a brown material in the abdominal region of the skeleton, whose composition was found to consist of cannabis seeds, mixed with fruits and other dried seeds. Archaeologists believe that the mixture was used as an aid in childbirth, a custom that prevailed in the area well into the 19th century. The find raises questions as to the extent and the purposes for which cannabis might have been used in this early Middle Eastern culture. In spite of these recent finds, most authorities seem to believe that cannabis came to the Middle East relatively later than it did to Central Asia, China, and India.

More intriguing, perhaps, has been the dispute as to whether cannabis products are mentioned in the Bible, which would, of course, place their use many centuries and even millennia earlier. The basic problem is whether words used in the Old Testament actually refer to cannabis or to some other type of plant. In I Samuel, 14, for example, Saul places a restriction on his people, telling them that they should not eat until they took vengeance upon his enemies. His son Jonathan did not hear that command, however, and when the army reached a wooded area, he

> . . . reached out the end of the staff that was in his hand and dipped it into the honeycomb. He raised his hand to his mouth, and his eyes brightened. (I Samuel 14: 27)

The question is whether there is more than meets the eye to this seemingly innocuous passage. According to one historian, there may in fact be. In a 1903 article on the passage, Dr. C. Creighton points out that the Hebrew words for "honey comb" used here—*yagarah hadebash*—probably should be translated as a type of flower stalk similar to that of cannabis, and that the "brightened eyes" may have been Jonathan's response to ingesting cannabis (Creighton 1903, 241; for an extended discussion of this point, also see Benet 1975). Other scholars take a more skeptical view of efforts to place the cannabis plant into biblical sources. One widely respected authority, for example, has criticized experts who have "tickled, teased, and twisted [Biblical texts] into surrendering secret references to marijuana that it never contained" (Abel 1982).

Cannabis in Africa (and Beyond)

The use of any form of cannabis on the African continent appears to have been a comparatively recent event. According to the best information now available, cannabis was probably introduced to the continent by Muslim sea traders who brought the plant to the eastern coast of Africa in the first century CE, after which it spread inland throughout most of southern Africa. There are a few scattered reports of ancient remnants of cannabis finds such as a discovery of prehistoric pollen samples dating to about 2300 BCE from the Kalahari Desert in Botswana, but these are rare, with most discoveries dating to only the first century CE or much later (Merlin 2003, 315–316). More commonly, the archeological record appears to confirm that tribesmen practiced a communal use of cannabis by, for example, "throwing hemp plants on the burning coals of a fire and staging what might today be called a 'breathe-in'" (Emboden 1972, 226, as cited in Spicer 2002).

A somewhat minor, but very interesting, note about the use of cannabis products in Africa has to do with a modern organization known as the Ethiopian Zion Coptic Church (EZCC).

Modern leaders of the church say that it has been in existence for a long time, with roots in Africa going back hundreds of years. Whatever its ancient history, the church was formulated in its modern form in the 1930s during the rise of the Rafastari movement in Jamaica. Rafastari (also known as Rasta, but not as Rafastarianism) is a religious movement that consists almost entirely of Christian descendants of slaves brought to the Western Hemisphere. They originally worshiped Haile Selassie I, emperor of Ethiopia from 1930 to 1974, as the reincarnation of Christ and God incarnate. Among the tenets of the church is a belief in the sacramental role of cannabis smoking as a way of communicating with God. One of the early leaders of the church, Louv Williams, said that the church was based on a new trinity consisting of "The Man, The Herb, and The Word" ("the herb" being cannabis) (Menelik 2009, 138). A defense for the fundamental principles of Rafastari and its basis in biblical teachings was laid out in a 1988 publication, *Marijuana and the Bible*, which contains dozens of specific citations in the Bible that purportedly allude to the use of cannabis in religious ceremonies. The church's fundamental teaching is that

> Herb (marijuana) is a Godly creation from the beginning of the world. It is known as the weed of wisdom, angel's food, the tree of life and even the "Wicked Old Ganja Tree." Its purpose in creation is as a fiery sacrifice to be offered to our Redeemer during obligations. (Marijuana and the Bible 1988)

In 1975, a branch of the EZCC consisting primarily of white Americans was incorporated in the state of Florida. Four years later, members of that group were arrested while unloading a very large shipment of marijuana from Jamaica, a shipment they said they intended to use in religious ceremonies. The question as to whether the use of marijuana was legal among the members of this religious denomination worked its way through the federal courts over a number of years. Members of the Rafastari argued that their right to use marijuana in their religious ceremonies was protected by the U.S. Constitution's "freedom of religion" clause, which prevents the government from interfering with the religious practices of individuals and denominations. (American Indians are permitted to use the mind-altering drug peyote under this provision of the law.) The U.S. and state governments responded to this argument by saying that the constitutional right to freedom of religion is not absolute, but is subject to overweening "public interest" factors, such as the risk of a particular drug. In the end, the government's argument won out in the highest court decisions on the Rafastari complaints, and the denomination's right to use marijuana in its ceremonies is not permitted (*United States v. Rush* 1984).

One interesting sidelight of this story emerged when an eminent psychiatrist Brian L. Weiss, chief of the Division of Psychiatry at Mount Sinai Medical Center in New York City, was asked to evaluate 14 members of the EZCC each in Miami and in Jamaica to determine their psychological, physical, and emotional states. Dr. Weiss reported that he was "surprised by the absence of positive findings" among members of both groups. In fact, the only positive finding he could report was that "the American Coptics are functioning at a much better level than they were prior to joining the Coptic Church." He noted that although the number of individuals examined was small, he felt he could conclude that "some people, at least, can smoke marijuana in high doses for sixteen hours daily for up to fifty years without apparent psychological or physical harm" (Weiss 1980).

Cannabis in Europe

As with other parts of the world, cannabis use appears to have a long history in Europe. Perhaps the earliest reference to such use dates to the third millennium BCE in a grave site near modern-day Bucharest. The grave site contained small vessels called *pipe cups* that contained burned cannabis seed. Similar finds have been recovered in other parts of Eurasia, prompting the noted Oxford archaeologist Andrew Sherratt to observe that the practice of burning cannabis as a narcotic is a tradition that goes back in this area some 5,000 or 6,000 years and was the focus of social and religious rituals of the pastoral peoples of central Eurasia in prehistoric and early historic times (Goodman, Lovejoy, and Sherratt 2007, 27).

One of the routes by which cannabis may have come to Europe was through the dispersion of the Scythians from their original home in Central Asia into Eastern Europe. Polish anthropologist Sula Benet (also known as Sara Benetowa) has studied this process in some detail. She has noted that the Scythians carried with them the use of cannabis for funerary ceremonies (similar to those described by Herodotus) out of their Central Asian homelands into southern Russia and Eastern Europe over centuries of migration. Some of those customs have been retained into modern times. One such example is the preparation of a soup made of cannabis seeds called *semieniatka* at Christmas time in Poland, Lithuania, and Russia as nourishment for dead souls who have come back to their families at the holidays (Benet 1975).

In his superb review of the history of cannabis, "Archaeological Evidence for the Tradition of Psychoactive Plant Use in the Old World," M. D. Merlin mentions a number of sites at which various forms of cannabis have been discovered in prehistoric Europe: locations of the Hallstatt and Laténe cultures of Hungary; a site at Vallensbæk in Denmark; in a region near Trier, Germany; and a location at Mikulčice in the Czech Republic, all dating to the Bronze or Iron Ages in Europe (Merlin 2003, 314).

The point at which cannabis reached Western Europe is not known with any certainty. The date most often mentioned for this event is about 500 BCE. An urn containing burnt cannabis seeds found near modern-day Berlin has been carbon-dated to about that period. In any case, a number of references suggest that the plant rapidly dispersed throughout the continent following that date and by the turn of the millennium was used in locations as far west as the British Isles. An instructive story that is often told is that Hieron II, the ruler of Syracuse from 270 to 215 BCE, decided to purchase the hemp he needed for his fleet's sails from producers in the Rhone Valley of Germany, rather than the much-closer Caspian Sea providers because the former were more skilled and could produce the best hemp available. This story suggests that German growers and producers of hemp must, even as early as the second century BCE, have become highly skilled at working with the plant (Abel 1982).

Cannabis probably reached the British Isles in the first century CE. Rope fragments made of hemp have been discovered as far north on the islands as Bar Hill, located between Glasgow and Edinburgh at a fort built by the Romans around 80 CE. By the fourth century CE, hemp was being grown throughout the British Isles (in contrast to its having been imported by the Romans earlier). At about the same time, the plant was being grown in Scandinavia, where it was being used by the Vikings for the production of sails and ropes. Also within the same period, hemp was apparently being grown and processed in France. This assumption is based on a famous discovery made in the early 1960s with the opening of tombs at the Cathedral of St. Denis in Paris. One of those tombs contained the body of Queen Arnegunde, second wife of King Clothar I, who died in 561. The queen's richly decorated body was wrapped in a cloth made of hemp (Booth 2005, 34–35).

Cannabis arrived in Western Europe by a second route. After the conquest of the Iberian Peninsula by the Moors in 711, the art of papermaking using hemp was brought to Europe from China by way of the new Muslim civilization. By 1150, the first paper mill in Western Europe that was using this technology was constructed in the town of Xatvia in the province of Valencia. Before long, it was exporting paper "to the East and West" (Balfour 1873, 381). Cotton-based paper was being developed at about the same time, but it was found to be generally inferior to hemp-based paper that, by the end of the century, had essentially replaced all cotton-based products. A 19th-century historian reported that some of those earliest hemp-based papers "possess their original qualities even to this day" (Balfour 1873, 381).

By the 16th century, hemp had reached its zenith in Europe, finding use in a host of applications. In the form of paper, it was the material on which important documents such as the Magna Carta and Gutenberg's first Bible were printed; in the form of canvas, it was the substance on which most great (and not-so-great) paintings were made; it was the basic material on which ship building depended for sails and ropes of every description; and in many countries, it had become the fabric of choice from which the clothing of commoners was made. A notable observation about the importance of hemp to the 16th-century world can be found in a 1562 book by William Bullein, a relative of King Henry VIII's second wife, Anne Boleyn. Bullein wrote that "no Shippe can sayle without Hempe. . . . No Plowe, or Carte, can be without ropes halters, trace, &c. The Fisher and Fouler must haue Hempe, to make their nettes. And no Archer can wante his bowe string: and the Malt man for his sackes. With it the belle is rong, to seruice in the Church, with many mo thynges profitable" (Shrank 2006).

The plant received some small measure of historical fame in a notable book by the French writer François Rabelais, *Gargantua and Pantagruel*, which devotes three whole chapters to the plant. Rabelais begins by presenting an extended and complete botanical description of the cannabis plant, and then provides a paean to its uses:

> Without this herb kitchens would be detested, the tables of dining-rooms abhorred, although there were great plenty and variety of most dainty and sumptuous dishes of meat set down upon them, and the choicest beds also, how richly soever adorned with gold, silver, amber, ivory, porphyry, and the mixture of most precious metals, would

without it yield no delight or pleasure to the reposers in them. . . . In what case would tabellions, notaries, copists, makers of counterpanes, writers, clerks, secretaries, scriveners, and such-like persons be without it? Were it not for it, what would become of the toll-rates and rent-rolls? Would not the noble art of printing perish without it? Whereof could the chassis or paper-windows be made? . . . The altars of Isis are adorned therewith, the Pastophorian priests are therewith clad and accoutred, and whole human nature covered and wrapped therein at its first position and production in and into this world. All the lanific trees of Seres, the bumbast and cotton bushes in the territories near the Persian Sea and Gulf of Bengala, the Arabian swans, together with the plants of Malta, do not all the them clothe, attire, and apparel so many persons as this one herb alone. Soldiers are nowadays much better sheltered under it than they were in former times, when they lay in tents covered with skins. It overshadows the theatres and amphitheatres from the heat of a scorching sun. It begirdeth and encompasseth forests, chases, parks, copses, and groves, for the pleasure of hunters. It descendeth into the salt and fresh of both sea and river-waters for the profit of fishers. By it are boots of all sizes, buskins, gamashes, brodkins, gambadoes, shoes, pumps, slippers, and every cobbled ware wrought and made steadable for the use of man. By it the butt and rover-bows are strung, the cross-bows bended, and the slings made fixed. And, as if it were an herb every whit as holy as the vervain, and reverenced by ghosts, spirits, hobgoblins, fiends, and phantoms, the bodies of deceased men are never buried without it. (Rabelais 1894)

In some regards, the most important application of hemp in Western Europe was in the shipbuilding industry. Except for the wood needed for the ship bodies themselves, arguably the most important raw material for ships was hemp, from which sails and ropes were made. Reflecting this importance was a law enacted by King Henry VIII in 1535. In order to provide an adequate supply of hemp for his fleet, Henry required that every landowner sow at least a quarter acre of land to hemp, or be fined for the failure to do so (see, as an example, Tudor: 1485 to 1558, 2007). Henry's daughter, Queen Elizabeth, renewed her father's decree in 1563, requiring that any landowner with more than 60 acres of land plant hemp (Deitch 2003, 12). The practice also spread to Spain, where King Philip announced a similar decree for the nation's widespread lands in both the Old and New Worlds (Cannabis Production and Markets in Europe 2012, 20; this is a widely cited statement for which a primary source does not appear to be readily available).

The cannabis plant arrived in Western Europe in a very different form—hashish—at a much later date. Hashish is a thick, sticky, dark-colored sap—like resin made from the flower of the female cannabis plant. It contains the highest THC concentration of any cannabis product, 20% or more (compared to about 5% for the average mild marijuana preparation). As with other aspects of the cannabis plant, little is known with certainty about the origins of hashish, although there is little doubt that it was first used in parts of the Middle East (Arabia), perhaps as early as the first century CE. The use of hashish by Qutb ad-Din Haydar (also Haidar or Haider), an early saint of the Sufi religion, is one of the best known, if not necessarily entirely accurate, tales of the introduction of hashish to human society. According to that story, Haydar, an ascetic monk who never left his home in the mountains, traveled one day into the nearby fields and came across the cannabis plant. When he returned to his home sometime later, his disciples hardly recognized him because of the "air of happiness and whimsey in his demeanor," which was totally inconsistent with his normal personality. He later explained that this change was a result of his having imbibed from the leaves of the cannabis plant, a discovery he ordered the disciples to keep within Sufism (O'Shaughnessy 1839).

In any case, the use of hashish soon spread throughout the Arab world, where it eventually became, as one writer has said, an "escape hatch for a large segment of Arab society," for whom alcohol was forbidden (Abel 1982, 56). The drug did not reach Europe, however, until the beginning of the 19th century. Some authorities suggest that the return of French soldiers from Napoleon's army in Egypt at the end of the 18th century was an important mechanism by which the substance was introduced into Europe. In any case, the hashish form of cannabis has never had quite the popularity of the weaker forms of the drug found in marijuana cigarettes. Historically, the most famous hashish-smoking episode has to do with a club of Parisian aristocrats and writers called Le Club des Hachichins (the Hashish Eater's Club), who met on a regular basis at the Hotel de Lauzun for regular hashish-smoking event. A number of famous men, including Jacques-Joseph Moreau, Theophile Gautier, Charles Baudelaire, Gérard de Nerval, Eugene Delacroix, and Alexandre Dumas, were members of the group. Baudelaire apparently used his experiences at the club as the basis for his later book, *Les Paradis artificiels* (*Artificial Paradises*), in which he described what it was like to be under the influence of opium and hashish, and argued for drug-taking as a way for humans to understand what a perfect world would be like (Club des Hashischins—The Hashish Club 2008).

Cannabis in North America

Most historians doubt that cannabis was native to the Western Hemisphere (probably not) or to North America (almost certainly not). They tend to believe that the plant arrived in North America by a variety of routes, one of which may have been across the Bering Strait from Siberia. At a time when a land bridge was available across the strait, wandering birds and animals could certainly have carried cannabis seeds with them to the New World (Booth 2005, 38). Some experts suggest that cannabis seeds or hemp products could also have been brought to North America by the Vikings or Chinese explorers dating as far back as the first millennium. The transfer of cannabis from the southern part of the continent (Mexico in particular) is also thought to have been a major route by which the plant entered the northern reaches of the continent. One of the first goals of the Spanish conquest of South America was to establish new plantations that would provide the vast amounts of hemp that could not be grown in the home country. Those efforts failed in large part because the climate was not suitable for hemp growing, and Spanish masters soon found that the narcotic effects of the plant provided natives with a reasonable excuse for performing poorly in growing and harvesting the crop (Booth 2005, 38).

A century later, a similar scenario was playing out in the new British colonies along the Atlantic coast of North America. Farmers in the mother country, by the early 17th century, could no longer supply even a fraction of the hemp Great Britain needed for its many industrial projects, especially the maintenance of a huge sea-going fleet. The solution seemed to be obvious: establish extensive hemp plantations in the American colonies. As a consequence, most colonial governments, either acting on their own or carrying out royal decrees, established requirements that all farmers or all land owners plant some portion of their property in hemp. In one of its first decrees, for example, the Virginia Company required all Jamestown colonists in 1619 to set 100 cannabis plants and the governor to set an additional 5,000 plants. The company also allotted 100 pounds to one Gabriel Wisher to hire men from Poland and Sweden to develop the hemp industry if they would emigrate to the new world (Abel 1982).

Similar laws sprung up throughout the colonies. For example, the General Court of Connecticut in 1640 ordered all families in the colony to plant one teaspoon of hemp seed. The rationale behind this order, interestingly enough, was not to meet British needs, but to meet the growing demands for hemp products in the colonies: "that we might in time have supply of linen cloth among ourselves," as the General Court order put it (Bishop 1861, 300). Indeed, as with the Spanish, the English plan to install mammoth hemp plantations in the colonies to meet the needs of the home country failed. As the American colonies themselves began to grow and prosper, they found that they were able to make use of a large fraction of the hemp they produced, with relatively little to ship back to England. For example, by 1630, half of the colonial population was being clothed in hemp products grown on this side of the Atlantic (Booth 2005, 40).

Other European countries were also interested in establishing hemp plantations in the New World. In 1606, the French explorer Samuel Champlain brought with him hemp seeds on his first trips to New France. There he assigned his botanist and apothecary, Louis Hébert, the task of determining how well the cannabis plant would grow in the new colony at Port Royal, Arcadia (now Nova Scotia). In fact, the French colonists were more concerned with growing enough food to survive, and hemp never became a favored crop in the French colonies (Abel 1982; also see Pickett and Pickett 2011, 164).

An ongoing question among historians is whether the cannabis plant was growing wild in North America when colonists first arrived in the first decade of the 17th century. By most accounts, it seems as if it was. For example, the French explorer Jacques Cartier, reporting on his journeys to North America between 1535 and 1541, noted that "the land groweth fulle of Hempe which groweth of it selfe, which is as good as possibly may be seen, and as strong" (The Third Voyage of Discovery Made by Captaine Jacques Cartier, 1541 2003). Other early explorers appeared to confirm this view. In 1719, for example, a Dutch farmer familiar with the cannabis plant reported on his visit to New Orleans that "hemp grows naturally on the lands adjoining to the lakes on the west of the Mississippi. The stalks are as thick as one's finger, and about six feet long. They are quite like ours in the wood, the leaf and the rind" (Le Page du Pratz 1758, 238). Still, many modern observers believe that such judgments were inaccurate and that the plants reported as growing so abundantly were really other species, such as wood nettle (*Laportea canadensis*) or Indian hemp (*Apocynum cannabinum*) (Kirk 2014, 3).

In any case, there can be little doubt that the cannabis plant had arrived in North America at a relatively early date and, perhaps more to the point, its intoxicating effects were well known to at least some cultures on the continent. For example, researchers have found stone and wooden pipes containing traces of cannabis dating back to 800 CE in the Ohio Valley (Bennett, Osburn, and Osburn 2001, 267–268). And some older members of Native American tribes recall the use of smoked cannabis in very old rituals (Spicer 2002).

The cannabis plant played an important role in American history in the three centuries following the foundation of the first colonies in Virginia and Massachusetts. In fact, American history is studded with interesting factoids about the role of both hemp and marijuana in American culture. For example, for a period of more than two centuries after the establishment of the Jamestown and Massachusetts Bay settlements, hemp was so widely grown and used that it was legal tender for payment of taxes and fines. Also, Virginia passed the Act for the Advancement of Manufactures in 1682, allowing the use of hemp, flax, wool, tar, and lumber as a form of remuneration, with each product assigned a specific value per weight unit. In the case of hemp, that value was four pence per pound of hemp. Other colonies eventually passed similar laws—Maryland in 1706, Rhode Island in 1721, and Massachusetts in 1737—so that hemp remained a legal form of tender for well over a century (Nelson 2016).

Some of the nation's leaders were so enamored of the plant that they either grew it themselves (George Washington and Thomas Jefferson) or used it in industries that they created (Benjamin Franklin). In the latter case, Franklin, who was instrumental in the establishment of at least 18 new paper mills, arranged for one such mill to use hemp to produce paper, thus reducing the colonies' dependence on England for a supply of the paper it needed for books, documents, and other purposes (Nelson 2011, Chapter 2). When the War of Independence placed severe demand on the rapid production of new uniforms for the colonies' soldiers, wives, sisters, and daughters banded together to have spinning bees to make cloth for their soldier husbands, sons, and brothers (Abel 1982).

The failure of the colonies to supply Mother England with the hemp it so desperately needed (see earlier discussion) eventually had historical significance in the relationship between the two countries. By the beginning of the 19th century, Russia had become the world's largest exporter of hemp, with neither England nor Spain nor, for that matter, the United States able to keep up with the demand for the product from their own domestic production. That imbalance of trade eventually had political consequences in 1807 with the signing of the Treaty of Tilset between Napoleon and Czar Alexander of Russia. One of the provisions of that treaty was that trade between Russia and England was no longer to be permitted. That provision was, of course, a disaster for England, which, at the time, was importing 90% of its hemp from Russia. As a way of getting around the provision, the English began commandeering American ships and crews, and sending them to Russia to purchase the hemp that the English needed. The controversy that developed over this issue between England and the United States eventually led to the outbreak of the War of 1812 (Herer 2001, Chapter 11).

As the United States developed after 1776, hemp production moved away from the East Coast, where it was replaced by more profitable crops, and began to develop in the Midwest. In particular, farms in Kentucky, Missouri, and Illinois began to supply the necessary hemp, primarily for the nation's sailing ships. The first hemp farms in the region were planted near Danville, Kentucky, in 1775, and their products were first advertised for sale 15 years later. Hemp was first grown in Missouri in 1835 and only five years later, the state was producing 12,500 tons of the product annually. The first hemp farms in

Illinois were planted somewhat later, after 1875, while other hemp farms were also attempted in Nebraska, Indiana, Texas, and a few other states (Dvorak 2004). By 1870, the U.S. Census showed that the primary hemp-producing states for that year were Kentucky (7,777 tons), Missouri (2,816 tons), and Tennessee (1,033 tons), with no other state producing more than 600 tons of the fiber (U.S. Census Bureau 1870, 85). The peak era for the production of hemp in the United States during the 19th century was probably the middle of the century. The census for 1850 found that, at the time, there were 8,327 plantations growing hemp for cloth, canvas, cordage, and a variety of other purposes. The total value of the hemp crop for 1850 was said to be $5,247,480, making it the 18th most popular agricultural crop behind corn, wheat, cotton, hay, oats, potatoes, wool, tobacco, and a number of other products (U.S. Census Bureau 1854, 176).

In spite of these apparently promising beginnings, hemp farming never really became as successful in the United States as its adherents had hoped. Growing and harvesting hemp was a labor-intensive activity, and most farmers were barely able to make a living growing the crop. Over time, hemp was gradually replaced on most farms by more profitable crops, such as cotton, jute, and sisal (Dvorak 2004). Political and cultural factors also had their effects. Just prior to and during the Civil War, the Confederate Congress prohibited the exportation of cotton, negating the use of the hemp ropes that had been a major use for hemps being grown in the Midwest. This disturbance in the hemp market was not relieved by the end of the war, and hemp farming never really recovered its earlier heights nor its proponents' most enthusiastic expectations (Abel 1980; Ehrensing 1998). By the end of the century, hemp farming had become a minor feature of the American agricultural industry, with the vast majority of the plant harvest being used to produce bird seed (still an important use of the product) and materials made from hemp seed oil, such as varnish.

The hemp industry in Canada ultimately did no better than its cousin business in the United States. As noted earlier, Samuel Champlain tried to encourage the growth of hemp in the new French colony, but his hopes were not realized. His successors, usually with equal enthusiasm for a new hemp empire in Canada, met similar discouragement, as did the English, when they took over the North American French colonies in 1763. The explanation for these failures was essentially the same as it was in the United States: farmers were simply not able to make a sufficient profit on hemp crops to justify the financial and labor costs of growing the crop. Even after a variety of appeals, including cash payments for raising the crops, grants of land on which to raise it, and appeals from church pulpits throughout the land, hemp farming continued to be a failure in Canada, as it was turning out to be in the United States (Abel 1980).

Hemp was not the only cannabis product that had reached the New World from Europe. Although its history is much different from that of hemp, marijuana also eventually became an important part of everyday life in the early United States during the mid-19th century. The impetus for that situation can be traced largely to the efforts of a single individual, the Irish physician William Brooke O'Shaughnessy. O'Shaughnessy served in India with the British East India Company from 1833 to 1841 and again from 1844 to 1860. While in India, he learned about the use of marijuana among native Indians for the treatment of a number of physical disorders. He attempted to formalize the use of marijuana for the treatment of his own patients by creating a variety of preparations and testing them on animals. He eventually became convinced of their value for the treatment of a variety of ailments, including pain and muscle spasms, as well as the vomiting and diarrhea associated with cholera that often led to a patient's death (O'Shaughnessy 1839; also see Mack and Joy 2001, 15–16).

O'Shaughnessy's research on marijuana interested and excited many of his colleagues, who designed and conducted their own experiments on the medical effects of the drug. Much of this research was summarized and analyzed toward the end of the century by a special committee appointed by the British government to study the reputed harmful effects on native Indians ingesting cannabis products. In their 1895 report, that committee, the Indian Hemp Drugs Commission, concluded that the use of hemp had no injurious physical, mental, or moral effects on users of the drug and that, in fact, it had a number of beneficial effects in the treatment of a variety of diseases and disorders (Young et al. 1894, 263–264).

The first medical conference in the United States devoted to the use of marijuana for medical purposes was held by the Ohio State Medical Society in 1860. The report of that meeting consists of a long list of personal testimonials by doctors who had had occasion to use the drug with patients or to perform experiments with the drug. Those reports covered a range from observations of frightening psychological events to almost miraculous cures of medical conditions that had been resistant to any other form of treatment (McMeens 1860).

Anecdotal reports from conferences like those of the Ohio State Medical Society were apparently sufficient to convince pharmaceutical companies to begin producing medications containing cannabis. Many histories of marijuana mention that some well-known pharmaceutical companies made available a variety of cannabis products beginning in the second half of the 19th century (e.g., Herer 2001). But the scope of that activity is difficult to envision. An invaluable source on this topic is the website, http://antiquecannabisbook.com/, which is a compendium of all known over-the-counter cannabis-containing medications available to the American public prior to adoption of the 1937 Marihuana Tax Act. The book lists more than 2,000 tinctures, extracts, home brews, corn remedies, anti-asthmatic cigarettes, cough syrups, migraine headache products, veterinary medicines, prescription drugs, and other products. Photographs of the containers for most of these products are also available, providing a better explanation as to their contents and their intended uses. A review of this work makes it abundantly clear that the use of cannabis-related products in the period between 1850 and 1937 was not somewhat rare and unusual but, instead, was a common component of the collection of medicines for treating a host of disorders (Antique Cannabis Book 2011).

From the perspective of the early 21st century, it is sometimes difficult to realize the extent to which cannabis products permeated the American marketplace in the late century. In his remarkable book, *Cannabis: A History*, Martin Booth points out that cannabis products were widely recommended for use by married couples in the last half of the 19th century. One author, the "quack" doctor Frederick C. Hollis, for example, wrote a wildly popular (more than 200 editions) book, *The Marriage Guide; Or, Natural History of Generation: A Private Instructor for Married Persons and Those about to Marry*, in which he encouraged readers to order from him an aphrodisiac in which hashish was a constituent (Booth 2005, 120–121). Perhaps most ironic of all was the effort by some members of the Women's Temperance Movement in the late 1800s to encourage men to replace their consumption of alcohol with the use of marijuana. The basis for this campaign was the belief that men would be less likely to abuse their wives and girlfriends if they were under the influence of marijuana rather than under the influence of alcohol (Booth 2005, 121).

Cannabis was present in a number of seemingly less innocuous products also. For example, beginning in the 1860s, the Gunjah Wallah Company of New York City began producing a "hasheesh candy" that it called the Arabian "Gunja" of Enchantment, which was a confectionized preparation of cannabis. Advertisements for the candy claimed that it was a "most pleasurable and harmless stimulant" that cured a number of medical conditions, including nervousness, weakness, and melancholy. It also "inspire[d] all classes with new life and energy" and acted as "a complete mental and physical invigorator" (Maple Sugar Hashish Candy 2016).

Industrial Hemp in the United States

Whatever appeals cannabis products may have had as patent medicines, tonics, marriage aphrodisiacs, or confectionary products, the greatest official public attention was always paid to hemp as an agricultural product. And statistical evidence suggests that that product had become a minor component of American agriculture by the end of the 19th century. As Table 1.2 shows, the amount of land devoted to hemp farming in the United States and the total amount of hemp produced remained relatively constant, and relatively small, from the last quarter of the 19th century to 1937, when the Marihuana

Table 1.2 Acreage Devoted to Hemp Farming and Hemp Production, 1876–1940

Period	Acreage (in acres)	Production (in tons)
1876–1880	15,000	7,000
1881–1885	11,000	5,000
1886–1890	16,000	7,500
1891–1895	11,000	5,000
1896–1900	10,000	4,500
1901–1905	12,000	5,500
1906–1910	10,000	4,500
1911–1913	10,000	4,500
1914–1918	10,500	8,500
1919–1923	8,600	3,800
1924–1928	4,300	1,800
1929–1933	1,200	500
1934–1938	7,100	600
1940	241	

Source: West, David P. "Industrial Hemp Farming: History and Practice." http://www.druglibrary.org/schaffer/hemp/indust/indhmpfr.htm. Accessed on May 11, 2016. West's data were apparently derived from J. Merritt Matthews and Herbert R. Mauersberger, *Matthews' Textile Fibers: Their Physical, Microscopical, and Chemical Properties*, 5th ed., New York: J. Wiley & Sons, 1947, which, in turn, apparently obtained its data from a U.S. Department of Agriculture Bulletin, B. B. Robinson and A. H. Wright, "Hemp, Its Production and Use as a Fiber Crop," 1941.

Tax Act (Chapter 2) was passed. For most of the 20th century, then, hemp farming was a largely insignificant component of the U.S. agricultural system.

For all intents and purposes, adoption of the Marihuana Tax Act of 1937 brought to an end the agricultural production of hemp in the United States. Although that act was aimed primarily at reducing the availability of marijuana as a recreational drug in the country, a side effect was the prohibition on the growing of cannabis plants that had any THC at all in them, and that included hemp plants. Even though the level of THC in hemp plants is very low (usually much less than 1%), it is not zero. This provision of the act accounts for the production of hemp in the country dropping to less than 250 tons by 1940.

World War II, however, created a challenge for the U.S. government with regard to the growing of hemp. A number of products important to the war effort, for example, sail canvas, rope, and military uniforms, had previously been made from imported hemp or other fibers from countries now occupied by the Japanese. To compensate for the loss of these fibers, the U.S. government decided to provide waivers from the 1937 act for farmers who were willing to start growing hemp again to meet wartime needs. In 1942, the U.S. Department of Agriculture (USDA) made a film *Hemp for Victory,* extolling the virtues of hemp as a farm crop and encouraging American farmers to start growing the crop as their contribution to the war effort. (The USDA and Library of Congress later denied that such a film was ever made, although they reversed that view when copies of the film were later donated to the library.) The film is in the public domain and can be viewed at a number of Internet sites (e.g., see Evans 1942).

The USDA campaign to increase hemp production was successful, with a huge upswing in the amount of land planted with the crop; the amount of hemp produced peaked during the middle of the war. (See Table 1.3.) However, the end of the war saw the reimposition of federal controls on the planting and harvesting of hemp, and production dropped essentially

Table 1.3   Hemp Production in the United States, 1931–1946

Year	Acreage Planted to Hemp	Production (long tons)
1931	320	122
1932	200	71
1933	140	47
1934	500	190
1935	700	273
1936	1,400	453
1937	1,300	465
1938	1,390	556
1939	1,440	572
1940	2,070	738
1941	7,400	3,308
1942	14,500	6,216
1943	146,200	62,803
1944	68,200	30,130
1945	6,500	2,232
1946	4,800	1,715

Source: *Agricultural Statistics*. 1948. Washington, DC: Government Printing Office, 1949, 327. Available online at http://usda.mannlib .cornell.edu/usda/nass/Agstat//1940s/1948/Agstat-04-23-1948.pdf. Accessed on May 11, 2016.

to zero over the following half century. A small hemp industry was maintained in Wisconsin until 1958, when it too was abandoned.

In response to pressure from producers of hemp products, however, that trend gradually began to change over time. While the federal government continued its ban on the production of cannabis in any form whatsoever, individual states have begun to consider ways in which the growing of hemp might be permitted. They have taken essentially two approaches to the problem, either allowing the planting of hemp crops for industrial purposes only (and risking federal objections to such laws and practices) or allowing the planting of such crops exclusively for research studies on hemp. The first such law was adopted in Vermont in 1996 when the state legislature adopted the Industrial Hemp Research Act, which became law without the governor's signature (or veto). Since that time, 28 states have taken some type of action allowing the growth of hemp for either industrial or commercial purposes or purposes of research on the plant (State Industrial Hemp Statutes 2016; [State Laws] 2015).

The federal government has also begun to change its views on industrial hemp, albeit much more slowly than have the states. In 2005, Representative Ron Paul (R-TX), with 11 co-sponsors, introduced the Industrial Hemp Farming Act. The bill never made it out of committee, but was re-introduced in 2007, 2009, and 2011, and in 2012, 2013, and 2014 in both the House and the Senate. None of these efforts made it through both houses of Congress, although a breakthrough did occur in 2014 with passage of the Farm Bill of 2013. That bill contained a section (Section 7606) that allowed states that had already adopted industrial hemp acts to carry out research programs on the growing of hemp. As of mid-2016, efforts are still proceeding in the Congress to adopt a more sweeping action that would allow the growing of industrial hemp with less than 0.3% THC ([Federal Law] 2015; [Section 7606] 2015).

Industrial Hemp Worldwide

Although the cultivation of hemp in the United States is still largely prohibited, the product is grown legally for industrial purposes in more than 30 other countries around the world, including Australia, Austria, Canada, Chile, China, France, Great Britain, North Korea, Russia, and Spain. Some of these countries never banned the growing and harvesting of hemp products, while others had such a ban at one time in the past, but have since revoked it (Johnson 2015). According to the latest data available from the UN Food and Agriculture Organization of the United Nations (FAO), the largest producer of hemp fiber in the world is China (16,000 tons in 2013), followed by North Korea (14,000 tons), Netherlands (10,273 tons), Chile (4,250 tons), and Romania (3,000 tons). France leads the world in the production of hempseed with a harvest of 48,264 tons in 2013, followed by China (16,000 tons), Chile (1,450 tons), and Ukraine (1,000 tons) ([Crop Data] 2015).

Conclusion

Humans have known about and grown the cannabis plant for more than 5,000 years. They have found a variety of uses for the plant, including the manufacture of clothing, sails, rope, and oils, as well as its inclusion in religious and ceremonial occasions. It has also been used by many cultures for many different medical applications. Finally, in the form of marijuana and hashish, humans have used the cannabis plant for recreational purposes. The United States as well as other nations and governmental units have banned some or all of these uses at one or another time in history. Over the centuries, the cannabis plant has gone from being a highly respected, sometimes holy object of veneration to one that is viewed with the greatest opprobrium by some cultures. Chapter 2 provides a review of how this dramatic change came about, and the issues the change has raised in modern societies around the world.

References

Abel, Ernest L. 1980. *Marijuana: The First Twelve Thousand Years.* New York: McGraw Hill. Available online at http://www.druglibrary.org/schaffer/hemp/history/first12000/abel.htm. Accessed on May 8, 2016.

Acomplia. 2016. Drugs.com. http://www.drugs.com/acomplia.html. Accessed on May 7, 2016.

"Antique Cannabis Book." 2016. http://antiquecannabisbook.com/. Accessed on May 11, 2016.

Backes, Michael. 2014. *Cannabis Pharmacy: The Practical Guide to Medical Marijuana.* New York: Black Dog & Leventhal Publishers.

Balfour, Edward Green. 1873. *The Cyclopaedia of India and of Eastern and Southern Asia, Commercial, Industrial, and Scientific: Products of the Mineral, Vegetable, and Animal Kingdoms, Useful Arts and Manufactures* (2nd ed.). London: B. Quaritch. (Text available through Google Books.)

Benet, Sula. 1975. "Early Diffusion and Folk Uses of Hemp." In Rubin, Vera, ed., *Cannabis and Culture.* The Hague: Mouton, 39–49. Also available online at http://khem-caigan.livejournal.com/3259.html. Accessed on May 8, 2016.

Bennett, Chris, Lynn Osburn, and Judith Osburn. 2001. *Green Gold: Marijuana in Magic & Religion.* Frazier Park, CA: Access Unlimited.

Bishop, J. Leander. 1861. *A History of American Manufactures from 1608 to 1860.* Philadelphia: Edward Young & Co. Available from Google Books. https://books.google.com/books?id=XAhFAQAAMAAJ&pg=PA300&lpg=PA300&dq=%22general+court+of+connecticut%22+hemp+1640&source=bl&ots=eSU5fvc8MM&sig=2fnuxWKa52hHdfR S4xYhCkFytQo&hl=en&sa=X&ved=0ahUKEwin9JazgN DMAhVDymMKHQimAnoQ6AEIMTAJ#v=onepage&q=%22general%20court%20of%20connecticut%22%20 hemp%201640&f=false. Accessed on May 10, 2016.

Booth, Martin. 2005. *Cannabis: A History.* New York: Picador Press.

Brecher, Edward M., and the Editors of Consumer Reports. 1972. *Licit and Illicit Drugs.* Mount Vernon, NY: Consumers Union.

"Cannabis Production and Markets in Europe." 2012. Luxembourg: Office for Official Publications of the

European Communities. Available online at http://www
.emcdda.europa.eu/attachements.cfm/att_166248_EN_
web_INSIGHTS_CANNABIS.pdf. Accessed on May 9,
2016.

"Cesamet." 2016. https://www.cesamet.com/patient-home
.asp. MEDA Pharmaceuticals. Accessed on May 7, 2016.

"Club des Hashischins—The Hashish Club." 2008. *420 Magazine*. https://www.420magazine.com/forums/cannabis-facts-and-information/74080-club-des-hashischins-hashish-club.html. Accessed on May 10, 2016.

Creighton, C. 1903. "On Indications of the Hachish-Vice
in the Old Testament." JANUS, Archives Internationales
pour l'Histoire de la Medecine et la Geographie Medicale,
Huitieme Annee. 1903: 241–246. Cited in http://www
.erowid.org/plants/cannabis/cannabis_spirit4.shtml.
Accessed on May 8, 2016.

["Crop Data"]. 2015. FAOSTAT. Food and Agriculture
Organization. http://faostat3.fao.org/download/Q/QC/E.
Accessed on May 12, 2016.

"DEA Clarifies Status of Hemp in the Federal Register."
2001. U.S. Drug Enforcement Administration. http://
www.justice.gov/dea/pubs/pressrel/pr100901.html. Accessed
on May 7, 2016.

"Definitions and Explanations." 2016. International
Association for Cannabinoid Medicines. http://www
.cannabis-med.org/science/science-definitions.htm. Accessed
on May 7, 2016.

Deitch, Robert. 2003. *Hemp: American History Revisited: The
Plant with a Divided History*. New York: Algora Publishing.

Dvorak, John. 2004. "America's Harried Hemp History."
http://www.hemphasis.net/History/harriedhemp.htm.
Accessed on May 11, 2016.

Ehrensing, Daryl T. 1998. "Feasibility of Industrial Hemp
Production in the United States Pacific Northwest." Station

Bulletin 681. Agricultural Experiment Station. Oregon State University. http://extension.oregonstate.edu/catalog/ html/sb/sb681/#History. Accessed on May 11, 2016.

Emboden, William A., Jr. 1972. "Ritual Use of *Cannabis sativa L.*" In Furst, Peter T., ed., *Flesh of the Gods.* New York: Praeger.

Evans, Raymond. 1942. "Hemp for Victory." https://archive .org/details/Hemp_for_victory_1942. Accessed on August 9, 2016.

["Federal Law."] 2015. Vote Hemp. http://www.votehemp .com/federal.html. Accessed on May 11, 2016.

Fleming, M. P., and R. C. Clarke. 1998. "Physical Evidence for the Antiquity of *Cannabis sativa* L. (Cannabaceae)." *Journal of the International Hemp Association.* 5(2). Available online at http://www.druglibrary.net/olsen/ HEMP/IHA/jiha5208.html. Accessed on May 8, 2016.

Freeman, Brian C., and Gwyn A. Beattie. 2008. "An Overview of Plant Defenses against Pathogens and Herbivores." APSnet. http://www.apsnet.org/edcenter/intro pp/topics/Pages/OverviewOfPlantDiseases.aspx. Accessed on May 7, 2016.

Goodman, Jordan, Paul E Lovejoy, and Andrew Sherratt. 2007. *Consuming Habits: Global and Historical Perspectives on How Cultures Define Drugs* (2nd ed.). London; New York: Routledge.

Green, Johnny. 2011. "Marijuana Cultivation Eradication in America Statistics." The Weed Blog. http://www.the weedblog.com/marijuana-cultivation-eradication-in-america-statistics/. Accessed on May 7, 2016.

Gumbiner, Jann. 2011. "History of Cannabis in India." *Psychology Today.* http://www.psychologytoday.com/blog/ the-teenage-mind/201106/history-cannabis-in-india. Accessed on May 8, 2016.

Hanuš, Lumir, and Raphael Mechoulam. 2008. "The Chemistry of Major New Players in Physiology." In Ikan, Raphael, ed., *Selected Topics in the Chemistry of Natural Products*. Singapore: World Scientific.

"Hashish." 2015. Drugs.com. http://www.drugs.com/hashish .html. Accessed on May 8, 2016.

Herer, Jack. 2001. *The Emperor Wears No Clothes* (11th ed.). Anaheim, CA: AH HA 2001. Also available online at http://www.jackherer.com/emperor-3/. Accessed on May 11, 2016.

"Hua Tuo." 2014. China Travel Guide. Famous Doctors. http://www.chinatraveldesigner.com/travel-guide/culture/ traditional-chinese-medicine/famous-doctors/hua-tuo.htm. Accessed on May 8, 2016.

Johnson, Renée. 2015. "Hemp as an Agricultural Commodity." Congressional Research Service. https://www.fas.org/sgp/ crs/misc/RL32725.pdf. Accessed on May 12, 2016.

Kirk, Don. 2014. *Hatches & Fly Patterns of the Great Smoky Mountains*. Mechanicsburg, PA: Headwater Books; Stackpole Books.

Le Page du Pratz, A. 1758. *History of Louisiana*. London: T. Becket. Available online at Google Books. https://books .google.com/books?id=o9YBAAAAMAAJ&pg=PA236& source=gbs_toc_r&cad=3#v=onepage&q=hemp&f=false. Accessed on May 10, 2016.

Li, Hui-Lin. 1974a. "An Archaeological and Historical Account of Cannabis in China." *Economic Botany*. 28(4): 437–448.

Li, Hui-Lin. 1974b. "The Origin and Use of Cannabis in Eastern Asia Linguistic-Cultural Implications." *Economic Botany*. 28(3): 293–301.

Lu, Xiaozhai, and Robert C. Clarke. 1995. "The Cultivation and Use of Hemp (*Cannabis sativa* L.) in Ancient China."

Journal of the International Hemp Association. 2(1): 26–30. Archived online at http://www.internationalhempassociation .org/jiha/iha02111.html. Accessed on May 8, 2016.

Mack, Alison, and Janet E. Joy. 2001. *Marijuana as Medicine?: The Science beyond the Controversy.* Washington, DC: National Academy Press.

"Maple Sugar Hashish Candy." 2016. ElectricEmperor. com. http://www.electricemperor.com/eecdrom/HTML/ EMP/12/ECH12_03.HTM. Accessed on May 11, 2016.

"Marijuana and the Bible." 1988. Ethiopian Zion Coptic Church. Available online at http://www.erowid.org/plants/ cannabis/cannabis_spirit2.shtml. Accessed on May 9, 2016.

"Marinol." 2016. AbbVie, Inc. http://www.marinol.com/. Accessed on May 7, 2016.

McMeens, R. R. 1860. "Report of the Ohio State Medical Committee on Cannabis Indica." *Transactions of the Fifteenth Annual Meeting of the Ohio State Medical Society at Ohio White Sulphur Springs, June 12 to 14, 1860.* Available online at http://www.onlinepot.org/medical/Dr_Tods_ PDFs/s3_1.pdf. Accessed on May 11, 2016.

Menelik, Girma Yohannes Iyassu. 2009. *Menelik Rastafarians: A Movement Tied with a [sic] Social and Psychological Conflicts.* [Munich]: GRIN.

Merlin, M. D. 2003. "Archaeological Evidence for the Tradition of Psychoactive Plant Use in the Old World." *Economic Botany.* 57(3): 295–323.

Nelson, Robert A. 2016. *A History of Hemp.* Rex Research. http://rexresearch.com/hhist/hhist2.htm#congress. Accessed May 10, 2016.

"98 Percent of All Domestically Eradicated Marijuana Is 'Ditch-weed,' DEA Admits." NORML. http://norml.org/news/ 2006/09/07/98-percent-of-all-domestically-eradicated-mari juana-is-ditchweed-dea-admits. Accessed on May 7, 2016.

Oner, S. T., ed. 2013. *Cannabis indica: The Essential Guide to the World's Finest Marijuana Strains* (2nd ed.). San Francisco: Green Candy Press.

O'Shaughnessy, W. B. 1839. "On the Preparations of the Indian Hemp, or Gunjah." Schaffer Library of Drug Policy. http://www.druglibrary.org/schaffer/history/e1850/gunjah.htm. Accessed on May 10, 2016.

Pickett, Margaret F., and Dwayne W. Pickett. 2011. *The European Struggle to Settle North America: Colonizing Attempts by England, France and Spain, 1521–1608.* Jefferson, NC: McFarland & Company.

Rabelais, Master Francis. 1894. *Five Books of the Lives, Heroic Deeds and Sayings of Gargantua and His Son Pantagruel.* Derby: Moray Press. Available at Project Gutenberg. http://www.gutenberg.org/files/1200/1200-h/p3.htm. Accessed on May 9, 2016.

Rudgley, Richard. 1998. *Encyclopedia of Psychoactive Substances.* London: Abacus.

["Section 7606"]. 2015. Vote Hemp. http://www.votehemp.com/2014_farm_bill_section_7606.html. Accessed on May 11, 2016.

Shrank, Cathy. 2006. "Bullein's Bulwark." (Originally, in full: Bullein's Bulwark of Defence against All Sickness, Soreness, and Wounds That Dooe Daily Assault Mankinde). http://www.hrionline.ac.uk/origins/DisplayServlet?id=Bullein4033&type=normal. Accessed on May 9, 2016.

Smith, Frederick Porter. 1911. *Chinese Materia Medica: Vegetable Kingdom.* Shanghai: American Presbyterian Mission Press. Available online at http://www.archive.org/stream/chinesemateriame00stuauoft/chinesemateriame00stuauoft_djvu.txt. Accessed on May 8, 2016.

Spicer, Leah. 2002. "Historical and Cultural Uses of Cannabis and the Canadian 'Marijuana Clash.' Report prepared for the Senate Special Committee on Illegal Drugs." http://

www.parl.gc.ca/Content/SEN/Committee/371/ille/library/
spicer-e.htm#2. Central Asia. Accessed on May 8, 2016.

Stafford, Ned. 2009. "Synthetic Cannabis Mimic Found in
Herbal Incense." Cannabis Culture. http://www.cannabis
culture.com/v2/news/synthetic-cannabis-mimic-found-
in-herbal-incense. Accessed on May 7, 2016.

Stanley, Alessandra. 1994. "Moscow Journal; Tattooed Lady,
2,000 Years Old, Blooms Again." *New York Times*. Available online at http://www.nytimes.com/1994/07/13/world/
moscow-journal-tattooed-lady-2000-years-old-blooms-
again.html. Accessed on May 8, 2016.

"State Industrial Hemp Statutes." 2016. National Conference
of State Legislatures. http://www.ncsl.org/research/agri
culture-and-rural-development/state-industrial-hemp-
statutes.aspx. Accessed on May 11, 2016.

["State Laws"]. 2015. Vote Hemp. http://www.votehemp
.com/state.html. Accessed on May 11, 2016.

"The Third Voyage of Discovery Made by Captaine Jacques
Cartier, 1541." 2003. Wisconsin Historical Society.
Available online at http://www.americanjourneys.org/pdf/
AJ-028.pdf. Accessed on May 10, 2016.

"Tudor: 1485 to 1558." 2007. http://www.johnhmoore
.co.uk/hele/tudor.htm. Accessed on May 9, 2016.

United States v. Rush. 1984. 738 F.2d 497. Opinion at http://
www.ethiopianzioncopticchurch.org/Cases/rush.aspx.
Accessed on May 9, 2016.

U.S. Census Bureau. 1854. *Statistical View of the United
States*. Washington, DC: Beverley Tucker, Senate Printer.
Available online at http://www2.census.gov/prod2/decen
nial/documents/1850c-06.pdf. Accessed on May 11,
2016.

U.S. Census Bureau. 1870. *The Statistics of the Wealth and
Industry of the United States*. Washington, DC: Government
Printing Office. Available online at http://www2.census

.gov/prod2/decennial/documents/1870c-02.pdf. Accessed on May 11, 2016.

Weiss, Brian L. 1980. [Summary of Psychiatric Examination of Ethiopian Zion Coptic Church Members]. http://www .ethiopianzioncopticchurch.org/Agency/amicus_19880713_ ex07.pdf. Accessed on May 9, 2016.

Young, W. Mackworth, et al. 1894. *Report of the Indian Hemp Drugs Commission, 1893–94.* [n.p.]: Government Central Printing Office, 1894. Also available online at http://www .drugtext.org/Table/Indian-Hemp-Commission-Report/.

The inspection was expected to be routine. For years, the Canadian company, Kenex, Ltd., had been shipping hemp seed to the Nutiva company in Sebastopol, California, for use in its bird seed for years. Jean Laprise, the president of Kenex, expected the present shipment of hemp seed to clear customs at the U.S. border without any problems. So Mr. Laprise was a bit shocked, to say the least, when U.S. custom agents impounded all 40,000 pounds of hemp seed and shipped them for storage in a Detroit, Michigan, warehouse. The hemp seed contained THC, custom agents said, so it could not be admitted to the United States under a provision of the 1970 Controlled Substances Act (CSA). The news was a surprise to Mr. Laprise at least in part because hemp growers in Canada have long been scrupulous in ensuring that their products contain a very low level of THC, always less than 1%. The hemp seed in question had been analyzed and was found to contain about 0.0014%, not enough, according to one observer, to "give a bird a buzz" (Wren 1999). What was the logic behind the decision to impound a legitimate agricultural product from Canada that has such a modest likelihood of being used as an illegal drug in the United States? (For additional examples of the U.S. campaign against hemp products, also see Barnett 2006; Bonné 2002.)

A woman puffs on a fake marijuana cigarette during the NYC Pride Parade in New York on June 26, 2016. (AP Photo/Seth Wenig)

History of Cannabis Prohibition

Throughout history, humans have had a profound love/hate relationship with the cannabis plant. On the one hand, it has provided a host of valuable materials in the form of hemp, which has been used for cloth, twine, rope, cordage, sails, yarn, body-care products, paper, pet foods, hemp seed oil, and, of course, bird seed. In the form of marijuana and hashish, it has provided a gateway to out-of-body experiences that have been understood as a simple "high"—an escape from the often less-than-pleasant humdrum of everyday life—or a window to the sacred. But many cultures have also viewed such experiences as too much of an escape from reality, too much like the tale of Icarus, who flew too far from Earth's surface and too close to the heavenly orb, losing his life in the process. And so, the history of *Cannabis sativa* is as much a story of caution, risk, and prohibition as it is of anything else.

Should the use of cannabis by humans be prohibited? If so, which forms of the plant and under what circumstances? These questions are as controversial in the early 21st century as they have been throughout human history. Some people argue that the choice of using or not using hemp, marijuana, and/or hashish is one that should be left to individuals; governments have no authority to prohibit the use of a plant that humans have used safely for millennia. Others are more cautious in their views, suggesting that hemp is certainly a harmless and valuable material, although other forms of cannabis are more problematic. Still others see useful applications of marijuana as a therapeutic agent, although its uses as a recreational drug pose more difficult issues. Finally, other individuals argue that the cannabis plant poses such great dangers—even to birds—that all forms should be banned under all circumstances. Understanding historical attitudes about prohibitions on the use of cannabis provides a perspective from which to understand today's debate about the plant.

Prohibitions on Cannabis: Ancient Cultures

Throughout most of human history, the use of cannabis products has not been a matter of controversy. Hemp has long been almost universally considered a valuable material for making a host of useful products. And healers of all kinds—from shamans to modern physicians—have commonly turned to marijuana as an important tool in their *materia medica*. Even the use of marijuana to achieve out-of-body experiences, as is done in religious ceremonies, has generally been more widely praised than condemned. In spite of this generally positive view of the cannabis plant, there have always been cultures in which negative attitudes outweighed positive beliefs, and the plant fell into disrepute among leaders of the society and/or the general public.

As an example, some historians believe that acceptance and/or tolerance for the use of marijuana in achieving psychoactive effects began to wane in China during the Han dynasty (206 BCE–220 CE) largely because Chinese society was developing a more rational outlook on life and saw a consequent reduction in dependence on shamanism (and hence, on psychoactive drugs). This change eventually resulted in the view that marijuana was a "disreputable" herb not worthy of use by true healers (Touw 1981, 23).

Early Islamists also seem to have taken a somewhat neutral view toward cannabis since it was apparently not specifically prohibited in the Qu'ran. Indeed, in view of the Prophet's specific prohibition of the use of alcohol, the use of cannabis seems to have become at first the psychoactive drug of choice within early Islamic society. That situation changed over time, however, as more and more scholars adopted the view that the traditional Qu'ranic prohibition of khamr (literally, "fermented grape") referred not only to alcoholic beverages, but also to any substance that "befogs the mind" (Naguib 2008). That interpretation obviously added cannabis to the list of substances forbidden to believers in Islam. (The controversy over the true interpretation of khamr and the implication of that interpretation remains a matter of some controversy today. See, for example, Is Marijuana Haram? 2016.) In spite of the Islamic position, however, cannabis appears far more likely to have been viewed as a beneficial (or, at least, a harmless) natural product until the early 20th century. Its worst effects generally seemed to be seen as erratic behavior when used in excess, especially by mentally unstable individuals already predisposed to antisocial actions.

International Concerns, 1910–1925

That situation changed significantly during the first two decades of the 20th century, when the world began to consider the potentially harmful (to individuals) and dangerous (to society) consequences of narcotic abuse, especially from derivatives of the coca plant (cocaine) and opiates such as opium and heroin. Similar fears about the risks and dangers of other drugs, such as alcohol, nicotine (tobacco), and caffeine (coffee) had largely run their course before the end of the 19th century. Such concerns had led to the bans, among many possible examples, on the drinking of coffee in Egypt in 1524, and on the use of tobacco throughout Christendom in 1624 (Christen et al. 1982, 825; Hanauer and Pickthall 2007, 291–292).

The first international meeting called to discuss and act on the (perceived) rising threat of narcotic drugs was the International Opium Commission, held in Shanghai in 1909. That meeting was held at the instigation of the U.S. government and was attended by representatives from 12 nations in addition to the United States: Austria-Hungary, China, France, Germany, Italy, Japan, Netherlands, Persia (now Iran), Portugal, Russia, Siam (now Thailand), and the United Kingdom. The meeting was careful not to call itself a conference, which would have permitted the drafting and signing of an official international treaty. It did, however, unanimously adopt a statement of principle in opposition to the trade of opium products among nations of the world (The Shanghai Opium Commission 2016).

One of the recommendations produced at the Shanghai meeting was that a follow-up conference be held to further consider the problem of narcotics trade and use around the world. That meeting was held in The Hague, the Netherlands, in 1912. It was chaired by Bishop Brent of the United States, who had also chaired the Shanghai meeting. Attendees included the same nations that had assembled in Shanghai, except for Austria-Hungary. The treaty entered into force two years later in five countries: China, Honduras, the Netherlands, Norway, and the United States. In 1919, the treaty received much wider acceptance when it became part of the Treaty of Versailles, which ended World War I. At that point, it took effect in 60 nations worldwide. The United States remained a signatory to the original Hague treaty, although it was not then (and never was) a member of the League of Nations, under which the treaty was administered.

An effort to include cannabis in the Hague Treaty had been made by the United States, which suggested that it be included among the narcotic drugs for which information would be exchanged among signatories to the treaty. (Marijuana is not a narcotic, but it has long been so labeled, especially by individuals and organizations that support increased control over its sale and use.) That proposal was rejected, however, as other members of the convention were not convinced that there was as yet enough information about the risks posed by cannabis or its use throughout the world. They did agree, however, to recommend that additional research be conducted on cannabis with a view to reconsider the U.S. recommendation at a later date. That research was never actually carried out (The Cannabis Problem: A Note on the Problem and the History of International Action 2016).

Cannabis finally received attention as a potentially harmful and dangerous drug at the international level just prior to the 1925 International Convention on Narcotics Control, sponsored by the League of Nations and held in Geneva, Switzerland. The subject of marijuana—then commonly known as

Indian hemp—was raised by delegates from Egypt and Turkey, who told spine-tingling tales of the disastrous consequences of its use in their countries. The Egyptian delegate, Dr. Mohamed Abdel Salam El Guindy, for example, claimed that the use of hashish was responsible for most of the cases of insanity occurring in his country. He described the typical cannabis user as follows:

> His eye is wild and the expression of his face is stupid. He is silent; has no muscular power; suffers from physical ailments, heart troubles, digestive troubles etc; his intellectual faculties gradually weaken and the whole organism decays. The addict very frequently becomes neurasthenic and eventually insane. (Pietschmann [2009], 54; also see Kendell 2003, 144–145)

Warnings such as these carried the day among the Geneva delegates, and they devoted two chapters of the final treaty (IV and V) to recommending a ban on all uses of cannabis except for medical and scientific uses, which were not defined. The actual claims about the effects of cannabis put forward by Dr. El Guindy—which differed dramatically from those contained in the 1894 Indian Hemp Drugs Commission Report— were not investigated before the Geneva delegates adopted the final treaty. The United States never signed the Geneva Convention because it was not a member of the League at the time and also because U.S. delegates thought that the conference's attitudes about and approach to the control of dangerous drugs was too lenient, certainly more lenient than policies then being developed at home.

Prohibition of Cannabis: The United States

Indeed, by the first decade of the 20th century, a number of U.S. politicians, law enforcement officials, social reformers, and members of the general public had become convinced that mind-altering drugs of all kinds posed a severe danger, not only to the individuals who used them, but far more importantly, to the stability of society itself. These individuals and the organizations they founded and/or represented were instrumental not only in calling the Shanghai and Hague meetings, but also, ultimately, in the adoption of the Eighteenth Amendment to the U.S. Constitution, prohibiting the sale of alcohol, in 1919, and adoption of the Harrison Narcotics Act of 1914, which established a tax on the production, manufacture, compounding, importation, distribution, and sale of cocaine in the United States. And, although the first federal law limiting the use of cannabis in the United States was not passed until 1937, a movement to label the drug as a dangerous narcotic had been well under way many years earlier. That movement did not develop in a vacuum in the United States but, instead, was deeply associated with a more general cultural trend toward the prohibition of any type of mind-altering substance. In their classic analysis of the process by which marijuana use was criminalized in the United States, Bonnie and Whitebread (1970) have pointed out that

> At each stage of its development marijuana policy has been heavily influenced by other social issues because the drug has generally been linked with broader cultural patterns. . . . In fact, the facility with which marijuana policy was initiated directly related to the astoundingly sudden and extreme alteration of public narcotics and alcohol policy between 1900 and 1920. (Bonnie and Whitebread 1970, Chapter 3)

Until the 1930s, concerns about the risks posed by "dangerous drugs" in the United States—as in the rest of the world—focused almost entirely on cocaine and the opiates; cannabis was rarely mentioned. In the United States, marijuana was not mentioned in any federal drug legislation until the Uniform Narcotics Drug Act was adopted in 1932. That act encouraged individual states to bring their drug laws into agreement with the 1922 Narcotic

Drug Import and Export Act, which had placed restrictions on the distribution of cocaine and opiates. (Cannabis was not mentioned in the act.) At the time, state drug laws differed widely from each other and from the restrictions included in the Narcotic Drug Import and Export Act. One of the provisions of the 1932 act dealt with cannabis, including it with cocaine and opiates, a provision that had not been included in the 1922 act. No explanation was given in the act as to the reason for this broadening, and the act was adopted with the addition of cannabis (Bonnie and Whitebread 1970, Chapter 4).

The legal status of cannabis at the state level during the first three decades of the 20th century was different from that at the national level. As early as 1913, some local communities and states had begun to adopt legislation criminalizing the growing, distribution, and/or use of cannabis products. What were the forces, Bonnie and Whitebread (1970) have asked, that motivated this trend toward the criminalization of marijuana, a trend that eventually became an aggressive national movement by the 1930s?

Their research points to three such factors: class and racial prejudices; concerns that drug users would switch from more tightly controlled drugs like cocaine and heroin to marijuana (the theory of "substitution"); and an international trend toward the criminalization of marijuana, as expressed in the 1912 Hague Convention and the 1925 Geneva Convention (Bonnie and Whitebread 1970, Chapter 3). Bonnie and Whitebread point out that the earliest laws criminalizing the use of marijuana were passed in the western states, at a time when Mexican immigration was increasing dramatically, largely because of the number of Mexican nationals who were fleeing the revolution of 1910 through 1920. At the time, marijuana was used almost exclusively by these immigrants, and that practice was quickly associated with a generally agreed-upon perception that Mexicans were poorly educated and of low moral character. Their use of marijuana as a recreational drug was *ipso facto*, an indication of the risks it posed. Bonnie and Whitebread provide a number of specific examples in which states passed anti-cannabis laws based on clearly racist views with little or no public debate, or even thoughtful discussion within legislatures. They cite a newspaper report of the debate in the Montana legislature in 1929 over criminalizing marijuana use. One legislator noted that a Mexican who has smoked marijuana "thinks he has just been elected president of Mexico so he starts out to execute all his political enemies." In response, "[e]verybody laughed and the bill was recommended for passage" (Bonnie and Whitebread 1970, Chapter 3). Based on the many examples they found, Bonnie and Whitebread concluded that "legislative action and approval [of anti-cannabis laws] were essentially kneejerk responses uninformed by scientific study or public debate and colored instead by racial bias and sensationalistic myths" (Bonnie and Whitebread 1970, Chapter 3). In any case, laws prohibiting the sale of marijuana swept through the United States between 1914 and 1931, with 26 states including some form of prohibition in their laws.

Such laws were not restricted to the western states, although the motivation for laws in the East was considerably different from those in the West. The most common basis for anticannabis laws in the East, Bonnie and Whitebread (1970) found, was fear that marijuana use would grow if laws related to cocaine and opiates were tightened (as was occurring at the time). The argument is one that is still heard today, namely that drug users will switch to a new drug (e.g., marijuana) as other drugs (e.g., cocaine and heroin) are more tightly controlled. This philosophy, Bonnie and Whitebread believe, was the primary basis for anticannabis laws passed in Maine, Massachusetts, Michigan, New York, Ohio, Rhode Island, and Vermont in the period between 1914 and 1947. For example, when New York City added marijuana to its list of prohibited drugs in 1914, the *New York Times* commented that users of cannabis "are now hardly numerous enough to count, but they are likely to increase as other narcotics become harder to obtain" (Sanitary Code Amendments 1914, 8).

Cannabis Legislation in the States

Legislators in the United States awakened to the (supposed) threat posed by cannabis began looking for ways of dealing with this new problem as early as the 1910s. Those efforts took two general approaches: taxation on the production, distribution, and (less commonly) use of marijuana, as a way of reducing demand for the drug, and outright bans on cannabis in any and all forms. The federal government was relatively timid in acting on the cannabis problem, not passing the first national law on the drug until 1937. A number of local communities and states, however, had begun to take action against cannabis much earlier. The first state law prohibiting the use of marijuana was adopted in California in 1913. The law was actually a technical amendment to the state's poison laws, proposed by the state's Board of Pharmacy. It was apparently inspired by concerns over the use of narcotic drugs by the state's Chinese residents (Gieringer 1999, 2). The law received essentially no public attention at the time, and historians often pass it over and point to a law adopted in Utah in 1915 as the first state law dealing with cannabis.

The Utah law has become the subject of considerable controversy among cannabis historians. According to some authorities, the motivation behind this law was somewhat different from that leading to other anticannabis laws in the West (xenophobia). These authorities suggest that a number of Mormon missionaries returning from assignments to Mexico in the mid-1910s brought with them the practice of smoking marijuana, a practice that they had learned in Mexico and that was quickly condemned by the church as opposed to doctrine (as was and is the use of all other kinds of psychoactive substances). In any case, according to this reading of history, the synod of the Mormon church banned the use of marijuana among all church members in August 1915, and two months later, the state legislature passed similar legislation (as was commonly the case with other church prohibitions at the time in the state). The classic statement of this view can be found in Whitebread (1995).

A number of observers have rejected this analysis of the origin of Utah's early drug law. They suggest that religious attitudes had little or nothing to do about its evolution. They argue that the Utah law may actually have been drafted on the model of the earlier California law, and that Utah legislators actually were barely familiar with cannabis when they adopted the law. According to one writer arguing for this view of history:

> There is no hint whatsoever that Utah's law—which, you now see, did not specially target marijuana, and did not even show any particular awareness of marijuana, but merely incorporated the language used by other entities to name marijuana among a whole host of regulated drugs— was spurred by religious concerns. There is no discussion of marijuana, no complaint about its use, no report of arrest for intoxicated behavior other than alcohol or Chinese opium use, no marijuana-related editorials, in Utah's newspapers before the passage of the 1915 law. (Parshell 2009)

Federal Cannabis Laws

During the first third of the 20th century, then, a movement developed throughout the United States in which the public's perception of cannabis was transformed from a medically useful, commercially valuable, relatively harmless recreational drug into a highly dangerous product on a par with cocaine, heroin, and opium. A key figure in that movement was Harry J. Anslinger, the first commissioner of the U.S. Treasury's Federal Bureau of Narcotics (FBN). Anslinger had attended (but not graduated from) Altoona (Pennsylvania) Business College and worked at the Pennsylvania Railroad. Physically ineligible for military service in World War I (he was blind in one eye), Anslinger volunteered instead to work at the War Department. He was later transferred to the State Department because of his fluency in German. After the war, he was transferred again, this time to the Department of the Treasury, where he became interested in problems related to the transport and use of illegal substances, such as alcohol (then illegal because of the Eighteenth Amendment), cocaine, and opiates. In 1929, Anslinger was appointed assistant commissioner in the U.S. Bureau of Prohibition (created by the Eighteenth Amendment), a position he held only briefly before being selected as the first commissioner of the newly created Federal Bureau of Narcotics in 1930. Anslinger remained at his post until 1970, five years before his death. Throughout that time, he remained an ardent and aggressive foe of all forms of mind-altering substances, including marijuana.

During this period of time, Anslinger continued to carry on an attack against the production, distribution, and use of cannabis that was strong on invective and weak on scientific accuracy. His broadsides against the use of marijuana carry strong racist tones of the type identified by Bonnie and Whitebread (1970), only focusing more strongly on the supposedly low moral character of African Americans. He also drew special attention to other supposedly corrupt groups of individuals, such as jazz musicians (who were generally also African American), whom "everyone acknowledged" as being of poor moral character. (See, for example, Guither 2012; Harry J. Anslinger's Quotes/Quotations 2010; Statement of H. J. Anslinger 2016; for an analysis of the racist basis of many of Anslinger's comment, see especially Moran 2011.) An example of the image that Anslinger attempted to portray of marijuana can be found in his testimony before the Ways and Means Committee of the U.S. House of Representatives during its consideration of the 1937 Marihuana Tax Act (which was later adopted). The drug, he said, first produces feelings of "well-being [and] a happy, jovial mood." However, he went on, that euphoria is soon replaced by much less salubrious emotions, including:

a more-or-less delirious state . . . during which [users] are temporarily, at least, irresponsible and liable to commit violent crimes . . . [and] releases inhibitions of an antisocial nature which dwell within the individual . . . Then follow errors of sense, false convictions and the predominance of extravagant ideas where all sense of value seems to disappear.

The deleterious, even vicious, qualities of the drug render it highly dangerous to the mind and body upon which it operates to destroy the will, cause one to lose the power of connected thought, producing imaginary delectable situations and gradually weakening the physical powers. Its use frequently leads to insanity. (quoted in Taxation of Marihuana 1937)

The Marihuana Tax Act of 1937

By the mid-1930s, Anslinger's efforts (and those of his colleagues in the fight against cannabis) had begun to bear fruit. The first concrete accomplishment in that fight was passage in 1937 of the Marihuana Tax Act. (Note that the modern spelling of the substance, *marijuana*, is of relatively recent origin, with an "h" instead of a "j" being more common historically.) Consideration of the act before the House Ways and Means Committee (presented first as H.R. 6385 and later re-designated as H.R. 6906) began on April 27, 1937, and ran for a total of six days. In his analysis of the hearings on the bill, marijuana historian and then professor of law at the University of Southern California Charles Whitebread has commented on the relatively brief amount of time spent in hearing testimony, "one hour, on each of two mornings," a surprisingly short time for consideration of a major bill (Whitebread 1995). During this period, testimony was received from three groups of individuals, representatives of the U.S. government, including especially Harry Anslinger, but also including the consulting chemist at the Department of the Treasury and the assistant general counsel at Treasury; representatives from the hemp industry, including rope-making, hemp seed oil, and other companies; and representatives from the medical community.

This testimony was almost universally supportive of the bill, especially, of course, from Anslinger and other government officials. Hemp company representatives were also supportive, arguing that they would have no problem obtaining hemp for their products from the Far East (a proposition that proved to be dubious with the start of World War II four years later) and replacements for hemp seed oil (the bird seed industry requested and received an exemption by promising to use only "denatured" seeds, that is, those that were free of THC) (Whitebread 1995). The only objection to the pending bill came from Dr. William C. Woodward, a representative of the American Medical Association (AMA), which had also submitted a letter to the committee opposing the bill. Woodward pointed out that there was no scientific evidence suggesting that marijuana is a harmful drug, so there was no reason to ban its manufacture and use.

Woodward's testimony was apparently not what the committee wanted to hear. During one of his appearances before the committee, one member observed: "Doctor, if you can't say something good about what we are trying to do, why don't you go home?" Immediately following that observation, a second member said, "Doctor, if you haven't got something better to say than that, we are sick of hearing you" (quoted in Whitebread 1995). Other testimony had apparently convinced the committee of the validity and necessity of H.R. 6385/ H.R. 6906, and the bill was adopted on October 1, 1937.

The bill that Congress finally passed did not specifically outlaw the production, sale, or consumption of marijuana, but it did impose a complex system of taxes and regulations. Anyone involved in any of these activities had to register with the federal government and pay a tax for each type of activity. For example, anyone who grew or processed a cannabis product had to pay a tax of $24 annually (equivalent to about $360 in current dollars). The tax for sale of a cannabis product to anyone who already held a license was $1 per transaction (about $15 in current dollars), but $100 (about $1,500 in current dollars) to anyone who did not hold such a license (Marihuana Tax Act of 1937 1937, Section 2).

Federal authorities did not take long to put the Marihuana Tax Act into effect. On October 1, 1937—the day the bill was adopted—they arrested two men in Denver, Colorado, for possession (Moses Baca) and selling (Samuel Caldwell) marijuana. Judge Foster Symes sentenced Baca to 18 months in jail, and Caldwell to four years at hard labor and a $1,000 fine ("The First Pot POW" 2016). Note that some observers dispute this story. (See, for example, Compilation of Publications, Interviews, Criminal Files and Photographs of Moses Baca & Samuel Caldwell 2010.)

1951 Boggs Amendment to the Harrison Narcotic Act

In the three decades following the adoption of the Marihuana Tax Act of 1937, Congress struggled to refine and improve U.S. drug laws to deal with two major questions: (1) What is the status of marijuana in comparison with other illegal drugs, such as cocaine and the opiates?, and (2) What is the most effective mechanism for reducing the spread of marijuana use among the general population? This struggle led to a number of legislative acts, the next most important of which chronologically was the Boggs Act, an amendment to the Narcotic Drugs Import and Export Act of 1932. The Boggs bill was inspired by an apparent increase in drug use among young people in the United States after the conclusion of World War II. Representative Boggs introduced into the Congressional Record reports from local media and authorities documenting this increase. He summarized these reports by saying that "[t]he most shocking part about these figures is the fact that there has been an alarming increase in drug addiction among younger persons. . . . We need only to recall what we have read in the papers in the past week to realize that more and more younger people are falling into the clutches of unscrupulous dope peddlers" (U.S. Congress 1951, 8198). Boggs went on to say that the solution to the mushrooming problem of youth drug addiction was the imposition by Congress of more severe penalties for drug use:

> Short sentences do not deter. In districts where we get good sentences the traffic does not flourish. . . . There should be a minimum sentence for the second offense. The commercialized transaction, the peddler, the smuggler, those who traffic in narcotics, on the second offense if there were a minimum sentence of 5 years without probation or parole, I think it would just about dry up the traffic. (U.S. Congress 1951, 8198; for a more completion discussion of this topic, see Bonnie and Whitebread 1970, Chapter 6)

The Boggs Act was passed by Congress and became law on November 2, 1951, as 21 U.S.C. 174. The Boggs Act was significant in a number of ways, primarily in the dramatic increase in penalties it provided for drug possession and use. It established a minimum mandatory sentence of two years for simple possession of marijuana, cocaine, or heroin, with a maximum sentence of five years; a minimum of 5 years and a maximum of 10 years for a second offense; and a minimum of 10 years and a maximum of 15 years for a third offense. In addition, the Boggs Act was significant in that it was the first time that marijuana, cocaine, and opiates had been included together in a single piece of federal legislation.

The Boggs amendment was important not only as a piece of federal legislation, but also because it served as a model that the federal government urged states to use for their own state laws. Many states took up the suggestion. Between 1953 and 1956, 26 states passed "mini-Boggs" bills. Some of the bills carried penalties significantly more severe than those in the federal bill. The law in Louisiana, for example, provided for a 5- to 99-year sentence without the possibility of parole, probation, or suspension of sentence for sale or possession of any illegal substance (Bonnie and Whitebread 1974, 210). Similarly, Virginia adopted a mini-Boggs law that made possession of marijuana the most severely punished crime in the state. While first-degree murder earned a mandatory 15-year minimum sentence and rape earned a mandatory 10-year sentence, possession of marijuana drew a mandatory minimum of 20 years, and sale of the drug drew a mandatory minimum of 40 years (Whitebread 1995).

Narcotics Control Act of 1956

One of the signature legislative events of the early 1950s was the appointment of the U.S. Senate Special Committee to Investigate Crime in Interstate Commerce, chaired by Senator Estes Kefauver (D-TN) and widely known, therefore, as the Kefauver Committee. The committee had been formed due to a growing concern in the U.S. Congress and throughout the United States about the growing threat posed by organized crime. The issue of narcotic drugs became involved in the committee's deliberations partly because a number of antidrug activists, such as Harry Anslinger, attempted to show that drugs were the primary cause of most crime in the United States and half of all crime in U.S. metropolitan areas (King 1972, Chapters 14 and 16).

The committee's final report included a total of 22 recommendations for action by the federal government, and 7 additional recommendations for state action. Of those recommendations, only one was ever enacted into law, the Boggs amendment of 1951 (discussed previously). Another, possibly more important long-term effect of the Kefauver Committee's deliberations was an increasing awareness of the nation's (supposed) growing drug problem. Interestingly enough, not everyone deemed drugs to be as much of a threat as did Anslinger, Boggs, and a number of other legislators. In the period following the Kefauver hearings, these individuals and the organizations they represented (e.g., the American Bar Association, the American Medical Association, and the U.S. Public Health Service) began to call for a relaxation in the battle against illegal drug use, even calling for the legalization of some types of drug use. This movement produced pro-decriminalization articles, such as "Make Dope Legal," "Should We Legalize Narcotics?," "We're Bungling the Narcotics Problem . . . How Much of a Menace Is the Drug Menace? . . . The Dope Addict-Criminal or Patient?," "This Problem of Narcotic Addiction–Let's Face It Sensibly," and "Let's Stop This Narcotics Hysteria!" (King 1972, Chapter 14). These articles often called for dealing with drug abuse as a medical, social, or psychological problem rather than as a crime. The Bureau of Narcotics and its allies, as would be expected, fought back vigorously against this view of substance abuse, with its own release of fact sheets, articles, and other publications reiterating the threat that illegal drug use posed to human health and public stability.

This battle came to a head in February 1955, when Senator Price Daniel (D-TX) submitted Senate Resolution 60, calling for the formation of a committee to investigate ways of expanding and improving the nation's laws that dealt with drug abuse. A year later, the Daniel subcommittee submitted its report to the full Senate. That report contained much of the verbiage that had been used when discussing drug abuse over the preceding two decades. It said that drug abuse was spreading with "cancerous rapidity" throughout the nation. It called for more severe penalties for drug abuse and for those who could not be cured of their habit, placement "in a quarantine type of confinement or isolation" (King 1972, Chapter 16). The subcommittee also devoted about half of its final report to disputing the position that drug abuse should be considered as something other than a criminal problem. It concluded that

> to permit a governmental institution to engage in the ghastly traffic in narcotics is to give the Government the authority to render unto its citizens certain death without due process of law. (quoted in King 1972, Chapter 16)

Congress was apparently convinced by these arguments, passing the Narcotic Control Act of 1956 without dissent. The act was signed by President Dwight D. Eisenhower on July 18, 1956. The key provisions of the act included even more severe penalties for the sale of and trafficking in illegal substances, with a mandatory minimum sentence of 5 years and a mandatory maximum of 10 years for all subsequent violations. In addition, judges were prohibited from suspending sentences or providing probation for convicted offenders (Hudon 1956). Finally, some of the more constructive recommendations of the Daniel subcommittee, such as developing an educational program to reduce youth drug use and the opening of federal narcotics hospitals to people who were addicted to drugs, did not make it into the final bill, essentially excluding prevention and treatment as possible options for dealing with drug abuse in the United States (King 1972, Chapter 16).

Controlled Substances Act of 1970

Between 1937 and 1969, the prohibition of marijuana distribution and use was enshrined in a cluster of legislations that included the Marihuana Tax Act of 1937, the 1951 Boggs Amendment to the Harrison Narcotic Act, the Narcotic Control Act of 1956, and a hodgepodge of state and local laws. In 1969, that system fell apart when the U.S. Supreme Court ruled that essential elements in the 1937 tax act were unconstitutional. The relevant case, *Leary v. United States*, arose as the result of the 1965 arrest of Dr. Timothy Leary, psychologist, writer, sometime Harvard University faculty member, and vigorous proponent of drug legalization. Leary, his girlfriend, and two children were returning from an extended visit to Mexico when federal agents found a small amount of marijuana in his daughter's clothing. Leary took responsibility for his daughter's having the drug and was charged with possession of an illegal drug, sentenced to 30 days in jail, and fined $30,000. Leary appealed the sentence, and the case worked its way to the highest court in the land, which handed down its decision on May 19, 1969. (The case was the first time the U.S. Supreme Court had acted on a case related to the nation's marijuana laws.)

In its decision, the Court ruled unanimously that the marijuana tax act was unconstitutional because it exposed an individual to self-incrimination, an act specifically prohibited by the Fifth Amendment of the U.S. Constitution. The justices reasoned that

> the Marihuana Tax Act compelled petitioner to expose himself to a "real and appreciable" risk of self-incrimination . . . [It further] required him, in the course of obtaining an order form, to identify himself not only as a transferee of marihuana, but as a transferee who had not registered and paid the occupational tax under §§4751-4753. Section 4773 directed that this information be conveyed by the Internal Revenue Service to state and local law enforcement officials on request.
>
> Petitioner had ample reason to fear that transmittal to such officials of the fact that he was a recent, unregistered transferee of marihuana "would surely prove a significant link in a chain' of evidence tending to establish his guilt" [footnote omitted] under the state marihuana laws then in effect. (*Leary v. United States* 1969, 16)

The Court then concluded that

> petitioner's invocation of the privilege against self-incrimination under the Fifth Amendment provided a full defense to the charge . . .
>
> Since the effect of the Act's terms were such that legal possessors of marihuana were virtually certain to be registrants or exempt from the order form requirement, compliance with the transfer tax provisions would have required petitioner, as one not registered but obliged to obtain an order form, unmistakably to identify himself as a member of a "selective group inherently suspect of criminal activities," and thus those provisions created a "real and appreciable" hazard of incrimination . . . (*Leary v. United States* 1969, 7)

For a very brief period of time, then, the United States had no federal policy regarding the use of marijuana. That situation was not, however, to last long. Even before the Supreme Court decision in *Leary v. United States*, politicians were beginning to grumble about the confused state of federal and state laws relating not only to marijuana, but to other dangerous drugs as well. In a special message delivered to Congress on February 7, 1968, for example, President Lyndon Johnson had described the nation's approach to drug control as "a crazy quilt of inconsistent approaches and widely disparate criminal sanctions" (Johnson 1968). Congress then began working on drug policy legislation in earnest, producing the Comprehensive Drug Abuse Prevention and Control Act of 1970. The act covered virtually every aspect of drug manufacture, distribution, registration, and use in the United States. Arguably its most important part is Title II, the Controlled Substances Act of 1970 (CSA), which for nearly five decades has provided the basic legislative framework for U.S. policy regarding illegal drug use (The Controlled Substances Act of 1970 2015).

The CSA included provisions that represented significant changes in the nation's policies toward drug use. The first of these changes was the decision to give up on taxation as a primary mechanism of drug policy and to adopt direct penalties and punishment as a way of controlling drug use. In the act, the United States abandoned the principle inherent in the 1937 Marihuana Tax Act that placing a tax on the manufacture, distribution, and use of drugs was an effective means of controlling the use of such products, and adopted the principle that prison and jail sentences and monetary fines issued directly for possession or distribution of drugs, instead, were likely to be more effective in reducing (or eliminating) drug use.

In adopting the CSA, Congress also expressed a very different view about the severity of punishment appropriate for drug use. Senator Thomas Dodd (D-CT) expressed this view in hearings on the (as it was known at the time) Controlled Dangerous Substances Act of 1969. He observed,

It had also become apparent that the severity of penalties including the length of sentences does not affect the extent of drug abuse and other drug-related violation. The basic consideration here was that the increasingly longer sentences that had been legislated in the past had not shown the expected overall reduction in drug law violations. The opposite had been true notably in the case of marihuana. Under Federal law and under many State laws marihuana violations carry the same strict penalties that are applicable to hard narcotics, yet marihuana violations have almost doubled in the last 2 years alone. (Controlled Dangerous Substances Act of 1969 1969, 2308)

Reflecting this new view of "the drug problem," the CSA eliminated many of the most severe penalties for drug abuse, including the harsh minimum sentences established by the Boggs amendment. Congress had apparently come to the conclusion that such penalties simply did not work.

The CSA also included provisions for prevention, treatment, and research programs for drug users, a striking change in the previous position that such individuals were dangerous criminals who needed to be punished and/or excluded from society. As an example, the act expanded the availability of methadone treatment for heroin addicts, which dramatically altered the way such individuals were handled in the United States. It also provided for the creation of the Special Action Office for Drug Abuse Prevention, which marked a promising new avenue to research on drug prevention and treatment.

Additionally, the act reversed a long-standing policy that included cannabis along with cocaine and opiates in drug laws and policies. Instead, Part F of the act established a commission to study in more detail the special and unique problems posed by cannabis use in the United States and to offer recommendations for dealing with those problems. That commission, chaired by Raymond P. Shafer, former governor of Pennsylvania, issued its report, "Marihuana: A Signal of Misunderstanding," in 1972. The report was an about-face from previous policy toward marijuana, recommending much more lenient penalties for possession of the drug and expanded programs of treatment, prevention, and research. The philosophy that motivated the committee's recommendations was enunciated at one point by Shafer, who said that

> we believe that the criminal law is too harsh a tool to apply to personal possession even in the effort to discourage use. It implies an overwhelming indictment of the behavior which we believe is not appropriate. The actual and potential harm of use of the drug is not great enough to justify intrusion by the criminal law into private behavior, a step which our society takes only "with the greatest reluctance." (U.S. Commission on Marihuana and Drug Abuse 1972, 176)

In some respects, the most significant long-term effect of the CSA was the creation of a system for classifying illegal substances under one of five *schedules*. This system of so-called controlled substances has dominated U.S. drug policy throughout the more than four decades since the adoption of the CSA. The schedules are based on three features of any given substance: (1) its potential for abuse, (2) its value in accepted medical treatment in the United States, and (3) its safety when used under medical supervision. Thus, substances placed in Schedule I were those that (1) have a high potential for abuse, (2) have no currently accepted use for medical treatments in the United States, and (3) cannot be safely used even under appropriate medical supervision. Drugs traditionally regarded as the most dangerous—cocaine, the opiates, and marijuana—were (and are) all classified under Schedule I of the act. Other examples of Schedule I drugs today are LSD, mescaline, peyote, and psilocybin. In contrast to Schedule I drugs, substances listed in Schedule V (1) have minimal potential for abuse, (2) have accepted medical applications in the United States, and (3) are generally regarded as safe to use under medical supervision (although they may have the potential to lead to addiction). Examples of Schedule V drugs are certain cough medications that contain small amounts of codeine and products used to treat diarrhea that contain small amounts of opium. In the first announcement of scheduled drugs in the *Federal Register* in 1971, 59 substances were listed in Schedule I, 21 in Schedule II, 22 in Schedule III, 11 in Schedule IV, and 5 in Schedule V (Title 21: Food and Drugs 1971, 7803–7805). Since that time, about 160 substances have been added to and dropped from one or more of the schedules (Controlled Substances Schedules 2016).

The Shafer Report

The National Commission on Marihuana and Drug Abuse ("the Shafer Commission") took its job seriously. It conducted by far the most comprehensive study of marijuana ever carried out in the United States, holding hearings that produced thousands of pages of testimony from public officials, community leaders, law enforcement officers, academicians, public health experts, and others with experience and expertise in the field of drug abuse. It also commissioned more than 50 studies on all aspects of marijuana use in the United States as well as on the status and effectiveness of existing marijuana laws. It eventually came to the conclusion, cited earlier, that the possession of marijuana by individuals for their own use should be decriminalized, that is, not penalized by either civil or criminal law (Nixon Tapes Show Roots of Marijuana Prohibition: Misinformation, Culture Wars and Prejudice 2002).

As in other instances before and since, the commission's report did not appear in a politically neutral climate. In fact, even as the committee was conducting its work, President Richard M. Nixon was making clear that he held very different views about the nation's drug problems. He was, in fact, envisioning a "war on drugs" that would be an essential element in his campaign for re-election and a keystone of his second administration. In tapes made while he was in office, for example, Nixon told his chief of staff, H. R. ("Bob") Haldeman, that he wanted "a drug thing every week" during the re-election campaign (Nixon Tapes Show Roots of Marijuana Prohibition: Misinformation, Culture Wars and Prejudice 2002). At the same time, Nixon was warning Shafer that he could not allow his committee to get out of hand and make recommendations that ran counter to what Congress and the general public wanted to hear. He warned Shafer to avoid adopting the views of "a bunch of muddle-headed psychiatrists" (at the U.S. Department of Health, Education, and Welfare) who let "their hearts run their brains." Nixon concluded his instructions to Shafer by advising him:

> You see, the thing that is so terribly important here is that it not appear that the Commission's frankly just a bunch of do-gooders, I mean, they say they're a bunch of old men [who] don't understand, that's fine, I wouldn't mind that, but if they get the idea you're just a bunch of do-gooders that are going to come out with a quote "soft on marijuana" report, that'll destroy it, right off the bat. I think there's a need to come out with a report that is totally oblivious to some obvious differences between marijuana and other drugs, other dangerous drugs . . . (Nixon Tapes Show Roots of Marijuana Prohibition: Misinformation, Culture Wars and Prejudice 2002, 2)

Within this setting, it is hardly surprising that the Shafer report went essentially nowhere. True, the report did have some important lasting contributions to make to the nation's effort to deal with drug abuse—it insisted for the first time, for example, to describe alcohol as a dangerous drug—but it had essentially no effect on changing the way the nation viewed marijuana as a "dangerous drug," a perception that has not essentially changed among government officials today. Even as the Shafer committee was conducting its studies, Nixon decided to strengthen the nation's battle against drug abuse by creating a new administrative office to deal with the problem, the Special Action Office for Drug Abuse Prevention. To lead that office, Nixon appointed a respected physician, Dr. Jerome Jaffe, the first of a series of national drug leaders who were later generally referred to as "drug czars."

The Carter Years

The years from 1977 to 1981 provided a brief respite in the "war against drugs" declared by Richard Nixon. During that period, President Jimmy Carter took a much softer approach to dealing with all psychoactive drugs, calling for reduced penalties for their use and an expanded and improved program of education, treatment, and prevention. With respect to marijuana, he notably observed in a 1977 message to Congress that "[p]enalties against possession of a drug should not be more damaging to an individual than the use of the drug itself" (Carter 1977). As recently as 2011, Carter repeated that message in an op-ed in the *New York Times* (Carter 2011, A35). Dr. Peter Bourne, Carter's drug czar, took a similar view toward marijuana. In a 2000 interview with PBS, Bourne remembered the Carter administration's attitude about marijuana:

> We did not view marijuana as a significant health problem—as it was not—even though there were people who wanted to construe it as being a public health problem. Nobody dies from marijuana smoking. (Interview Peter Bourne 2000)

The Nixon administration's policy toward marijuana use, Bourne observed, was motivated by something other than public health issues:

> Smoking marijuana [in the 1960s] became very important as a symbolic gesture against the government. . . . We're

really talking more about cultural wars than we are talking about drug wars. (Interview Peter Bourne 2000)

Federal Legislation since the Controlled Substances Act, 1970–2010

The one-term Carter administration represented only a brief interlude in the much longer aggressive campaign (the "war on drugs") that lasted from the Nixon administration to (arguably) the most recent administration of President Barack Obama. With the election of President Ronald Reagan in 1981, national policy reverted once again to a militaristic theme in which all of the nation's resources were marshaled in an effort to reduce or eliminate the use of illegal drugs in the United States. In one of his earliest speeches in office, Reagan announced that "we're taking down the surrender flag that has flown over so many drug efforts; we're running up a battle flag" (Reagan 1982). An indication of the sincerity with which Reagan attempted to pursue the drug war was the words and actions of his first drug czar, Carlton Turner. Turner argued that smoking marijuana was more than just a recreational activity with young people of the 1980s. It was instead, he told an interviewer with *Government Executive* magazine in 1982, a "behavioral pattern" that "sort of tagged along" with an "anti-military, anti-nuclear power, anti- big business, anti-authority" attitude that refused to accept civic responsibility (quoted in Kick 2002, 150; also see Schlosser 1997). When it was discovered in 1983 that federal agents had illegally sprayed marijuana plants from the air with toxic paraquat herbicide, Turner appeared on television to say that anyone who died of ingesting the herbicide probably got what he or she deserved. Two years later, at a gay pride parade in Atlanta, Turner also suggested that convicted drug dealers should receive the death penalty (Herer 1993, Chapter 15). When Turner said a year later that marijuana caused homosexuality which, in turn, caused HIV/AIDS, Reagan apparently had heard enough and fired Turner from his position

(Herer 1993, Chapter 15; for a recent expression of Turner's views on marijuana, see Turner 2016).

The tenor of congressional attitudes toward drugs in general and marijuana in particular in the 1980s was illustrated by passage of the Anti-Drug Abuse Act of 1986. Apparently the primary impetus for that act was an attempt by the Democratic Party to convince the nation that it was "tough on drugs," a position traditionally taken by its opponents in the Republican Party, especially at election time (as it was in 1986). In an attempt to prove that the party could be "tough on drugs," Democrats pushed through legislation that reinstated minimum penalties for possession of drugs (Sterling 1999). The penalties established for "harder" drugs, such as cocaine, heroin, and amphetamines, were relatively large, compared to those established for marijuana. For example, conviction for possession of 5 grams of crack cocaine, or 500 grams of powder cocaine, or 1 gram of LSD resulted in a minimum sentence of five years without possibility of parole. Possession of 10 times those quantities called for a minimum sentence of 10 years without possibility of parole. By contrast, a five-year prison sentence without possibility of parole was established for possession of 100 cannabis plants or 100 kilograms of marijuana, and a 10-year sentence for 1,000 plants or 1,000 kilograms of marijuana (Sterling 1999). In addition to re-establishing minimum penalties, the law provided $1.7 billion for drug enforcement efforts, $200 million for drug education programs, and $241 million for drug treatment programs (Public Law 99-570 2016, Title IV).

By 1986, then, federal laws on possession, cultivation, and distribution had essentially been established. The modern expression of those laws is summarized in Table 2.1.

State Marijuana Laws

As might be expected, marijuana laws vary considerably from state to state. One way to compare these laws is simply to prepare a chart like Table 2.1 for each state and try to decide which states are "most severe" in their laws and which are "less severe."

Table 2.1   Federal Marijuana Laws

Possession

Amount	Level	Incarceration	Fine (in dollars)
Any (first offense)	Misdemeanor	1 year	1,000
Any (second offense)	Misdemeanor	15 days*	2,500
Any (third offense)	Misdemeanor or felony	90 days–3 years*	3,500

Sale or Cultivation

Less than 50 plants or 50 kilograms (first offense)	Felony	Not more than 5 years	250,000
50–99 plants or 50–99 kilograms (first offense)	Felony	Not more than 20 years	1,000,000
100–999 plants or 100–999 kilograms (first offense)	Felony	5–40 years	2,000,000–5,000,000
1,000 or more plants or 1,000 or more kilograms (first offense)	Felony	10 years–life	4,000,000–10,000,000
Sale to a minor	Felony	Double penalty	Double penalty
Sale within 1,000 feet of a school	Felony	Double penalty	Double penalty

*Mandatory minimum penalty.

Source: Adapted from "Federal Laws and Penalties." 2016. NORML. http://norml.org/laws/item/federal-penalties-2?category_id=833. Accessed on May 15, 2016, and summarized from Subchapter I—Control and Enforcement. 2016. Office of Diversion Control. http://www.deadiversion.usdoj.gov/21cfr/21usc/841.htm. Accessed on May 15, 2016.

An excellent way of making such a comparison can be found on the NORML website, which lists marijuana laws for all 50 states (State Laws 2016). As this site indicates, states with the most severe penalties include those that assess a one-year prison term for possession of a relatively small amount of marijuana (typically 20 to 35 grams, or about an ounce or less) and a fine ranging from $1,000 to $5,000. States that fall into this category include Florida, Indiana, Kansas, Maryland, Missouri, Oklahoma, Rhode Island, South Dakota, and Tennessee (State Laws 2016).

By contrast, a number of states have decriminalized the possession of small amounts of marijuana. Decriminalization typically means that possession of small amounts of marijuana is treated in the same way as a minor traffic offense. There is no prison time or monetary fine assessed, and the offense may not be recorded in a person's legal records. As of 2016, states that have decriminalized the possession of small amounts of marijuana include Alaska (1 ounce or less), California (28.5 grams or less), Colorado (2 ounces or less), Connecticut (0.5 ounce or less), Delaware (175 grams or less), District of Columbia (2 ounces or less), Maine (usable amount with proof of physician's prescription), Maryland (less than 10 grams), Massachusetts (1 ounce or less), Minnesota (less than 42.5 grams), Mississippi (30 grams or less), Missouri (less than 35 grams), Nebraska (1 ounce or less), Nevada (less than 1 ounce), New York (25 grams or less), North Carolina (0.5 ounce or less), Ohio (less than 100 grams), Oregon (less than 1 ounce), Rhode Island (less than 1 ounce), and Vermont (less than 1 ounce) (States That Have Decriminalized 2016).

Most of the laws in states that have decriminalized the possession of small amounts of marijuana closely follow a model law suggested by the Marijuana Policy Project. That model law specifies that first-time possession of less than an ounce of marijuana by a person over the age of 18 should be considered to be a civil offense with no jail or prison time and a fine of $100. Individuals under the age of 18 should be assessed the fine (without jail or prison time) only if they do not complete a drug awareness program (Model State Civil Fine Bill 2016).

Patterns of Marijuana Use in the United States

Efforts to obtain valid and reliable estimates of the number of boys and girls, men and women, who use marijuana in the United States go back to the early 1970s, largely, at first, in response to provisions of the Controlled Substances Act of 1970, which required the collection of such statistics. Research on the prevalence of marijuana use and related topics originated with two studies commissioned in 1971 and 1972 by the National Commission on Marihuana and Drug Abuse (NCMDA). Those studies were then continued by the National Institute on Drug Abuse (NIDA) under the title of the National Household Survey on Drug Abuse (NHSDU), which was later renamed the National Survey on Drug Use and Health (NSDU) and which continues to carry out annual surveys of drug use.

At the outset (and, to some extent, up to the present time), it should be noted that such data were relatively difficult to collect because, of course, marijuana was, and still is, an illegal drug, so an individual might be reluctant to be entirely forthcoming as to his or her use of the substance. (See, for example, Gettman 2007.) Nonetheless, researchers worked diligently to make an estimate of the number of marijuana users. Such studies commonly divided users into a number of categories, many of which were, of course, demographic: by age, gender, and, sometimes, racial or ethnic background. Also, researchers attempted to distinguish individuals who had tried the drug only once ("one-time users"), who used it occasionally ("within the past year/month/week"), or who used it regularly.

Much of the earliest research focused on the use of marijuana by young people, possibly because of the widespread publicity at the time about the threat posed by drug abuse among teenagers and young adults. In a series of studies commissioned by the NIDA, for example, researchers found in 1974 that 52.8% of 18- to 21-year-olds and 47.2% of 22- to 25-year-olds had used marijuana at least once in their lifetime. In 1976, the rates were 50.4% and 51.6% and they were 56.8% and 60.3% in 1977 (Richards 1981, Table 1, 44). Researchers in 1976 and 1977 further subdivided marijuana users into finer categories of gender, race, and geographic locations, as shown in Table 2.2.

Table 2.2   Classification of Marijuana Users by Gender, Race, and Geographic Location, 1976 and 1977

Subgroup	1976 (in percentage)	1977 (in percentage)
Females	43.6	54.4
Males	59.8	64.5
White	53.6	60.1
Nonwhite	46.3	54.4
Large metropolitan	58.1	62.7
Other metropolitan	57.5	63.2
Nonmetropolitan	36.2	47.8

Source: Richards, Louise G, ed. Demographic Trends and Drug Abuse, 1980–1995. NIDA Research Monograph 35. Washington, DC: Government Printing Office. May 1981. Table 4, 45.

Finally, researchers asked respondents to their surveys about the frequency of their marijuana use. The results of that question are summarized in Table 2.3.

The longest continuing study of marijuana use and attitudes toward marijuana use has been the Monitoring the Future (MTF) program, known originally as the National High School Senior Survey, funded by the National Institute on Drug Abuse and conducted by the Institute for Social Research at the University of Michigan. The study originally focused on about 16,000 high school seniors in approximately 130 schools. In 1976, the study was expanded to include populations beyond high school students and to cover a greater variety of topics than drug use. Finally, in 1991, the survey was extended again, this time to include samples of 8th and 10th graders.

As with many marijuana use studies, MTF researchers have traditionally asked students how frequently they use the drug: (1) at any time in their life, defined as *lifetime prevalence*, (2) during the last year, defined as *annual prevalence*, and (3) during the last 30 days, defined as *30-day prevalence*. The long-term trends of annual prevalence among 8th, 10th, and 12th graders

Table 2.3   Frequency of Marijuana Use, 1974, 1976 and 1977 (percentage)

Category	Current Use*			Regular Use			Occasional Use		
	1974	1976	1977	1974	1976	1977	1974	1976	1977
18- to 21-year-olds	30.3	25.6	30.4	10.8	6.9	13.0	27.0	22.3	23.7
22- to 25-year-olds	20.4	25.7	24.2	6.7	6.5	10.7	21.6	27.4	22.6
18- to 25-Year-Olds									
Females	**	19.6	20.8	**	4.4	**	**	20.2	21.3
Males	**	31.4	35.1	**	**	7.0	**	29.2	25.8
White	**	26.3	20.4	**	8.9	12.2	**	26.2	23.7
Nonwhite	**	23.8	24.1	**	6.5	10.5	**	20.2	22.0

*Use within the past month.

**Not asked.

Source: Richards, Louise G, ed. Demographic Trends and Drug Abuse, 1980–1995. NIDA Research Monograph 35. Washington, DC: Government Printing Office. May 1981. Tables 10 and 12, 48–49.

have ranged from a low of 21.1% in 1992 to a high of 37.8% in 1997. Since that year, lifetime prevalence has dropped off to about 30%, reaching 30.0% in 2015. As one might expect, marijuana use in all categories (lifetime, annual, and 30-day) is always highest among 12th graders and lowest among 8th graders, with frequency of use generally about three times as great among older students as among younger students (Johnston et al. 2016, Tables 1 and 5, pages 54 and 58).

Data for annual and 30-day use of marijuana follow a roughly similar pattern to those for lifetime use. The lowest rates for all three age groups were lowest in 1992 at 14.3% and 7.7% and highest in 1997 at 30.1% and 17.9%. Since that peak year, both annual and 30-day use has decreased among all three age groups to the mid-20% range for annual use and the high teen percentage in the 30-day range. In 2015, those rates were 23.7% for annual use and 14.0% for 30-day use (Johnston et al. 2016, Tables 2 and 3, pages 55 and 56; this study contains detailed data on many aspects of marijuana use among 8th, 10th, and 12th graders from 1991 through 2015).

Attitudes about Marijuana Use

A number of studies (including the Monitoring the Future study) have also attempted to discover how adolescent and young adult attitudes about the use of marijuana have changed over time in the United States. One of the most comprehensive of those studies was conducted by researchers at the University of Texas, St. Louis University, and the University of Michigan in 2015. In that study, subjects from the age of 12 to 25 who were regular-, occasional-, or nonsmokers of marijuana were asked about their approval or disapproval of using the drug. Researchers found that younger subjects were more likely to have increased their disapproval of the use of marijuana by a small, but significant, amount between 2002 and 2013. For example, 83.91% of 12-year-olds disapproved of the use of marijuana in 2002, a number that increased to 86.59% in 2013. For 13-year-olds, those numbers were 75.49% in 2002 and 81.67% in 2013.

Similar trends were not observed among older subjects, however. Among subjects over the age of 16, disapproval of marijuana use actually decreased, by a modest amount among younger subjects and by large amounts by older subjects. Among 17-year-olds, for example, disapproval of marijuana use decreased from 43.36% in 2002 to 34.92% in 2013, and among 24/25-year-olds from 40.74% in 2002 to 21.46% in 2013 (Salas-Wright et al. 2015, Tables 4 and 5, pages 397 and 402).

The effect of using marijuana on a regular or occasional basis on one's general approval or disapproval of the drug was difficult to determine from this study. In general, younger adults, age 12 to 17, who used marijuana on either an occasional or regular basis seemed more willing to approve of the use of the drug in 2013 than was the case in 2002. That pattern held for regular ("lifetime") users of the drug among those 18 to 25, but not for those who were only occasional (past year) users of the drug (Salas-Wright et al. 2015, Tables 4 and 5, pages 397 and 402). Even with the extensive data in studies such as this one, it is difficult to say how adolescents' and young adults' attitudes toward the use of marijuana have changed in the past decade, and how demographic factors have affected that change.

The vast majority of public opinion polls about marijuana ask a very different type of question of respondents, namely whether they believe that the use of marijuana should be legalized or not. That is, one might personally disapprove of the use of marijuana for medical and/or recreational purposes, but still feel that the drug should be legalized for one or the other (or both) purposes.

The Gallup Poll, for example, has been asking in its public opinion surveys for more than 40 years about attitudes toward the legalization of marijuana in the United States. Those surveys suggest that the public has gradually become more accepting toward the legalization of marijuana. When Gallup first asked in 1970 whether the drug should be legalized, only 12% of respondents answered in the affirmative, with 84% expressing opposition to legalization. Those numbers have gradually changed, until, in October 2011, pollsters found for the first time a preponderance of those favoring legalization (50%) versus those opposing legalization (46%). That trend has continued through the decade, with 58% of respondents supporting legalization of the drug for recreational purposes in 2015 (Jones 2015). Other public opinion polls have shown similar trends over the years with regard to legalization of marijuana, with even larger majorities supporting legalization of marijuana for medical purposes ("Illegal Drugs" 2016).

Current Controversies about Marijuana Use

Two questions dominate most discussions about marijuana today both in the United States and in other parts of the world.

The first question is whether or not the possession and use of marijuana should continue to be criminalized, as it currently is in most parts of the world. For a number of years now, many individuals and organizations have been arguing that there are sound reasons for changing existing policies and allowing the possession and use of small amounts of marijuana without legal penalty. The second question is whether the possession and use of marijuana is decriminalized or not, whether the drug should be permitted to be used for legitimate medical purposes.

Legalization and Decriminalization of Marijuana
In the United States and most other parts of the world today, the possession and use of marijuana (along with its production and distribution) are criminal acts. That means anyone who is found in possession of marijuana can be prosecuted for a misdemeanor or felony crime, conviction for which may result in a jail or prison sentence along with a monetary fine. People who object to this type of policy usually suggest that possession and use of marijuana (but generally not production and distribution of the drug) be either decriminalized or legalized. The terms have different meanings. Decriminalization means that the most severe penalties currently assessed for possession of marijuana would be eliminated. A person might still be fined or required to perform some public service, for example, if convicted of possessing the drug, but he or she would not be sentenced to prison. Legalization is an even more extreme action, in which all legal penalties of any kind against use of the drug would be eliminated. People who favor legalization often suggest that one or more controls be established over the use of the drug, as is the case with other addictive substances, such as tobacco and alcohol. They might recommend special labels on marijuana cigarettes, as is the case with tobacco cigarettes; restrictions on all or various types of advertising; age limits for purchasers of marijuana; or restrictions on the amount of marijuana that might be purchased at any one time. Individuals and organizations that argue for decriminalization or legalization

often do not specifically say which form of reform they prefer, but simply suggest that current sentencing policies be revised or eliminated.

Arguments in Favor of Decriminalization or Legalization

This section lists the major arguments offered in support of the decriminalization or legalization of marijuana possession. Following this section is a list of arguments used to refute these suggestions and to support existing policies on possession of the drug.

The War on Marijuana Is Far Too Costly

The nation's so-called war on drugs officially began in 1969 when newly elected president Richard M. Nixon submitted a budget to the Congress requesting $81.4 million for drug treatment, education, research, and law enforcement. Five years later, that budget had increased nearly tenfold, reaching $760 million (Goldberg 1980). Those costs continued to rise over the next four decades, reaching a total federal expenditure in 2016 of $30.6 billion (National Drug Control Budget 2016, 2). And these numbers reflect only federal spending. The cost of fighting drug abuse on state and local levels adds substantially to these totals. According to one study conducted in 2010, states and local municipalities had spent $25,684,407,000 in 2008 on drug enforcement programs, almost twice the total spent by the federal government ($13.7 billion) for that year (Miron and Waldock 2010, Table 3, p. 35; National Drug Control Strategy 2008, 1)

In an earlier study, Miron had focused on the cost of the war, on marijuana in particular, and the savings that could be achieved by legalization of the drug. That study, conducted in 2005, concluded that legalizing the possession of marijuana would save the U.S. government about $2.4 billion per year and state and local governments a total of $5.3 billion per year. Miron's calculations included all expenses involved in carrying out laws against marijuana, including costs of police, the judiciary, and corrections facilities. In an interesting extension of the study, Miron also analyzed the economic effects of assessing a tax on the purchase of marijuana at the rate used for most other goods or, alternatively, at the usual rates for alcohol and tobacco. He found that under the former arrangement, marijuana taxes would annually generate $2.4 billion and $6.2 billion in revenue annually, respectively (Miron 2005; this study contains detailed tables for both federal and state costs as well as potential tax returns). In response to Miron's report, more than 500 economists signed a petition to the president, Congress, governors, and state legislators urging a renewed debate on the benefits of legalizing the possession of marijuana (Hardy 2005).

Two other studies contemporaneous with Miron's research also dealt with the problems of financing the war against marijuana. In their 2005 report, "Efficacy & Impact: The Criminal Justice Response to Marijuana Policy in the US," Jason Ziedenberg and Jason Colburn pointed out that the cost of the nation's war against drugs had risen by about 307% between 1988 and 2003, while the rate of marijuana use had remained essentially the same during that period. (It decreased from about 5,000 per 100,000 individuals to less than 4,000 per 100,000 in the early 2000s, but then returned to 5,000 per 100,000 by 2003, for no net change during the period [Zidenberg and Colburn 2005, 7].) Also in 2005, the organization Citizens against Government Waste (CAGW) conducted a study, attempting to assess the success (or lack of it) of federal campaigns against marijuana. The CAGW focused in particular on the work of the White House Office of National Drug Control Policy (ONDCP) and found that that office "burns through tax dollars by funding wasteful and unnecessary projects." The CAGW also concluded that "the drug czar created a $2 billion national anti-drug campaign, produced expensive propaganda ads that failed to reduce drug use among America's youth, and in the process, violated federal law"

(French 2005). Finally, the CAGW claimed that ONDCP used the nation's $226.5 million High Intensity Drug Trafficking Areas Program (HIDTA) that had become a "cash cow for members of Congress to bring home the bacon for their constituents" (French 2005).

The War on Marijuana Has Not Been Effective

This point was discussed in some detail earlier in this chapter. The main argument is that the United States has spent more than $1 trillion in four decades in the battle against drugs, the most common of which by far is marijuana, with little or no decrease in use. During the same time, the lives of tens or hundreds of thousands of individuals have been ruined by incarceration for marijuana use. For probably the only time in U.S. history, except for the administration of President Jimmy Carter, an American president has taken a public stand on this position. On a number of occasions, both as a candidate for the presidency and as president, Barack Obama has suggested that drug use in general and marijuana use in particular should be treated as a public health problem, rather than a crime. In 2010, Obama's director of the ONDCP, Richard Gil Kerlikowske, told reporters that "in the grand scheme, it [the U.S. drug war] has not been successful. Forty years later, the concern about drugs and drug problems is, if anything, magnified, intensified" (War on Drugs Unsuccessful, Drug Czar Says 2010). (In point of fact, however, Obama's actions did not match his words. He raised spending on drug enforcement efforts every year he was in office except one, 2013, and made his highest ever request for fiscal year 2017, $31,071.4 million [National Drug Control Budget 2016, Table 3, Page 19].)

The Use of Marijuana Is Not Associated with Serious Health Problems

Probably the most contentious issue in the debate over legalization or decriminalization of marijuana is the risk it may or may not pose to an individual's physical, psychological, and social health as well as to the safety of society in general. Opponents of decriminalization and legalization routinely point to a host of negative consequences that may result from marijuana use, often claiming that the use of even small amounts of the drug can have serious results. This argument is in the long tradition of the warnings of drug prohibitionists like Harry Anslinger in the United States and other crusaders around the world, although today's opponents of decriminalization generally present their position in much less propagandistic language and with much more scientific evidence for their case.

By contrast, proponents of decriminalization commonly cite a wide number of scientific studies dating back more than a hundred years indicating that the risks to health and society, although not zero, are acceptably low. In fact, proponents and opponents of decriminalization sometimes cite the same scientific research, but draw different conclusions from that research. Some of the most comprehensive of health effects reviews of marijuana use are the Indian Hemp Drugs Commission report of 1894, the Panama Canal Zone Military Investigations into Marijuana (1916–1929), the LaGuardia Report of 1944, the report of the British Advisory Committee on Drug Dependency (the Wooton Report) of 1968, the Canadian Government's Commission of Inquiry (the Le Dain Report) of 1970, the National Commission on Marihuana and Drug Abuse (the Shafer Report) of 1973, the National Academy of Sciences' Analysis of Marijuana Policy of 1982, and the Academy's *Marijuana and Medicine: Assessing the Science Base* (1999), arguably the most comprehensive review of the marijuana-related scientific literature ever produced in the United States. Almost without exception, these reports came to the conclusion that moderate use of marijuana produces no serious, long-term consequences for individuals or for the general society. Some of the conclusions reported in the 1999 National Academy of Sciences report (Joy, Watson, and Benson 1999), for example, were:

- Marijuana is not a completely benign substance. It is a powerful drug with a variety of effects. However, except for the harms associated with smoking, the adverse effects of marijuana use are within the range of effects tolerated for other medications. (Joy, Watson, and Benson 1999, 5)
- A distinctive marijuana withdrawal syndrome has been identified, but it is mild and short lived. (Joy, Watson, and Benson 1999, 6)
- There is no conclusive evidence that the drug effects of marijuana are causally linked to the subsequent abuse of other illicit drugs. (Joy, Watson, and Benson 1999, 6)
- The short-term immunosuppressive effects are not well established but, if they exist, are not likely great enough to preclude a legitimate medical use. (Joy, Watson, and Benson 1999, 5)

Proponents of legalization often focus on scientific studies dealing with specific claims made by their opponents about the health effects of marijuana use on the brain, the respiratory system, or other body systems, or on the development of specific diseases, such as cancer. For example, they sometimes point to a study conducted in 2003 by Igor Grant, at the Department of Psychiatry at the University of California-San Diego and his colleagues, that showed that long-term use of marijuana apparently has no permanent effect on brain function, a result the researchers found "surprising." In a review of 15 previous studies on the problem, Grant's team found "very small" impairment of memory and learning (Grant et al. 2003, 686). A similar result was reported in a 2005 study of the relationship between marijuana use and cancer. In a retrospective review of 14 earlier studies on this relationship, Donald P. Tashkin at the University of California-Los Angeles (UCLA), Geffen School of Medicine, and his colleagues found no association between marijuana use and a variety of types of cancers, a result that they—like Grant—found "surprising." They concluded that, although "there is every reason to expect some adverse effect of marijuana use on aerodigestive tract cancers, . . . results of cohort studies have not revealed an increased risk of tobacco-related cancers among marijuana smokers" (Hashibe et al. 2005, 273). A recent study also found that the relationship between marijuana smoking and pulmonary function is not strong, with marijuana smokers actually having somewhat better lung function than cigarette smokers. The study followed more than 5,000 individuals who smoked marijuana regularly over a period of two decades—the equivalent of up to one joint per day over seven years—and found that they suffered no measurable impairment on a standard lung function test (Pletcher et al. 2012).

When hundreds, if not thousands, of scientific studies on the health effects of marijuana have been conducted over the years, the selection of any specific group of studies may seem somewhat arbitrary. However, these three examples do provide a flavor of the types of results that have been obtained in many research efforts.

The Health Effects of Marijuana Are Less of a Concern Than Are Those of Alcohol and Tobacco

Proponents of marijuana decriminalization often point to what might appear to be the dramatic difference in the way society views three psychoactive substances: marijuana, tobacco, and alcohol, the latter of two of which are legal in the United States and most other parts of the world, at least for adults. Studies have shown that the health effects of marijuana use are no greater than, and often are considerably less serious than, those of tobacco use and alcohol use. For example, a review of the extant literature on alcohol and marijuana effects on brain function conducted in 2009 by researchers at the San Diego State University/University of California-San Diego Joint Doctoral Program in Clinical Psychology found that heavy drinking of alcohol by adolescents resulted in significant abnormalities in brain structure, while similar heavy use of marijuana caused "some subtle anomalies too, but generally not the same degree of divergence from demographically similar non-using adolescents" (Squeglia, Jacobus and Tapert 2009, 31). In a similar review of studies on the relative effects of smoking tobacco and smoking marijuana over the period between 1988 and 1994, researchers found that tobacco smoking was more detrimental to respiratory health than marijuana smoking on one of nine measures ("shortness of breath"), while marijuana smoking was more detrimental than tobacco smoking in one other measure ("wheezing"), with the two practices having essentially the same effects on seven other measures (Moore et al. 2005, Table 3). How can we justify criminalizing the use of marijuana, some observers ask, when its health effects are no worse than those associated with the use of other legal substances, such as tobacco and alcohol?

The War on Marijuana Results in an Imposition on Individual Liberties

A quite different, but powerful, argument against the war on drugs that the United States has been fighting for half a century is that it has resulted in a broad and intense attack on the personal liberties of American citizens. One of the most eloquent statements of this view has come from Steven Wisotsky, professor of law at Nova Southeastern University. In a white paper on the drug war for the Cato Institute in 1992, Wisotsky described the ways in which the drug war had empowered law enforcement officials at all levels to insert themselves into the private lives of American citizens, virtually without restriction. He noted:

> the War on Drugs is necessarily a war on the rights of all of us. It could not be otherwise, for it is directed not against inanimate drugs but against people . . . all of whom try to keep their actions secret. . . . And because nearly anyone may be a drug user or seller of drugs or an aider and abettor of the drug industry, virtually everyone has

become a suspect. All must be observed, checked, screened, tested, and admonished—the guilty and innocent alike. (Wisotsky 1992)

In support of his argument, Wisotsky cites a number of both legislators and jurists, including Peter Rodino, former chair of the House Judiciary Committee ("We have been fighting the war on drugs, but now it seems to me the attack is on the Constitution of the United States") and Supreme Court justice Anton Scalia (the "immolation of privacy and human dignity in symbolic opposition to drug use"). Wisotsky concludes his essay by citing another jurist, Judge William Schwarzer: "It behooves us to think that it may profit us very little to win the war on drugs if in the process we lose our soul" (Wisotsky 1992).

The War on Marijuana Has Increased Pressure
on Prison Populations

As Table 2.4 shows, the consequence of the nation's marijuana laws has been a significant increase in the number of men and women in federal, state, and local prisons and jails. The most recent report on U.S. prison populations, for example, notes that individuals incarcerated for drug offenses account for the largest single category of federal prisoners as of September 30, 2014, the most recent date for which information is available. An estimated 96,500 inmates, 89,100 men and 7,400 women, fell into that category. Drug offenders accounted for just over half (50.1%) of all federal prison inmates, compared to those convicted of immigration-related offenses (10.6%), sex offenses (6.1%), burglary and related offenses (3.9%), robbery (3.8%), and homicide, aggravated assault, and kidnaping (2.8%) (Carson 2015, Table 12, page 17). Of all drug-related crimes represented in the prison population, marijuana was among the least common, accounting for a total of 11,553 arrests, or 12.4% of all such crimes in the prison population in 2012, the most recent year for which data are available (Taxy, Samuels, and Adams 2015, Table 2, page 2).

Table 2.4   Arrests for Marijuana Possession in the United States, 1965–2009

Year	Number of Arrests
1965	18,815
1966	31,119
1967	61,843
1968	95,870
1969	118,903
1970	188,682
1971	225,828
1972	292,179
1973	420,700
1974	445,000
1975	416,100
1976	441,100
1977	457,600
1978	445,800
1979	391,600
1980	405,600
1981	400,300
1982	455,600
1983	406,900
1984	419,400
1985	451,100
1986	361,800
1987	378,700
1988	391,600
1989	399,000
1990	326,900
1991	287,900
1992	342,300
1993	380,700
1994	481,100
1995	589,000
1996	641,600
1997	695,200

(continued)

Table 2.4   (continued)

Year	Number of Arrests
1998	682,900
1999	704,800
2000	734,500
2001	723,600
2002	697,100
2003	755,200
2004	771,600
2005	786,500
2006	829,600
2007	872,700
2008	847,863
2009	858,408

Source: These data are collected from a variety of sources, including Marijuana Research: Uniform Crime Reports—Marijuana Arrest Statistics; Drugs and Crime Facts: Drug Law Violations and Enforcement, United States Bureau of Justice Statistics; Marijuana Arrests Drop for First Time since 2002, Marijuana Policy Project; Paul Armentano, Incarceration Nation—Marijuana Arrests for Year 2009 Near Record High; Drug War Facts. Common Sense for Drug Policy.

Data for drug- and marijuana-related offenses in state prisons tend to be significantly different from that in federal prisons. According to the Bureau of Prisons 2015 report on federal and state prison populations, 15.7% inmates in state prisons had been convicted of drug-related crimes, compared to 53.2% for violent crimes such as murder, rape and sexual assault, and robbery; 19.3% for property crimes, such as burglary and auto theft; and 11.0% for public order, such as driving under the influence. (No data are available specifically for marijuana-related offenses) (Carson 2015, Table 11, page 16).

Other Arguments

A number of other arguments have been offered for the decriminalization and legalization of marijuana possession and use in small amounts. These arguments include the following:

- The war on drugs has ruined more lives than have drugs themselves.
- Marijuana has been safely used by people all over the world for millennia.
- Legalization of marijuana use could result in a lower price for the drug, thus reducing crimes committed to obtain the money needed to buy the drug.
- Drug dealers would be put out of business if marijuana were available legally.
- The quality of marijuana, its sale and advertising, and other commercial adjuncts to the use of marijuana could be brought under the control of federal and state agencies, such as the U.S. Food and Drug Administration (FDA).
- Individuals arrested for the possession and/or sale of small amounts of marijuana would be less likely to become part of the criminal system, which could ruin their lives and add to federal, state, and local law enforcement costs.
- Smoking marijuana may be, for some people, one of "life's little pleasures" over which the government should have no control.
- Legalizing marijuana may provide a significant benefit to the environment, since the current need to grow the plant surreptitiously does serious damage to the ecosystems in which it is planted.
- In a democracy, adults should be allowed to take part in activities (e.g., smoking marijuana) that does no demonstrable harm to others. (Half-Baked Idea?: Legalizing Marijuana Will Help the Environment 2011; Should Marijuana Be Legalized under Any Circumstances? 2011; Vance 2011)

Arguments in Opposition to Decriminalization or Legalization

Opposition to the decriminalization and legalization of marijuana has been strong among many individuals and organizations. International, national, state, and local governmental agencies, as well as independent organizations, such as Drug Watch International, Drug Free American Foundation, Keep Our Kids Off Drugs, and Save Our Society have marshaled a list of reasons that marijuana and other drugs should not be legalized. In the United States, the White House Office of National Drug Control Policy (ONDCP) and the National Institute on Drug Abuse (NIDA) have spearheaded the drive to counter arguments made by proponents of drug decriminalization and legalization. Here are some of the arguments these organizations have offered.

Marijuana Is Harmful to Human Health in a Number of Different Ways

One of the most common and strongest arguments made by those opposed to decriminalization of marijuana is precisely the opposite of one of the arguments presented earlier in this chapter. It is that marijuana, far from being safe to use, has many deleterious effects on human health. Opponents of legalization often cite dozens or hundreds of scientific studies indicating that the drug harms the brain, the respiratory system, and other body systems, as well as possibly being carcinogenic. A fact sheet produced by the NIDA, for example, claims that the use of marijuana can cause "altered perceptions and mood, impaired coordination, difficulty with thinking and problem solving, and disrupted learning and memory." The drug also has long-term effects on brain function, according to the NIDA, that may "last a long time or even be permanent" (Marijuana 2014). The same NIDA fact sheet points out that studies have detected a relationship between chronic marijuana use and a variety of mental illnesses, such as hallucinations, paranoia, schizophrenia, depression, anxiety, suicidal thoughts, and personality disturbances (Marijuana 2014; other NIDA publications with similar information are Marijuana 2015 and Marijuana 2016b).

Statements like these are repeated in different forms by other government agencies and private organizations at all levels of society. For example, in its drug fact sheet on marijuana, the U.S. Drug Enforcement Administration (DEA) reports that marijuana use may include "sedation, blood shot eyes, increased heart rate, coughing from lung irritation, increased appetite, and decreased blood pressure . . . bronchitis, emphysema, and bronchial asthma . . . suppression of the immune system . . . increase[d] . . . risk of cancer of the head, neck, lungs and respiratory track . . . and headache, shakiness, sweating, stomach pains and nausea, as well as behavioral signs including restlessness, irritability, sleep difficulties and decreased appetite." Some effects on the brain are said to include "apathy, impairment of judgment, memory and concentration, and loss of motivation, ambition and interest in the pursuit of personal goals . . . mental confusion, panic reactions and hallucinations . . . an increased risk of depression; an increased risk and earlier onset of schizophrenia and other psychotic disorders" (Drug Fact Sheet: Marijuana 2016).

A reasonable person might, at this point, ask which view of marijuana one should accept, that is generally harmless to human health if used in moderation, or that it has a significant variety and range of deleterious health effects on many body systems. Even trying to answer that question is difficult because reputable organizations have very different views, predicated to at least some extent on their own biases about the dangers of using marijuana. Even organizations that one would hope and expect to be unbiased about the scientific evidence may be selective or even imaginative about the data they choose to present to the general public. That having been said, a handful of sources have conducted extensive surveys of the health effects of marijuana on the human body. Two of those of special interest are a website that focuses on nutritional and supplement products, Examine.com, and a report from the state of Colorado on marijuana health effects

(Marijuana 2016a; Retail Marijuana Public Health Advisory Committee 2015).

Marijuana Is a "Gateway" Drug, Whose Use Leads to Increased Risk for Using Other Illegal Substances

This argument is a very old and simple one. It suggests simply that people who start out using illegal drugs by smoking marijuana are more likely to then continue drug use, only with even more dangerous substances, such as cocaine and heroin. Some organizations, in support of this argument, cite a 1994 study that found that adolescents who smoke marijuana are 85 times more likely to go on to use cocaine than are those who do not smoke marijuana, while 60% of adolescents who start smoking marijuana before the age of 15 then move on to cocaine (The Truth about Marijuana 2016; also see Is Marijuana a Gateway Drug? 2016a).

The debate over marijuana's possible role as a gateway drug is now at least two decades old and not much closer to resolution than it was when the 1994 study mentioned earlier was published. In 2016, for example, the *New York Times* sponsored an online debate among four experts in the field of marijuana studies who presented their own views on the current status of the question (Is Marijuana a Gateway Drug? 2016b).

Legalization of Marijuana Could Lead to a Significant Increase in Drug-Related Violent Crime

In a paper opposing the California Regulate, Control and Tax Cannabis Act of 2010, which would have legalized the use of small amounts of marijuana, Charles Stimson, of the Center for National Defense, listed a number of objections to the initiative, one of which was that legalizing marijuana would greatly increase the rate of violent crime in the state. Stimson noted that "an astonishingly high percentage of criminals are marijuana users," and that, therefore, legalization of the drug would "increase demand for the drug and almost certainly exacerbate drug-related crime, as well as cause a myriad of unintended but predictable consequences." Any income that might be achieved by taxing marijuana sales, the author goes on, would be minuscule compared to the costs of fighting this new wave of crime (Stimson 2010).

Marijuana Use Cannot Be Compared to Tobacco or Alcohol Use

Stimson goes on to say that comparisons between the effects of marijuana and tobacco or alcohol are invalid for a number of reasons. For example, he says, marijuana is far more addictive than alcohol, its use usually leads to intoxication (not the case with alcohol), it has no known health benefits (as does alcohol), and it is deleterious to one's health (which alcohol is not) (Stimson 2010). That viewpoint, while supported by many critics of marijuana use, is by no means held unanimously or even by the majority of experts in the area. A review of the long and complex debate over the relative harm caused by marijuana, alcohol, and tobacco can be found at Boffey 2014.

The War on Marijuana Has Been Effective

Opponents of drug legalization strongly dispute critics' claims that programs designed to reduce marijuana use in the United States have been a failure. They often point to a significant decrease in the marijuana use rate among young people, as expressed, for example, in the annual Monitoring the Future survey. According to that survey, the percentage of high school students who use marijuana at any level of frequency have decreased substantially since the 1990s. A report by the Institute for Behavior and Health, for example, argued that "[t]he decline in illegal drug use is a major public health success and should be recognized as such" (Perspectives on Drug Policy 2012). For many years, federal and state drug enforcement agencies also tried to support this view, sometimes pointing, for example, to their increased success in reducing the availability of marijuana and other drugs to potential American consumers. The U.S. Drug Enforcement Administration (DEA), for example, has often touted the success of its marijuana eradication program in reducing the supply of that drug to the American public. (See, for example, The DEA Position on Marijuana 2013, 54.) In recent years, such claims have, however, become much less common as evidence for the success of the nation's war on drugs has become more and more difficult to produce.

Only a Minuscule Number of Marijuana Users Ever Receive Jail or Prison Time for Using the Drug

Proponents of decriminalization often argue that individuals arrested for marijuana possession make a disproportionately large share of federal, state, and local prison and jail inmates. Their opponents disagree and point to statistics that would appear to prove otherwise. In its informational booklet Speaking Out against Drug Legalization, for example, the DEA says that only 2.7% of inmates in state prisons are there because of marijuana offenses of all kinds, 0.7% are there because of possession convictions only, and 0.3% are there because of first-time possession convictions. Statistics are similar for federal prisons, according to the DEA, where only 186 people (2.3% of all those convicted to of drug-related crimes) were sentenced for simple possession, and, of that number, only 63 individuals actually spent time behind bars (Speaking Out against Drug Legislation 2010, 61–62).

Other Arguments

As with the pro-legalization side of this dispute, a number of other arguments have been presented in opposition to the legalization of marijuana. They include the following:

- Decriminalization or legalization of marijuana will inevitably lead to increased levels of use and addiction.
- The use of illegal drugs, such as marijuana, is generally associated with increased levels of violence and criminal activity.

- Comparisons of U.S. policies with regard to marijuana to those of Europe are misinformed because the history, social structures, and politics of the two regions are very different from each other.

- Even nonusers of marijuana are placed at risk by those who do use the drug. For example, nonusers are at risk of being injured or killed in automotive accidents when another driver is "high" on marijuana.

- Legalization of marijuana will increase the likelihood that underage boys and girls may be able to gain access to the drug, as is now the case with alcohol and tobacco.

- The notion that adults should be free to smoke marijuana or not in a democracy is a fallacy because the practice can harm others, and some rights do trump other rights.

- The United States and many other countries have radically changed their approach to the use of marijuana, more strongly emphasizing prevention and treatment programs which, however, must be accompanied by continued strong enforcement of drug laws. (DuPont 2010; Hartnett 2005; McCrimmon 2012; Should Marijuana Be Legalized? 2010; Stimson [2010])

Legalization of Marijuana for Medical Uses

The second major issue related to marijuana in the United States in the early 21st century is its use for a variety of medical purposes. On one side, some groups and individuals argue that marijuana is a useful tool in treating a number of medical problems, while, on the other side, other groups and individuals say that the scientific evidence for that position is weak or nonexistent.

Arguments in Favor of Legalizing Medical Marijuana

As reported earlier in this book, marijuana has been used in many parts of the world for thousands of years to treat a variety of medical conditions. Many pharmacopoeia, textbooks, and other medical resources have recommended the use of cannabis. Proponents of medical marijuana today often point to this long history, in which some of the finest medical minds in history have recommended using marijuana in medical practice. In addition, modern physicians and researchers also point to peer-reviewed scientific studies that appear to support the use of marijuana for the treatment of diseases and disorders such as glaucoma, pain due to a variety of conditions, cancer, HIV/AIDS, multiple sclerosis, epilepsy and other seizure disorders, spasticity disorders, Crohn's disease, and hepatitis C.

The first point that needs to be made at the beginning of this discussion is that many authorities agree that a large database of research on the medical effects of marijuana is now available, and there is abundant evidence to support almost any claim made in the field, either in favor of or opposed to the use of cannabis for medical purposes. For example, NORML has published a review of some of the most important of the 22,000 peer-reviewed studies on medical aspects of cannabis (Armentano 2016), and the group Americans for Safe Access has published a similar review of 15,000 such studies (Report on Medical Cannabis Research History: What the Science Says 2016).

With such a vast array of data to choose from, it seems possible that the positions taken by individuals and groups vis-à-vis the use of marijuana for medical purposes may be based not only on scientific evidence, but also on other factors, such as one's general attitude about the use of marijuana under any circumstances whatsoever.

A few large studies have been conducted to sort through the myriad claims for the medical benefits of marijuana. One of the most important of these studies was conducted by a committee of the U.S. Institute of Medicine (IOM) in 1999. The committee's report was also published in the form of a book entitled *Marijuana and Medicine: Assessing the Scientific Base* (Joy, Watson, and Benson 1999). The committee claimed to have summarized and analyzed "what is known about the medical use of marijuana." Its report was taken as the gold standard of scientific research on medical marijuana for a decade. Although impossible to summarize briefly, the report suggests overall that compounds present in marijuana, especially THC, have "potential therapeutic value" for "pain relief, control of nausea and vomiting, and appetite stimulation." The committee points out, however, that "smoked marijuana . . . is a crude THC delivery system that also delivers harmful substances" (Joy, Watson, and Benson 1999, 3).

As public interest in the use of cannabis for the treatment of medical conditions increased during the first decade of the 21st century, other research groups repeated and extended studies of the type conducted by the IOM in 1999. (See, for example, Bagshaw and Hagen 2002; Ben Amar 2006.) The most recent of these studies was published in *JAMA*, the *Journal of the American Medical Association*, in June 2015 (Whiting et al. 2015). Space does not permit a detailed examination of these studies, but the conclusions drawn by the *JAMA* researchers may be of interest. "There was," they said, "moderate-quality evidence to support the use of cannabinoids for the treatment of chronic pain and spasticity." In addition, "[t]here was low-quality evidence suggesting that cannabinoids were associated with improvements in nausea and vomiting due to chemotherapy, weight gain in HIV infection, sleep disorders, and Tourette syndrome." Finally, they observed that "[c]annabinoids were associated with an increased risk of short-term Aes [adverse events]" (Whiting et al. 2015).

Among the conditions for which marijuana is most commonly recommended are the following:

- Cannabinoids may reduce intraocular pressure, thus offering some relief from glaucoma, although the drug's effects are generally no better than those produced by other available medications.
- Smoked marijuana may provide relief from pain resulting from injuries or surgical procedures when other more conventional pain-relieving medications are ineffective.

- Marijuana may help relieve the symptoms of multiple sclerosis, such as pain, spasticity, depression, fatigue, and incontinence.
- The use of marijuana may ameliorate some side effects of HIV/AIDS, such as anxiety, loss of appetite, and nausea.
- Treatment with marijuana has resulted in slowing the progression of Alzheimer's disease in some experimental animals.
- Marijuana may exhibit antibacterial action that will allow its use in the treatment of certain infections that are resistant to other antibiotics, such as methicillin-resistant *Staphylococcus aureus* (MRSA).
- Some patients with hepatitis C have used marijuana not only to treat the disease itself, but also to ameliorate the side effects of antiviral treatments used with the condition. (For citations for these conditions and further information on the therapeutic effects of medical marijuana, see Armentano 2016.)

A question that often arises with regard to the use of marijuana for medical purposes it how safe it is. Drugs used in the United States must be proved not only to be efficacious, but also safe for users. Studies have been conducted on this issue, none of which appear to show that marijuana is especially risky as a medication beyond the supposed harm it may cause in and of itself. (See discussion earlier in this chapter about possible physical risks associated with the use of marijuana.) For example, the organization ProCon.org in 2005 requested from the U.S. Food and Drug Administration (FDA) data regarding the relative safety in therapeutic situations of marijuana versus 17 other FDA-approved drugs. Those data showed that between January 1, 1997, and October 14, 2005, no deaths related to the use of marijuana in medical treatments had been recorded. During the same period, 10,008 deaths were attributed to the use of the 17 FDA-approved drugs. A second finding of that study was that 9,908 deaths were attributed to the use of FDA-approved drugs for conditions for which marijuana could have been used in its place (thus, presumably, saving some of those 9,908 lives) (Deaths from Marijuana v. 17 FDA-Approved Drugs 2009).

Arguments in Opposition to Legalizing Medical Marijuana

Critics of medical marijuana say that the drug is listed as a Schedule I for a reason, namely that it (1) is harmful to individuals and (2) has no generally accepted use in the medical community. One would never recommend the use of cocaine, heroin, or methamphetamines for the treatment of medical disorders, they say, so how can one justify the use of an equally dangerous substance, marijuana? For example, the DEA position statement on medical marijuana says simply that "smoked marijuana has not withstood the rigors of science—it is not medicine, and it is not safe" (DEA Position on Marijuana 2013, 1).

That view is echoed over and over again by opponents of the therapeutic use of medical marijuana. For example, the ONDCP has flatly stated its current position on medical marijuana:

> Marijuana and other illicit drugs are addictive and unsafe especially for use by young people. The science, though still evolving in terms of long-term consequences, is clear: marijuana use is harmful. (Strengthen Efforts to Prevent Drug Use in Our Communities 2016)

In debates over the use of marijuana for medical purposes, opponents of the practice tend to offer expert opinion and peer-reviewed research that contradict the claims made by proponents of medical marijuana. They point out, for example, that "no major medical association has come out in favor of smoked marijuana for widespread medical use" (Strengthen Efforts to Prevent Drug Use in Our Communities 2016). Such statements are often accompanied by an important caveat, however, namely that certain components of marijuana, or cannabis, or their chemical analogs may have medical benefit. For example, a chemical known as dronabinol may have therapeutic effects similar to those of smoked marijuana, without the potentially harmful side effects that many critics associate with the drug itself. Dronabinol is a synthetic product that contains Δ^9-tetrahydrocannabinol (THC), the major component of marijuana. Dronabinol has now been approved for medical use by the FDA under the trade name of Marinol. It is approved for use primarily for the treatment of anorexia in patients who have HIV/AIDS and for the nausea and vomiting experienced by individuals undergoing chemotherapy. In 2006, the FDA approved for limited use a similar chemical analog of THC known as nabilone (Cesamet).

Two other THC analogs now available for use are Canasol and Sativex, both derivatives of natural cannabis. Canasol was first developed by two Jamaican doctors and approved for use in that nation in 1987 for treatment of intraocular pressure in late-stage glaucoma. The drug has since been approved also in the United Kingdom, the United States, Canada, and other Caribbean nations. Sativex was first approved in Canada in 1995 for the treatment of neuropathic pain related to muscular sclerosis. It was later approved by the FDA, as well as a number of European nations, to treat cancer-related pain.

Current Status of Medical Marijuana in the United States

Marijuana is now permitted for use for at least some therapeutic purposes in a handful of nations around the world, including Canada, Israel, Netherlands, Czech Republic, Croatia, Mexico, Uruguay, Romania, Germany, Jamaica, Australia, Colombia, and Switzerland (Sherer 2015). In the United States, 28 states, the District of Columbia, and Guam have approved the use of marijuana for medical purposes. Those states are Alaska, Arizona, Arkansas, California, Colorado, Connecticut, Delaware, Florida, Hawaii, Illinois, Maine, Maryland, Massachusetts, Michigan, Minnesota, Montana, Nevada, New Hampshire, New Jersey, New Mexico, New York, North Dakota, Ohio, Oregon, Pennsylvania, Rhode Island, Vermont, and Washington (State Medical Marijuana Laws 2016; Steinmetz 2016).

A fundamental issue related to the legalization of medical marijuana in individual states is that the drug is still listed by the federal government as a Schedule I substance, making its use illegal under any circumstances. Various federal officials have attempted to deal with this conflict in one way or another, either by threatening to arrest any healthcare provider who prescribes marijuana for therapeutic purposes, or, on the other hand, largely turning a blind eye to the practice in individual states. The most important federal documents dealing with this issue have been a series of memoranda from the office of the U.S. Attorney General. The first of those memos (the *Ogden Memo* of October 19, 2009) seemed to lay out the general philosophy of the Obama administration with regard to the state-federal conflict over marijuana use. It began by emphasizing that the administration still held to the position that marijuana is "a dangerous drug, and the illegal distribution and sale of marijuana is a serious crime" which it intended to prosecute. On the other hand, the memo went on, the Department of Justice had limited resources, and it had to prioritize the crimes it chose to pursue. In general, therefore, investigators were directed to concentrate on marijuana-related crimes that met certain criteria, namely those that involved

- unlawful possession or unlawful use of firearms;
- violence;
- sales to minors;
- financial and marketing activities inconsistent with the terms, conditions, or purposes of state law, including evidence of money laundering activity and/or financial gains or excessive amounts of cash inconsistent with purported compliance with state or local law;
- amounts of marijuana inconsistent with purported compliance with state or local law;
- illegal possession or sale of other controlled substances; or
- ties to other criminal enterprises. (Memorandum for Selected United States Attorneys 2009)

Most observers viewed the Ogden memo as a signal that federal agents would largely keep hands off legitimate use of medical marijuana in states where such use had been approved. Two years later, however, the Obama administration felt it necessary to issue a second memorandum clarifying (or, some say, reversing) its position on the issue. That memo, the so-called *Cole Memorandum* of 2011 (Cole 2011) pointed out that the Ogden memo was not meant to imply that the federal government was simply going to turn its back on marijuana prosecutions. It was, Cole 2011 went on, "never intended to shield such activities from federal enforcement action and prosecution, even where those activities purport to comply with state law" (Memorandum for United States Attorneys 2011) The gates appeared to be open to more aggressive attacks by federal agents on state medical marijuana facilities, which shortly appeared to be the case as the number of such raids soon began to increase (Riggs 2011).

Fast forward two more years, and the situation has appeared to change one more time. In a second memorandum by Deputy Attorney General James M. Cole (Cole 2013), the administration repeats the apparent message of the Ogden memo, namely that the Department of Justice has decided to focus its limited resources on only certain types of marijuana-related activities, roughly corresponding with the list provided earlier (Memorandum for All United States Attorneys 2013). This most recent memo, then, appears to indicate that the Obama administration has decided essentially to ignore activities related to the use of marijuana for medical purposes in states where such use has been approved. (For a detailed background on the history of this issue, see Grim and Reilly 2013.)

Legalization of Recreational Marijuana

Progress toward the legalization of marijuana for recreational use has occurred more slowly than it has for medical marijuana. The earliest steps in that direction took place in the 1970s when a handful of states decriminalized the use of marijuana for recreational purposes. The first such action, the Oregon

Decriminalization Bill of 1973, made possession of one ounce of marijuana a violation (not a crime) punishable by a fine of $500 to $1,000 (Blachly 1976). Over the next four years, 10 more states—Alaska, California, Colorado, Maine, Minnesota, Mississippi, Nebraska, New York, North Carolina, and Ohio—followed Oregon's lead in decriminalizing the use of recreational marijuana (Austin [n.d.]; Scott 2010).

It took nearly 40 years, however, to take the next step: outright legalization of marijuana. Then, in the general elections of November 2012, two states, Colorado and Washington, adopted legislation legalizing the recreational use of up to one ounce of marijuana. Then, on November 4, 2014, two more states, Alaska and Oregon, and the District of Columbia also voted to legalize the use of small amounts of marijuana for recreational purposes. A major breakthrough occurred in November 2016, when four more states—California, Maine, Massachusetts, and Nevada—approved the use of marijuana for recreational purposes. (Arizona voters defeated a similar proposal.) The precise wording of laws in each of the eight states and the District varies to some extent (Ferner 2015; a detailed description of marijuana laws in all 50 states and the District of Columbia is available at State Laws 2016). A "betting game" is now going on among observers and commentators as to which states are most likely to become the next sites where marijuana is declared to be legal for recreational purposes (for example, see Rough 2016).

The legalization of recreational marijuana in these eight states and the District states has permitted the conduct of a "grand experiment" about certain long-standing and fundamental questions regarding marijuana consumption, such as:

- How does legalization affect the prevalence and incidence of marijuana use in the general population?
- What is the effect of legalization on marijuana use among children and adolescents?
- How does legalization affect patterns of physical, mental, and other forms of health in the general population?

- To what extent are accident rates (such as vehicle crashes) affected by legalization?
- Are financial benefits to states, such as taxes on marijuana sales, comparable to those predicted by supporters of legalization?

None of these questions are easy to answer, and, as of late 2016, it is still too early to know what those answers might be. Nonetheless, officials in all four states are aware of the importance of such questions and the need to collect data about them. In Colorado, for example, the state legislature adopted legislation in 2013 requiring the state Division of Criminal Justice and the Department of Public Safety to collect data and prepare a report on the effects of marijuana legalization in a variety of fields. The following data are summarized from a report released in March 2016 pursuant to that charge. Among the trends noted in the report are the following (all data from Reed 2016, 5–9):

- The total number of marijuana-related arrests dropped from 12,894 in 2012 (the last year before legalization) to 7,004 (the first year after legalization), a decrease of 46%. The number of arrests for possession was reduced by half (47%) and for sales by a quarter (24%) with essentially no change for production (–2%).
- The number of court filings for marijuana-related cases dropped by 81% between 2012 and 2015, from 10,340 to 1,954. The rate for juveniles 10 to 17 fell 69%, for young adults 18 to 20 by 78%, and for adults 21 and over, by 86%.
- The number of summons issued by the Colorado State Police for marijuana-related offenses decreased by 1% between 2014 and 2015.
- The number of marijuana-related hospitalizations increased from 803 per 100,000 in the period 2001–2009 to 2,413 per 100,000 in the period 2014–June 2015.
- The number of marijuana-related visits to emergency departments increased by 29%, from 739 per 100,000 in

the period 2010–2013 to 956 per 100,000 in the period 2014–June 2015.

- The Healthy Kids Colorado Survey found a "slight decline" in the number of "30-day use" respondents after legalization of the drug.
- The rate of juvenile arrests for marijuana-related crimes increased by 2% (from 598 to 611) between 2012 and 2014.
- Total state revenue from taxes, licenses, and fees increased by 77% from calendar year 2014 to 2015, going from $76,152,468 to $135,100,465. Essentially all of this increase resulted from marijuana-related activities.
- Tax revenue from marijuana-related activities in 2015 was $35,060,590, an increase of 163% over 2014 revenues of $13,341,001. Of the 2015 total, $8,626,922 was distributed to local schools.

Other states have prepared reports similar to Colorado's (see Dilley 2016; Monitoring Impacts of Recreational Marijuana Legalization: 2015 Baseline Report 2015), with results roughly similar to those from Colorado. Stronger statements about the effects on society of legalization marijuana, however, await the passage of time and more detailed studies of the issue.

Resistance to Legalization

As can be expected in the progress of any important social issue, the adoption of new laws or decisions by courts do not necessarily mark the end of the dispute over such issues (see, for example, the debates over abortion and same-sex marriage in the United States). Such has also been the case with the legalization of marijuana. The adoption of legislation permitting the use of marijuana for recreational purposes in these entities has not meant that opponents of legalization have ended their battle against the practice. In one instance, for example, residents of Pueblo County filed a law suit against the state because an adjacent crop of marijuana plants allegedly blocked their view. In another suit, a Holiday Inn hotel in Frisco, Colorado, filed a RICO (Racketeer Influenced and Corrupt Organizations Act) suit against the state because, it claimed, a marijuana dispensary scheduled to open next to the property would interfere with its normal business activities. In yet a third case, a group of sheriffs and other law enforcement officials from Colorado, Kansas, and Nebraska sued the state, claiming that the legalization of marijuana violated state law, the Colorado constitution, and the U.S. constitution. Plaintiffs lost in all three of these cases (Warner 2016).

The case that perhaps drew the greatest attention nationally was *Nebraska and Oklahoma v. Colorado* (U.S. Supreme Court docket #220144), in which Nebraska and Oklahoma sued Colorado. The two states argued that the legalization of marijuana in Colorado was likely to result in an increase in drug-related crimes in their own states and that the new Colorado law was, therefore, unconstitutional. In April 2016, the Supreme Court declined to hear the case, essentially bringing to an end this type of complaint about the new Colorado marijuana law (*Nebraska and Oklahoma v. Colorado* 2016). While the legal history of challenges to marijuana law have universally failed thus far, it is still early days in the history of marijuana legalization, and additional challenges in other states on a variety of issues are to be expected. (See, for example, Mapes 2015.)

Conclusion

Attitudes with regard to the use of marijuana for recreational and medical purposes have evolved in the United States over the past two decades at a fairly remarkable rate. Indications are that this change is likely to continue in the near future. Still, strong arguments exist for moving with caution in changing the legal status of the drug that has, for more than a century, been regarded largely as a dangerous, and probably gateway, substance that should not be available to the general public under any circumstances. With legalization efforts in some states now under way, our understanding of marijuana and the effects it has on a myriad of ways in everyday life is likely to improve, thus making decisions about the status of marijuana better informed in the future.

References

Armentano, Paul. 2016. "Emerging Clinical Applications for Cannabis and Cannabinoids: A Review of the Recent Scientific Literature, 2000–2015," 7th ed. http://norml .org/pdf_files/NORML_Clinical_Applications_for_ Cannabis_and_Cannabinoids.pdf. Accessed on May 20, 2016.

Austin, James. [n.d.] "The Decrim. Movement." NORML. http://norml.org/component/zoo/category/ rethinking-the-consequences-of-decriminalizing-marijuana. Accessed on May 22, 2016.

Bagshaw, Sean M., and Neil A. Hagen. 2002. "Medical Efficacy of Cannabinoids and Marijuana: A Comprehensive Review of the Literature." *Journal of Palliative Care*. 18(2): 111–122.

Barnett, Erica A. 2006. "Hold the Waffles." http://www .seattleweekly.com/2002-02-06/news/hold-the-waffles/. Accessed on May 12, 2016.

Ben Amar, Marine. 2006. "Cannabinoids in Medicine: A Review of Their Therapeutic Potential." *Journal of Ethnopharmacology*. 105(1–2): 1–25.

Blachly Paul H. 1976. "Effects of Decriminalization of Marijuana in Oregon." *Annals of the New York Academy of Sciences*. 282(1): 405–415.

Boffey, Philip M. 2014. "What Science Says about Marijuana." *New York Times.* http://www.nytimes.com/2014/07/31/ opinion/what-science-says-about-marijuana.html?_r=0. Accessed on May 19, 2016.

Bonné, Jon. 2002. "For Hemp Foods, A Decisive Moment." *Cannabis News.* http://cannabisnews.com/news/12/ thread12467.shtml. Accessed on May 12, 2016.

Bonnie, Richard J., and Charles H. Whitebread, II. 1970. "The Forbidden Fruit and the Tree of Knowledge: An Inquiry into the Legal History of American Marijuana Prohibition." *Virginia Law Review.* 56(6): 971–1203. Also available online at http://www.druglibrary.org/schaffer/ library/studies/vlr/vlrtoc.htm (not paginated). Accessed on May 13, 2016.

"The Cannabis Problem: A Note on the Problem and the History of International Action." 2016. UN Office on Drugs and Crime. http://www.unodc.org/unodc/en/ data-and-analysis/bulletin/bulletin_1962-01-01_4_ page005.html. Accessed on May 12, 2016.

Carson, E. Anne. 2015. "Prisoners in 2014." Bureau of Justice Statistics. http://www.bjs.gov/content/pub/pdf/p14.pdf. Accessed on May 18, 2016.

Carter, Jimmy. 1977. "Drug Abuse Message Top Congress." http://www.presidency.ucsb.edu/ws/index .php?pid=7908#axzz1PSLOq2Hj. Accessed on May 15, 2016.

Carter, Jimmy. 2011. "Call Off the Global Drug War." *New York Times.* June 17, 2011, A35. Also available online at http://www.nytimes.com/2011/06/17/opinion/17carter .html. Accessed on May 15, 2016.

Christen, Arden G., et al. 1982. "Smokeless Tobacco: The Folklore and Social History of Snuffing, Sneezing, Dipping, and Chewing." *Journal of the American Dental Association.*

105: 821–829. Also available online at http://www .modernsnuff.com/books/journal_article_by_Christen.pdf. Accessed on May 12, 2016.

Cole, James M. 2011. "Memorandum for United States Attorneys." U.S. Department of Justice. https://www .justice.gov/sites/default/files/oip/legacy/2014/07/23/ dag-guidance-2011-for-medical-marijuana-use.pdf. Accessed on August 9, 2016.

Cole, James M. 2013. "Memorandum for All United States Attorneys." U.S. Department of Justice. https://www .justice.gov/iso/opa/resources/3052013829132756857467 .pdf. Accessed on August 9, 2016.

"Compilation of Publications, Interviews, Criminal Files and Photographs of Moses Baca & Samuel Caldwell." 2010. Uncle Mike's Library. http://www.unclemikesresearch.com/ u-s-district-court-denver-colorado-imposes-first-federal-ma rihuana-law-penalties/. Accessed on May 13, 2016.

"Controlled Dangerous Substances Act of 1969." 1969. Committee on the Judiciary. U.S. Senate. Senate Report No. 613, 91st Congress, 1st Session. https://bulk.resource .org/gao.gov/91-513/000050F5.pdf. Accessed on May 14, 2016.

"The Controlled Substances Act of 1970." 2015. Catholic University of America. http://counsel.cua.edu/fedlaw/ csa1970.cfm. Accessed on May 14, 2016.

"Controlled Substances Schedules." 2016. Office of Diversion Control. Drug Enforcement Administration. http://www .deadiversion.usdoj.gov/schedules/. Accessed on May 15, 2016.

"The DEA Position on Marijuana." 2013. U.S. Department of Justice. Drug Enforcement Administration. http://www .dea.gov/docs/marijuana_position_2011.pdf. Accessed on May 19, 2016.

"Deaths from Marijuana v. 17 FDA-Approved Drugs." ProCon.org. http://medicalmarijuana.procon.org/view .resource.php?resourceID=000145. Accessed on May 20, 2016.

Dilley, Julia, et al. 2016. "Marijuana Report: Marijuana Use, Attitudes and Health Effects in Oregon." Oregon Public Health Division. https://public.health.oregon .gov/PreventionWellness/marijuana/Documents/ oha-8509-marijuana-report.pdf. Accessed on May 23, 2016.

"Drug Fact Sheet: Marijuana." 2016. U.S. Drug Enforcement Administration. http://www.dea.gov/druginfo/drug_data_ sheets/Marijuana.pdf. Accessed on May 19, 2016.

DuPont, Robert L. 2010. "Why We Should Not Legalize Marijuana." ILCAAAP. http://ilcaaap.org/2011/06/22/why- we-should-not-legalize-marijuana/. Accessed on May 19, 2016. Original site (unaccredited): http://www.cnbc .com/id/36267223. Accessed on May 19, 2016.

Ferner, Matt. 2015. "Alaska Becomes Fourth State to Legalize Marijuana." *Huffpost Politics*. http://www.huffingtonpost .com/2014/11/05/alaska-marijuana-legalization_n_594 7516.html. Accessed on May 22, 2016.

"The First Pot POW." 2016. NORML. http://norml.org/ component/zoo/category/the-first-pot-pow. Accessed on May 13, 2016.

French, Angela. 2005. "Up in Smoke: Office of National Drug Control Policy's Wasted Efforts in the War on Drugs." Citizens against Government Waste. http://cagw .org/sites/default/files/pdf/2005/up_in_smoke.pdf. Accessed on July 17, 2016.

Gettman, John. 2007. "Lost Taxes and Other Costs of Marijuana Laws." DrugScience.org. http://www.drug science.org/Archive/bcr4/2Usage.html. Accessed on May 16, 2016.

Gieringer, Dale H. 1999. "The Forgotten Origins of Cannabis Prohibition in California." *Contemporary Drug Problems.* 26(2): 237–288. Also available online at http://canorml .org/background/caloriginsmjproh.pdf, as revised in February 2000, December 2002, March 2005, and June 2006. Accessed on May 13, 2016.

Goldberg, Peter. 1980. "The Facts about Drug Abuse." The Drug Abuse Council. Available online at http://www .druglibrary.org/schaffer/library/studies/fada/fada1.htm. Accessed on May 17, 2016.

Grant, Igor, et al. 2003. "Non-Acute (Residual) Neurocognitive Effects of Cannabis Use: A Meta-Analytic Study." *Journal of the International Neuropsychological Society.* 9(5): 679–689.

Grim, Ryan, and Ryan J. Reilly. 2013. "Obama's Drug War: After Medical Marijuana Mess, Feds Face Big Decision on Pot." *Huffpost Politics.* http:// www.huffingtonpost.com/2013/01/26/obamas- drug-war-medical-marijuana_n_2546178.html. Accessed on May 21, 2016.

Guither, Pete. 2016. "Why Is Marijuana Illegal?" Drug War Rant.com. http://www.drugwarrant.com/articles/ why-is-marijuana-illegal/. Accessed on May 13, 2016.

"Half-Baked Idea?: Legalizing Marijuana Will Help the Environment." *Scientific American,* May 20, 2011. http://www.scientificamerican.com/article.cfm?id= would-legalizing-pot-be-good-for-environment. Accessed on May 18, 2016.

Hanauer, J. E., and Marmaduke William Pickthall. 2007. *Folk-Lore of the Holy Land: Moslem, Christian and Jewish.* Charleston, SC: BiblioBazaar. Reprint of original 1907 edition. Also available online at http://www .sacred-texts.com/asia/flhl/flhl37.htm. Accessed on May 12, 2016.

Hardy, Quentin. 2005. "Milton Friedman: Legalize It!" *Forbes.* http://www.forbes.com/2005/06/02/cz_qh_06 02pot.html. Accessed on May 17, 2016.

"Harry J. Anslinger Quotes/Quotations." 2010. Uncle Mike's Library. http://www.unclemikesresearch.com/harry-j-anslinger-quotesquotations/. Accessed on May 13, 2016.

Hartnett, Edmund. 2005. "Drug Legalization: Why It Wouldn't Work in the United States." *Police Chief.* http://www.policechiefmagazine.org/magazine/index.cfm?fuseaction=display_arch&article_id=533&issue_id=32005. Accessed on May 19, 2016.

Hashibe, Mia et al. 2005. "Epidemiologic Review of Marijuana Use and Cancer Risk." *Alcohol* 35(3): 265–275. Also available online at https://www.researchgate.net/publication/7690899_Epidemiologic_review_of_marijuana_use_and_cancer_risk. Accessed on May 17, 2016.

Herer, Jack. 1993. *The Emperor Wears No Clothes.* Van Nuys, CA: Hemp Publishing Company. Available online at http://www.hampapartiet.se/25.pdf. Accessed on August 9, 2016.

Hudon, Edward Gerard. 1956. *Narcotic Control Act of 1956: Legislative History of Public Law 84-728.* Washington, DC: U.S. Supreme Court Library.

"Illegal Drugs." 2016. PollingReport.com. http://www.pollingreport.com/drugs.htm. Accessed on May 16, 2016.

"Interview Peter Bourne." 2000. *PBS Frontline.* http://www.pbs.org/wgbh/pages/frontline/shows/drugs/interviews/bourne.html. Accessed on May 15, 2016.

"Is Marijuana a Gateway Drug?" 2016a. National Institute on Drug Abuse. https://www.drugabuse.gov/publications/research-reports/marijuana/marijuana-gateway-drug. Accessed on May 19, 2016.

"Is Marijuana a Gateway Drug?" 2016b. *New York Times.* http://www.nytimes.com/roomfordebate/2016/04/26/is-marijuana-a-gateway-drug. Accessed on May 19, 2016.

"Is Marijuana Haram?" 2016. Ummah Forum. http://www
.ummah.com/forum/showthread.php?88214-Is-marijuana-
Haram/page5. Accessed on May 12, 2016.

Johnson, Lyndon B. 1968. "Special Message to the Congress
on Crime and Law Enforcement: 'To Insure the Public
Safety.'" The American Presidency Project. http://www
.presidency.ucsb.edu/ws/?pid=29237#axzz1k1QdB1Wg.
Accessed on May 14, 2016.

Johnston, Lloyd D., et al. 2016. *Monitoring the Future
National Survey Results on Drug Use, 1975–2015:
Overview, Key Findings on Adolescent Drug Use.* Ann
Arbor: Institute for Social Research, The University of
Michigan.

Jones, Jeffrey. 2015. "In U.S., 58% Back Legal Marijuana
Use." Gallup. http://www.gallup.com/poll/186260/
back-legal-marijuana.aspx. Accessed on May 16, 2016.

Joy, Janet E., Stanley J. Watson, Jr., and John A. Benson, Jr.,
eds. 1999. *Marijuana and Medicine: Assessing the Science
Base.* Washington, DC: National Academy Press. Available
online at http://www.nap.edu/download.php?record_id=
6376. Accessed on May 17, 2016.

Kendell, Robert. 2003. "Cannabis Condemned: The
Proscription of Indian Hemp." *Addiction.* 98(2): 143–151.

Kick, Russell. 2002. *Everything You Know Is Wrong: The
Disinformation Guide to Secrets and Lies.* New York: The
Disinformation Company.

King, Rufus. 1972. *The Drug Hang Up: America's Fifty-Year
Folly.* Springfield, IL: Charles C. Thomas, 1972. Also
available online at http://www.druglibrary.net/special/king/
dhu/dhumenu.htm. Accessed on May 14, 2016.

Leary v. United States, 395 U.S. 6 (1969). Text available at
http://supreme.justia.com/cases/federal/us/395/6/.

Mapes, Jeff. 2015. "Oregon Marijuana Law Could Face Legal
Challenge, City and County Associations Say." *Oregon Live.*

http://www.oregonlive.com/mapes/index.ssf/2015/03/
oregon_marijuana_law_could_fac.html. Accessed on
May 30, 2016.

"The Marihuana Tax Act of 1937." 1937. Schaffer Library of
Drug Policy. http://www.druglibrary.org/schaffer/hemp/
taxact/mjtaxact.htm. Accessed on May 13, 2016.

"Marijuana." 2014. Drug Facts. National Institute on
Drug Abuse. https://www.drugabuse.gov/sites/default/
files/drugfactsmarijuana2014.pdf. Accessed on May 19,
2016.

"Marijuana." 2015. Facts for Teens. National Institute on
Drug Abuse. https://www.drugabuse.gov/sites/default/files/
marijuana_teens.pdf. Accessed on May 19, 2016.

"Marijuana." 2016a. Examine.com. http://examine.com/
supplements/Marijuana/. Accessed on May 19, 2016.

"Marijuana." 2016b. NIDA for Teens. National Institute
on Drug Abuse. https://teens.drugabuse.gov/drug-facts/
marijuana. Accessed on May 19, 2016.

McCrimmon, Katie Kerwin. 2012. "Research Shows Adverse Effects of Marijuana on Teens as Drug Use among
Students Appears to Be Rising." Chalkbeat. http://www
.chalkbeat.org/posts/co/2012/02/22/research-shows-
adverse-effects-of-marijuana-on-teens-as-drug-use-among-
students-appears-to-be-rising/#.Vz40kvkrJD8. Accessed
on May 19, 2016.

"Memorandum for All United States Attorneys." 2013. U.S.
Department of Justice. https://www.justice.gov/iso/opa/
resources/3052013829132756857467.pdf. Accessed on
May 21, 2016.

"Memorandum for Selected United States Attorneys." 2009.
U.S. Department of Justice. https://www.justice.gov/sites/
default/files/opa/legacy/2009/10/19/medical-marijuana
.pdf. Accessed on May 21, 2016.

"Memorandum for United States Attorneys." 2011. U.S. Department of Justice. https://www.justice.gov/sites/default/files/oip/legacy/2014/07/23/dag-guidance-2011-for-medical-marijuana-use.pdf. Accessed on May 21, 2016.

Miron, Jeffrey A. 2005. "The Budgetary Implications of Marijuana Prohibition." http://www.prohibitioncosts.org/mironreport/. Accessed on May 17, 2016.

Miron, Jeffrey A., and Katherine Waldock. 2010. "The Budgetary Impact of Ending Drug Prohibition." Washington, DC: Cato Institute. Available online at http://object.cato.org/sites/cato.org/files/pubs/pdf/DrugProhibitionWP.pdf. Accessed on May 17, 2016.

"Model State Civil Fine Bill." 2016. Marijuana Policy Project. https://www.mpp.org/issues/decriminalization/model-state-decriminalization-bill/. Accessed on May 15, 2016.

"Monitoring Impacts of Recreational Marijuana Legalization: 2015 Baseline Report." 2015. Forecasting and Research Division. Washington State Office of Financial Management. http://www.ofm.wa.gov/reports/marijuana_impacts_2015.pdf. Accessed on May 23, 2016.

Moore, Brent A., et al. 2005. "Respiratory Effects of Marijuana and Tobacco Use in a U.S. Sample." *Journal of General Internal Medicine.* 20(1): 33–37.

Moran, Thomas J. 2011. "Just a Little Bit of History Repeating: The California Model of Marijuana Legalization and How It Might Affect Racial and Ethnic Minorities." *Washington and Lee Journal of Civil Rights and Social Justice.* 17(2): 557–590.

Naguib, Hussein. 2008. "Alcohol and Intoxicants in Islam." Through Muslim Eyes. http://islam42.blogspot.com/2008/09/alcohol-and-intoxicants-in-islam.html. Accessed on May 12, 2016.

"National Drug Control Budget." 2016. Office of National Drug Control Policy. https://www.whitehouse.gov/sites/default/files/ondcp/press-releases/fy_2017_budget_high lights.pdf. Accessed on May 17, 2016.

"National Drug Control Strategy." 2008. Office of National Drug Control Policy. https://www.whitehouse.gov/sites/default/files/ondcp/Fact_Sheets/FY2009-Budget-Summary-February-2008.pdf. Accessed on May 17, 2016.

Nebraska and Oklahoma v. Colorado. 2016. SCOTUSblog. http://www.scotusblog.com/case-files/cases/nebraska-and-oklahoma-v-colorado/. Accessed on May 30, 2016.

"Nixon Tapes Show Roots of Marijuana Prohibition: Misinformation, Culture Wars and Prejudice." 2002. CSDP Research Report. http://proxy.baremetal.com/csdp.org/research/shafernixon.pdf. Accessed on May 15, 2016.

Parshell, Ardis E. 2009. "The Great Mormon Marijuana Myth." The Keepapitchinin. http://www.keepapitchinin.org/2009/01/09/the-great-mormon-marijuana-myth/. Accessed on May 13, 2016.

"Perspectives on Drug Policy." 2012. Institute for Behavior and Health. http://mnoa.com/IBH.pdf. Accessed on May 19, 2016.

Pietschmann, Thomas, et al. [2009]. "A Century of International Drug Control. Vienna: UN Office on Drugs and Crime. Available online at https://www.unodc.org/documents/data-and-analysis/Studies/100_Years_of_Drug_Control.pdf. Accessed on May 13, 2016.

Pletcher, Mark J., et al. 2012. "Association between Marijuana Exposure and Pulmonary Function over 20 Years." *JAMA.* 307(2): 173–181.

Public Law 99-570. 2016. Available at https://www.gpo.gov/fdsys/pkg/STATUTE-100/pdf/STATUTE-100-Pg3207.pdf. Accessed on May 15, 2016.

Reagan, Ronald. 1982. "Remarks on Signing Executive Order 12368, Concerning Federal Drug Abuse Policy Functions." June 24, 1982. http://www.presidency.ucsb.edu/ws/index .php?pid=42671%23axzz1P5p1SNqO. Accessed on May 15, 2016.

Reed, Jack K. 2016. "Marijuana Legislation in Colorado: Early Findings." Colorado Department of Public Safety. http://cdpsdocs.state.co.us/ors/docs/reports/2016-SB13-283-Rpt.pdf. Accessed on May 23, 2016.

"Report on Medical Cannabis Research History: What the Science Says." 2016. Americans for Safe Access. http:// www.safeaccessnow.org/medical_cannabis_research_what_ does_the_evidence_say. Accessed on May 20, 2016.

Retail Marijuana Public Health Advisory Committee. 2015. "Literature Review on Marijuana Use and Health Effects." https://drive.google.com/folderview?id=0BxqXhstk92Dbd 1ZoMG5OaFpJdUU&usp=sharing#. Accessed on May 19, 2016.

Richards, Louise G., ed. 1981. *Demographic Trends and Drug Abuse, 1980–1995.* NIDA Research Monograph 35. Washington, DC: Government Printing Office. Available online at https://archives.drugabuse.gov/pdf/ monographs/35.pdf. Accessed on May 16, 2016.

Riggs, Mike, 2011. "Obama Administration Overrides 2009 Ogden Memo, Declares Open Season on Pot Shops in States Where Medical Marijuana Is Legal." Reason.com. http://reason.com/blog/2011/06/30/white-house-overrides-2009-mem. Accessed on May 21, 2016.

Rough, Lisa. 2016. "What States Are Most Likely to Legalize Cannabis in 2016?" *Leafly.* https://www.leafly.com/news/ headlines/what-states-are-most-likely-to-legalize-in-2016. Accessed on May 22, 2016.

Salas-Wright, Christopher P., et al. 2015. "Trends in the Disapproval and Use of Marijuana among Adolescents and

Young Adults in the United States: 2002–2013." *American Journal of Drug and Alcohol Abuse.* 41(5): 392–404. Also available online at http://www.tandfonline.com/doi/abs/10.3109/00952990.2015.1049493. Accessed on May 16, 2016.

"Sanitary Code Amendments." 1914. Topics of the Times. *New York Times,* July 30, 1914, 8. Available online at http://query.nytimes.com/mem/archive-free/pdf?res=9B07E1DB1438EF32A25753C3A9619C946596D6CF. Accessed on May 13, 2016.

Schlosser, Eric. 1997. "More Reefer Madness." *Atlantic Online.* http://www.theatlantic.com/past/docs/issues/97apr/reef.htm. Accessed on January 22, 2012.

Scott, Emilee Mooney. 2010. OLR Research Report. https://www.cga.ct.gov/2010/rpt/2010-R-0204.htm. Accessed on May 22, 2016.

"The Shanghai Opium Commission." 2016. UN Office on Drugs and Crime. http://www.unodc.org/unodc/en/data-and-analysis/bulletin/bulletin_1959-01-01_1_page006.html. Accessed on May 12, 2016.

Sherer, Steph. 2015. "Global Patient Populations Need International Medical Cannabis Policies to Evolve." Americans for Safe Access. http://www.who.int/medicines/access/controlled-substances/StephShererAmericansforSafeAccessCannabisStatementECDD2015.pdf. Accessed on May 20, 2016.

"Should Marijuana Be Legalized under Any Circumstances?" 2011. Balanced Politics. http://www.balancedpolitics.org/marijuana_legalization.htm. Accessed on May 18, 2016.

"Speaking Out against Drug Legislation." 2010. [U.S. Department of Justice. Drug Enforcement Administration.] http://www.ibhinc.org/pdfs/DEASpeakingOutAgainstDrugLegalization2010.pdf Accessed on May 19, 2016.

Squeglia, L. M., J. Jacobus, and S. F. Tapert. 2009. "The Influence of Substance Use on Adolescent Brain Development." *Clinical EEG and Neuroscience.* 40(1): 31–38.

"State Laws." 2016. NORML. http://norml.org/laws/. Accessed on May 15, 2016.

"State Medical Marijuana Laws." 2016. National Conference of State Legislatures. http://www.ncsl.org/research/health/state-medical-marijuana-laws.aspx. Accessed on May 21, 2016.

"Statement of H. J. Anslinger." 2016. Schafer Library of Drug Policy. http://www.druglibrary.org/SCHAFFER/hemp/taxact/anslng1.htm. Accessed on May 13, 2016.

"States That Have Decriminalized." 2016. NORML. http://norml.org/aboutmarijuana/item/states-that-have-decriminalized. Accessed on May 15, 2016.

Steinmetz, Kary. 2016. "These States Just Legalized Marijuana." Time. http://time.com/4559278/marijuana-election-results-2016/. Accessed on November 9, 2016.

Sterling, Eric E. 1999. "Drug Laws and Snitching: A Primer." http://www.pbs.org/wgbh/pages/frontline/shows/snitch/primer/. Accessed on May 15, 2016.

Stimson, Charles. [2010]. "Legalizing Marijuana: Why Citizens Should Just Say No." http://www.heritage.org/research/reports/2010/09/legalizing-marijuana-why-citizens-should-just-say-no. Accessed on May 19, 2016.

"Strengthen Efforts to Prevent Drug Use in Our Communities." 2016. Office of National Drug Control Policy. https://www.whitehouse.gov/ondcp/strengthen-efforts-to-prevent-drug-use-in-our-communities/. Accessed on May 20, 2016.

"Taxation of Marihuana." 1937. U.S. House of Representatives, Committee on Ways and Means, Hearings, 4 May 1937. As cited in "The Marihuana Tax

Act of 1937." http://www.druglibrary.org/schaffer/hemp/
taxact/t10a.htm. Accessed on May 13, 2016.

Taxy, Sam, Julie Samuels, and William Adams. 2015. "Drug
Offenders in Federal Prison: Estimates of Characteristics."
Bureau of Justice Statistics. http://www.bjs.gov/content/
pub/pdf/dofp12.pdf. Accessed on May 18, 2016.

"Title 21: Food and Drugs." 1971. Rules and Regulations.
Federal Register. 36 (80; April 24): 7776–7826.

"The Truth about Marijuana." 2016. Foundation for a Drug-
Free World. http://www.drugfreeworld.org/drugfacts/
marijuana/on-the-road-to-drug-abuses.html. Accessed on
May 19, 2016.

Touw, Mia. 1981. "Use of Cannabis in China, India, and
Tibet." *Journal of Psychoactive Drugs.* 13(1): 23–34.

Turner, Carlton E. 2016. "The Medical Marijuana Con Job."
http://nacdac.org/wp-content/uploads/The%20Con%20
Job%20of%20Medical%20Marijuana(1).pdf. Accessed on
May 15, 2016.

U.S. Commission on Marihuana and Drug Abuse. 1972.
"Marihuana, A Signal of Misunderstanding. The Report of
the National Commission on Marihuana and Drug Abuse."
New York: New American Library. Also available online at
https://babel.hathitrust.org/cgi/pt?id=mdp.390150156475
58;view=1up;seq=1. Accessed on May 14, 2016.

U.S. Congress. 1951. Congressional Record. 97th Congress.
Washington, DC: Government Printing Office.

Vance, Laurence M. 2011. "The 40-Year War on Freedom."
The Future of Freedom Foundation. http://fff.org/
explore-freedom/article/40year-war-freedom/. Accessed on
May 18, 2016.

"War on Drugs Unsuccessful, Drug Czar Says." 2010. *CBS
News.* http://www.cbsnews.com/stories/2010/05/13/
politics/main6480889.shtml. Accessed on May 17, 2016.

Warner, Joel. 2016. "Marijuana Legalization Movement Just Won Multiple Courtroom Battles, But Will That Be Enough to Quash Future Legal Threats?" *International Business Times*. http://www.ibtimes.com/marijuana-legalization-movement-just-won-multiple-courtroom-battles-will-be-enough-2342055. Accessed on May 30, 2016.

WGME. 2016. "Maine Voters Narrowly Endorse Recreational Marijuana Use." On Your Side WGME. http://wgme.com/news/local/maine-voters-approve-recreational-marijuana-use. Accessed on November 9, 2016.

Whitebread, Charles. 1995. "The History of the Non-Medical Use of Drugs in the United States: A Speech to the California Judges Association 1995 Annual Conference." http://www.druglibrary.org/olsen/DPF/whitebread.html#TOC. Accessed on May 13, 2016.

Whiting, Penny F., et al. 2015. "Cannabinoids for Medical Use: A Systematic Review and Meta-Analysis." *JAMA*. 313(24): 2456–2473. Also available online at http://jama.jamanetwork.com/article.aspx?articleid=2338251. Accessed on May 20, 2016.

Wisotsky, Steven. 1992. "A Society of Suspects: The War on Drugs and Civil Liberties." Cato Institute. http://www.cato.org/pubs/pas/pa-180.html. Accessed on May 18, 2016.

Wren, Christopher C. 1999. "Bird Food Is a Casualty of the War on Drugs." *New York Times*. http://www.nytimes.com/1999/10/03/us/bird-food-is-a-casualty-of-the-war-on-drugs.html. Accessed on May 12, 2016.

Ziedenberg, Jason, and Jason Colburn. 2005. "Efficacy & Impact: The Criminal Justice Response to Marijuana Policy in the US." Justice Policy Institute. http://www.justicepolicy.org/images/upload/05-08_REP_EfficacyandImpact_AC-DP.pdf. Accessed on May 17, 2016.

Introduction

Marijuana is a topic that has elicited opinions over a wide range for centuries. Individuals have written and spoken about its wonderful healing properties, its gate to a world beyond the normal five senses, its key to understanding that goes beyond normal intelligence, its risks to physical and mental health, and many other benefits and risks. This chapter provides a venue in which those expressions of opinion can continue as nine authors of varying experience and understanding about the drug present their own specific views on some specific aspects of the topic of this book.

Marijuana Is Not Safe and Is Not Medicine
Peter Bensinger

Suggestions and legislative proposals continue to emerge on what to do about marijuana use in the United States. Proposed options range from full marijuana legalization to providing marijuana as a "medicine," to making penalties for marijuana use and/or possession a noncriminal offense payable with a fine like a traffic ticket. These are all bad ideas from a healthcare

---

A spokesperson for a marijuana retail and grow facility answers questions as a contingent of Nevada lawmakers tour two operations for both medical and recreational marijuana in Denver, Colorado, on April 25, 2015. (AP Photo/David Zalubowski)

ductivity, and crime prevention point of view.

Legalizing marijuana reminds me of the efforts in Britain in the early 1970s to make heroin available to heroin users. Those who registered to use heroin went to chemists shops (drugstores) and received their dosages at purity levels that were well within lower nonlethal limits. The anticipated results of this policy were to limit the negative effects of heroin use (e.g., overdose), to reduce heroin use, and to limit law enforcement needs. In reality, the heroin addicts purchased the more powerful and more lethal variety of heroin still sold on the streets. Rather than reducing its narcotics force, Scotland Yard doubled the number of investigators because illegal heroin imports tripled. Using this example, we must ask, if marijuana were legalized, at what purity would it be sanctioned—at 3% THC, the typical potency of marijuana in the 1970s; at 5–6%, typical today; or 11–12%, found in the "sensimillia" high potency marijuana? What age group could be buyers, 21 and older? The big market today is between the ages of 15 and 25 (Results from the 2008 National Survey on Drug Use and Health: National Findings 2009, 1–2).

Marijuana has 468 different chemicals and 40% more cancer-causing agents and four times the tar of tobacco cigarettes (Health, Education, Safety Experts Join White House Drug Czar to Educate Parents about Risks of Youth Marijuana Use 2003). If marijuana is made more available, users will compromise their lungs and incur higher rates of cancer and emphysema. Any taxes collected from marijuana cigarettes will pale in comparison to the social costs of the health and safety consequences of wider use and increased dependence. State and federal taxes on tobacco cigarettes bring in $1.25–$1.85 per pack but the social costs of smoking tobacco cigarettes exceed $7 per pack (Speaking Out against Drug Legislation 2010).

In addition to enabling marijuana users to further compromise their health, permitting marijuana users to smoke with no criminal sanction or serious disincentive would pose major problems on our highways and in our workplaces. A recent epidemiological review showed that marijuana use significantly increases the risk of motor vehicle crash (Li et al. 2011). One of the major deterrents to using marijuana and other illegal drugs over the last 30 years has been the adoption by employers, the military, and government agencies of fitness for duty as a condition of employment. What would happen to workplace safety and productivity if marijuana were legal and/or its use acceptable or permitted for medical reasons?

In California, a state with a long history of "medical" marijuana, less than 10% of individuals with marijuana cards have cancer, AIDS, glaucoma, or muscular dystrophy, the most serious and most common conditions for which "medical" marijuana is promised to help through these laws (Medical Marijuana 2009). Over 500,000 Californians have "medical" marijuana cards, most of them aged between 18 and 35 and almost all of them free of serious medical conditions. The professional associations representing those identified by legislators as needing smoked marijuana are all opposed to "medical" marijuana.

After my appointment as administrator of the U.S. Drug Enforcement Administration (DEA) by President Ford in 1976, I received repeated requests to authorize marijuana for individuals claiming to need it for personal use and well-being. I asked what the view of the Food and Drug Administration (FDA) was on this issue and the answer was that marijuana was not safe or effective as medicine and should not be made available except for special research. That view has not changed. The World Health Organization and the United Nations Commission on Drugs oppose classifying marijuana as anything but an illicit substance (Cannabis 'Safer Than Alcohol and Tobacco' 1998).

Legislators influenced by anecdotal experiences from some constituents and by large campaign contributions from pro marijuana organizations and lobbyists should not decide what constitutes an acceptable medical product. That should be a scientific determination by the agency responsible by law for determining safe and effective medicines, the FDA.

Some believe that U.S. prisons are filled with unjustly incarcerated marijuana users. In fact, less than 1% of inmates in American prisons have been sent there solely for the use or possession of marijuana (Who's Really in Prison for Marijuana? 2005). There are thousands of marijuana arrests each month, but the offenders are not spending time in jail or prison unless there are more serious charges. Cook County Jail in Chicago houses approximately 9,500 prisoners every day; on a recent day a total of 90 were held overnight for possession of small amounts of marijuana, fewer than 40 others were out on electronic monitoring. Drug courts hold great promise for drug offenders. Under drug court supervision, offenders can stay out of jail, be subject to drug testing which will clearly discourage use, and if after six months they stay clean and out of trouble, their arrest record can be expunged. The recidivism rate for our nation's 2,400 drug courts is 16%, one-third the rate for offenders who do not go through this process (Rowan, Townsend, and Bhati 2003). Legislators should think about the value of intervention that comes with a criminal sanction so users can get treatment. Many drug users, including marijuana users, will not seek treatment unless compelled to do so.

Marijuana use has increased over the last decade as more states have enacted "medical" marijuana laws, but there are fewer individuals using illegal drugs today than the peak in the late 1970s. In 1978, approximately 25 million Americans used an illegal drug in the past month in a population of 225 million. In 2009, there were 22 million monthly users of illegal drugs in a population of 305 million U.S. citizens, constituting a drop in use from 11% of our population to 7% (Results from the 2011 National Survey on Drug Use and Health 2011).

Marijuana use, particularly for American youth, is a serious problem. It may be tempting to try to find an easy answer, calling for legalization or decriminalization, but such a path would be a fool's choice. The leading admission category in public-funded treatment centers in Los Angeles is for marijuana, not alcohol, with most for patients in their teens and early 20s. Keeping marijuana illegal and out of the hands of the youth is in the public interest. Removing sanctions and disincentives to use will only contribute to higher healthcare costs, continued criminal activity, expanded dependency and compromised safety and productivity at work and at school.

References

"Cannabis 'Safer Than Alcohol and Tobacco.'" 1998. *BBC News.* http://news.bbc.co.uk/2/hi/science/nature/58013 .stm. Accessed on June 2, 2016.

"Health, Education, Safety Experts Join White House Drug Czar to Educate Parents about Risks of Youth Marijuana Use." 2003. U.S. Drug Enforcement Administration. http://cannabisnews.com/news/15/thread15683.shtml. Accessed on June 2, 2016.

Li, Mu-Chen, et al. 2011. "Marijuana Use and Motor Vehicle Crashes." *Epidemiological Reviews.* 34(1): 65–72.

"'Medical' Marijuana." 2009. Save Our Society from Drugs. http://www.saveoursociety.org/our-issues/ medical-marijuana. Accessed on June 2, 2016.

"Results from the 2008 National Survey on Drug Use and Health: National Findings." 2008. Rockville, MD: Substance Abuse and Mental Health Services Administration, 2009. http://www.dpft.org/resources/ NSDUHresults2008.pdf. Accessed on June 2, 2016.

"Results from the 2011 National Survey on Drug Use and Health: Summary of National Findings." 2011. U.S. Department of Health and Human Services. (Office of National Drug Control Policy). https://www.whitehouse .gov/sites/default/files/ondcp/policy-and-research/nsduh results2011.pdf. Accessed on June 2, 2016.

Rowan, John, Wendy Townsend, and Avinash Singh Bhati. 2003. "Recidivism Rates for Drug Court Graduates: Nationally Based Estimates, Final Report." https://www .ncjrs.gov/pdffiles1/201229.pdf. Accessed on June 2, 2016.

"Speaking Out against Drug Legalization." 2010. U.S. Drug Enforcement Administration. http://www.dea.gov/pr/multimedia-library/publications/speaking_out.pdf. Accessed on June 2, 2016.

"Who's Really in Prison for Marijuana?" Office of National Drug Control Policy. http://www.prisonpolicy.org/scans/whos_in_prison_for_marij.pdf. Accessed on June 2, 2016.

Peter Bensinger is president and chief executive officer of Bensinger, DuPont & Associates (BDA), a privately owned professional services company that provides a wide range of consultation, training, and employee assistance program services. He previously served as the administrator of the U.S. Drug Enforcement Administration (DEA), as director of the Illinois Department of Corrections, and as chairman of the Illinois Youth Commission.

The Waiting Game
Mary Jane Borden

As I was waiting to present my testimony before the Ohio Senate, my mind wandered back to the last time Ohioans could make a legal claim for the medicinal use of cannabis. It was 1997 when this same body repealed a "get-out-of-jail-free" affirmative defense against criminal charges, its last legislative action on medical marijuana until today, 2016. For some, the wait for safe, legal access has been excruciating, if not deadly. After securing the promise of improvements to the bill—including the affirmative defense—I left to visit my doctor, one whom I hadn't seen for a while. Several years ago, her exam room walls entertained long waiting times with an abundance of accoutrements from the pharmaceutical industry.

To my surprise, wait times had decreased. Just as I sat down, the nurse called me in. She took my vitals and asked me a few questions, typing my answers into her laptop before leaving the room to get the doctor. I figured I'd have a few moments to gaze at the posters on the wall. To my surprise, there were none. Just informational guidelines from the Centers for Disease Control and Prevention and a reminder to get a flu shot.

I queried the doctor when she arrived. No pharma posters? No logo notepads? No Celexa calendars? "No" was indeed the answer. Apparently, the hospital had adopted a policy banning advertising by pharmaceutical companies on its premises.

This healthcare facility, along with others, has followed suit with the American Medical Association (AMA) and its recent call for a ban on direct-to-consumer advertising (DTCA). The AMA said such a ban "reflects concerns among physicians about the negative impact of commercially-driven promotions" and that DTCA "inflates demand for new and more expensive drugs, even when these drugs may not be appropriate" (AMA Calls for Ban on Direct to Consumer Advertising of Prescription Drugs and Medical Devices 2015).

DTCA is the practice whereby drugs are promoted, not only to the physicians who prescribe them, but also directly to the patients who use them. The theory behind DTCA holds that it improves compliance, raises awareness of various diseases, and increases patient flow into physician offices; this witnessed by the 30% of Americans who have asked their doctors about the drugs they have seen advertised. DTCA may also be responsible for the exorbitant rise in deaths and serious outcomes from these drugs—almost 124,000 deaths in 2014 alone.

Like a thief in the night, where did DTCA go once it was banned? Look no further than your favorite TV show. There you will see a long legged girl brushing her hair as she whispers soft words about her man. Or, the cute little red stuffed bladder that likes to hold hands. Or, the jingly firefighter who happy dances "Low Rider" because his number is down. Or, those prancing, painting, punching body of proof people. Or, maybe a golfing legend honing his game with a blood thinner.

And if these slow-motion smiles weren't enough, each DTCA pitch is followed by the drug's side effects in excruciating detail. That frightening "four-hour" window. Diabetes, muscle pain and kidney failure. Fatal bleeding. Life-threatening infections, including tuberculosis. Unusual cancers and lymphoma. Severe fungal infections. Red, scaly patches or raised, pus-filled bumps. Degeneration of the lower spine. Makes you wonder what all of the prancing was about.

The United States has a drug problem. More drugs are consumed here than anywhere else in the world. Americans are spending more and getting less. While advertising directly to consumers may build sales for pharmaceutical companies, it carries a host of side effects for patients, families, and physicians.

In contrast, cannabis as medication has been therapeutically used by millions for 10,000 years. More research has been conducted on it than any of those drugs named by their side effects. And its side effects are comparatively few, as one judge on the subject ruled in 1988, "Marijuana, in its natural form, is one of the safest therapeutically active substances known to man. By any measure of rational analysis marijuana can be safely used within a supervised routine of medical care" (Young 1988).

As I left my doctor's office, I reflected on waiting, bans, and ads. The AMA's recent call reveals the core problem: alternative medicines like cannabis have been banned for almost a century, reverting medical treatment to more dangerous and deadly drugs that must be advertised to generate consumer use. Physician concerns like those articulated by the AMA over DTCA can be ameliorated, not only with an advertising ban, but also by safe, legal access to alternatives like medical marijuana.

The Ohio Senate indeed passed the bill with the affirmative defense and much, much more, allowing my home state to join a tipping point of 25 others in legalizing the medicinal use of this therapeutic plant. Perhaps on my next visit, I'll ask my doctor, not about a drug I saw advertised, but about cannabis. For that, I can't wait.

References

"AMA Calls for Ban on Direct to Consumer Advertising of Prescription Drugs and Medical Devices." 2015.

American Medical Association. http://www.ama-assn
.org/ama/pub/news/news/2015/2015-11-17-ban-
consumer-prescription-drug-advertising.page.
Accessed on June 13, 2016.

Young, Francis J. 1988. *In the Matter of Marijuana
Rescheduling Petition*. United States Department of
Justice. Drug Enforcement Administration. http://
medicalmarijuana.procon.org/sourcefiles/Young1988
.pdf. Accessed on June 14, 2016.

*Mary Jane Borden is a writer, artist, advocate, and internationally
recognized expert in cannabis policy from Westerville, Ohio. She
holds a B.A. from Otterbein University, an MBA from the University of Dayton and the prestigious Accredited in Public Relations
(APR) certification from the Public Relations Society of America
(PRSA). Her diverse background spans 30 years and includes
9 years as a pharmaceutical industry analyst, co-authoring four
proposed medical cannabis amendments to the Ohio Constitution,
and lobbying for six medical marijuana bills, the last and the most
noted of which was signed into law in June 2016.*

An Effective Public Health Approach to Reduce Marijuana Use
Robert L. DuPont

Now that recreational marijuana is legal in some states and
medical marijuana is legal in many others, the contentious
debate about marijuana continues to make headlines. There
is continued funding from drug policy "reformers" that are
seeking to further legalize the use, sale, production, and commercialization of this widely abused drug for recreational and
medical purposes. The ongoing state and national legalization campaigns are also backed by massive new funding from
marijuana entrepreneurs. Concurrently scientific research is
showing abundant reasons why marijuana use, and marijuana
legalization, is not a good idea. There are significant social and

health costs (e.g., Volkow et al. 2014). In many states there are criminal sanctions associated with marijuana possession, sale, and use.

Some suggest that because marijuana is so widely used, criminal sanctions against its use should be suspended and only the health problems resulting from its use should be a matter of public concern. In this view the criminal justice system should not be involved, and thus, the answer to handling marijuana is to legalize it ("tax and regulate").

The consequences of such state policy changes are being documented in the states of Colorado and Washington where recreational and medical marijuana are legal. The Rocky Mountain and Northwest High Intensity Drug Trafficking Areas (HIDTAs) serving these two states have released powerful reports highlighting the significantly negative impacts of these policies. These reports document increases in underage and adult marijuana use, marijuana-impaired driving and traffic deaths, marijuana-related emergency room and hospital admissions, marijuana-related poison control center calls, and significant diversion of marijuana both within and out of these states (Northwest High Intensity Density Trafficking Area 2016; Rocky Mountain High Intensity Density Trafficking Area 2015). In 2014 the states of Alaska and Oregon as well as the District of Columbia legalized marijuana for adults age 21 and older, and it is expected that similar changes will occur in these locations.

Marijuana is not a single drug. The explosive and exploitative commercialization of marijuana in these states has produced a seemingly endless array of high-potency products, including waxes/oils and edible products such as candy, cookies, and sodas. Strong action is needed now to monitor the local, state, and national impact of these initiatives to inform future policy decisions for public health and safety (Institute for Behavior and Health, Inc. 2016).

Nationally the rates of marijuana have not been static. They have changed significantly over the last four decades, rising sharply, then falling in response to pushback, then rising once again. The impact is clearly documented in the high school population. Marijuana use among 12th graders reached its peak in 1978 when 37.1% used it in the past 30 days. This figure reached a low in 1992 at 11.9%, reflecting an increase in perceived risk of harm from marijuana use and a rise in social disapproval of marijuana use. Since that time, marijuana use has increased. In 2015, 21.2% of high school seniors reported past month marijuana use (Johnston et al. 2016). Marijuana use among adults has also increased in recent years (Center for Behavioral Health Statistics and Quality 2015). This rise in marijuana use and corresponding increase in public support for legalization (Motel 2015) are no doubt the result of the pro-marijuana campaigns which portray marijuana use as harmless and even beneficial, as well as the increasingly permissive state laws regarding marijuana, including the legalization of marijuana for recreational and "medical" uses.

Research from the National Institute on Drug Abuse (NIDA) clearly states that marijuana use is a health threat, particularly to youth (Volkow et al. 2014). The nation's public health marijuana policy must focus first on youth because almost all drug use begins in the teenage years and, because the teen brain is not fully developed, this age is especially vulnerable (National Institute on Drug Abuse 2016). Marijuana policy must commit to mobilizing parents, schools, health care professionals, and others concerned with the health and well-being of youth to help them grow up drug-free. It must set the goal for young people to not use alcohol, tobacco, marijuana, or other drugs, all of which are illegal for youth (DuPont 2016). A sound public health policy limits the harm caused by drug use, including marijuana use. The best way to do that is to dramatically reduce drug use. Marijuana legalization makes the drug more accessible and more socially acceptable.

Keeping marijuana illegal is an important public health strategy that reinforces all prevention messages. The criminal justice system is a strong force not only for prevention but also for intervention to stop marijuana use. Few people are incarcerated for marijuana use now, but many are arrested each year. I encourage modest fines and community service requirements for those arrested for marijuana possession or use, with expungement of such criminal records after a few years.

For people on parole or probation for crimes other than marijuana possession or use brief incarceration is appropriate primarily for the criminal offenders who fail drug tests, including for marijuana use, during the period that they are under community supervision. This type of monitoring has been successfully implemented in drug courts (Marlowe 2010) and by innovative probation strategies, including HOPE Probation for felony probationers (Hawken and Kleiman 2009; Institute for Behavior and Health, Inc. 2015) and South Dakota's 24/7 Sobriety for repeat DUI offenders (Kilmer et al. 2013). These monitoring strategies produce excellent outcomes. They reduce drug and alcohol use, they reduce criminal recidivism, and they reduce incarceration.

A better way to deal with marijuana and other drugs has been widely and wrongly presented as a choice between treatment and incarceration. This is a false choice. The systems of health care and criminal justice do not compete when it comes to drugs. A better drug policy is achieved when criminal justice and health care work together to achieve outcomes that neither can accomplish alone (DuPont and Humphreys 2011). The public health is best served by keeping marijuana use, production, and sale illegal because it discourages marijuana use, an important public health objective.

References

Center for Behavioral Health Statistics and Quality. 2015. "Behavioral Health Trends in the United States: Results from the 2014 National Survey on Drug Use and Health." HHS Publication No. SMA 15-4927, NSDUH Series H-50. Rockville, MD: Substance Abuse and Mental Health

Services Administration. http://www.samhsa.gov/data/sites/default/files/NSDUH-FRR1-2014/NSDUH-FRR1-2014.pdf. Accessed on May 5, 2016.

DuPont, R. L. 2016. "Drug Abuse Prevention Should Be about Health: No Use of Alcohol, Tobacco, Marijuana and Other Drugs for Reasons of Health." *Coalitions.* May 2016.

DuPont, R. L., and K. Humphreys. 2011. "A New Paradigm for Long-Term Recovery." *Substance Abuse.* 32(1): 1–6.

Hawken, A. and M. Kleiman. 2009. "Managing Drug Involved Probationers with Swift and Certain Sanctions: Evaluating Hawaii's HOPE." Washington, DC: National Institute of Justice, Office of Justice Programs, U.S. Department of Justice.

Institute for Behavior and Health, Inc. 2015. "State of the Art of HOPE Probation." Rockville, MD: Institute for Behavior and Health, Inc. http://ibhinc.org/pdfs/StateoftheArtofHOPEProbation.pdf. Accessed May 5, 2016.

Institute for Behavior and Health, Inc. 2016. "A Strategy to Access the Consequences of Marijuana Legalization." Rockville, MD: Institute for Behavior and Health, Inc. http://ibhinc.org/pdfs/IBHAStrategytoAssesstheConsequencesofMarijuanaLegalization.pdf. Assessed May 5, 2016.

Johnston, L. D., et al. 2016. "Monitoring the Future National Survey Results on Drug Use, 1975–2015: Overview, Key Findings on Adolescent Drug Use." Ann Arbor: Institute for Social Research, The University of Michigan.

Kilmer, B., et al. 2013. "Efficacy of Frequent Monitoring with Swift, Certain, and Modest Sanctions for Violations: Insights from South Dakota's 24/7 Sobriety Project." 103(1): e37–43.

Marlowe, D. B. 2010. "Need to Know: Research Update on Adult Drug Courts." Alexandria, VA: National Association of Drug Court Professionals. http://www.nadcp.org/sites/default/files/nadcp/Research%20Update%20on%20Adult%20Drug%20Courts%20-%20NADCP_1.pdf. Accessed on July 26, 2012.

Motel, S. 2015. "6 Facts about Marijuana." Washington, DC: Pew Research Center, April 14, 2015. http://www.pewresearch.org/fact-tank/2015/04/14/6-facts-about-marijuana/. Accessed on May 24, 2016.

National Institute on Drug Abuse. 2016. "Marijuana Abuse." Research Report Series, NIH Pub. Number: 16-3859. Bethesda, MD: U.S. Department of Health and Human Services, National Institutes of Health, National Institute on Drug Abuse. https://www.drugabuse.gov/sites/default/files/mjrrs_3_2016.pdf. Accessed on May 5, 2016.

Northwest High Intensity Drug Trafficking Area. 2016. "Washington State Marijuana Impact Report." Seattle, WA: Author. http://www.mfiles.org/home/nw-hidta/marijuana-impact-report. Accessed on May 5, 2016.

Rocky Mountain High Intensity Drug Trafficking Area. 2015. http://www.rmhidta.org/html/2015%20FINAL%20LEGALIZATION%20OF%20MARIJUANA%20IN%20COLORADO%20THE%20IMPACT.pdf. Accessed on May 5, 2016.

Volkow, N.D., et al. 2014. "Adverse Health Effects of Marijuana Use." *New England Journal of Medicine.* 370(23): 2219–2227.

Robert L. DuPont, M.D. is president of the Institute for Behavior and Health, Inc., a nonprofit organization that works to identify and promote effective new strategies to reduce illegal drug use. He also is clinical professor of psychiatry at Georgetown Medical School. He was the first director of the National Institute on Drug Abuse and served as the second White House Drug Chief.

Government Research Support and Marijuana Legalization Brightens the Spotlight on the Endocannabinoid System
Rachele Hendricks-Sturrup

Introduction

Cannabis sativa, or the naturally occurring plant better known as marijuana, has been used for thousands of years by humans and, historically, for a multitude of living purposes that include medicinal therapy. Marijuana's primary and active chemical compound is called Δ^9-tetrahydrocannabinol (Δ^9-THC). Δ^9-THC is "psychoactive" in that it has the ability to change or manipulate brain function, resulting in alterations of perception, mood, or consciousness (National Institute on Drug Abuse 2016). Ecologists have hypothesized that Δ^9-THC evolutionarily served the marijuana plant as a deterrent against its herbivore predators (Pate 1994). In the 1990s, scientists confirmed that Δ^9-THC interacts with the human endocannabinoid system, and binds to receptors called CB1 and CB2 that are located on cells of almost every organ (Alger, 2013; Matsuda et al., 1990; Munro et al., 1993).

The discovery of the endocannabinoid system triggered an incredible amount of scientific research interest in understanding how Δ^9-THC can be used to produce medically beneficial effects in humans, as well as commercialization efforts. For example, Δ^9-THC is currently prescribed to patients under the brand name Marinol, a synthetic Δ^9-THC compound that is generically called dronabinol, and both state and federal governments monetarily support exploratory endocannabinoid system research using other natural and synthetic forms of Δ^9-THC. Thus, this narrative describes (1) an overview of the current prescribed use of dronabinol and current clinical studies examining its ability to treat other medical indications, (2) scientific research that has explored and discovered new insights into the endocannabinoid system, and (3) examples of how certain states and the federal government currently support exploratory research into the endocannabinoid system and on Δ^9-THC.

Prescription Marinol

Marinol, or dronabinol, is a form of prescription medical marijuana that contains synthetic Δ^9-THC as its active ingredient. Today, doctors may prescribe Marinol to cancer patients suffering from cancer drug-related side effects of persistent nausea and vomiting, or to stimulate the lost appetite of patients suffering from acquired immune deficiency syndrome (AIDS) (AIDSinfo 2016; Bellum 2012;). Dronabinol is also under scientific investigation to determine its drug abuse potential, and its ability to treat other diverse ailments and disorders such as neuropathic pain (pain from nerve damage) and obstructive sleep apnea syndrome (ClinicalTrials.gov, 2012, 2014, 2016).

The Endocannabinoid System: New Insights

Studies show that the endocannabinoid system is a cell-signaling system that supports homeostasis and modulates behavior in mammals. For example, the endocannabinoid system modulates stress, energy intake, storage, and utilization (metabolism), immunity, and circadian rhythm (day/night behavior cycle) in mammals (Hillard 2014; Mazier et al. 2015; Pandey, et al. 2009; Vaughn et al. 2010). Very recent animal studies also, and interestingly, show that the endocannabinoid system has the ability to modulate alcohol-induced behavior, and that alcohol increases endocannabinoid levels (Henderson-Redmond et al. 2016). Thus, these findings open a new door in behavioral and substance abuse research.

State and Federal Research

States that have approved medical and/or recreational marijuana, such as Colorado, have also taken an initiative to provide state-level funding to support medical marijuana and/or exploratory research into the endocannabinoid system. For example, the Colorado Department of Public Health and Environment provided a total of $9 million in state funding to support a diverse array of medical marijuana research projects that either are or will be conducted by various research teams at the University of Colorado School of Medicine, Children's Hospital Colorado, and other medical research facilities. Further, the University of Michigan currently grows and supplies medical marijuana to the National Institute on Drug Abuse (NIDA), a federal government research institute with an expressed mission to "lead the Nation in bringing the power of science to bear on drug abuse and addiction" (National Institute of Health n.d.). The NIDA is responsible for providing and allocating hundreds of millions of dollars in federal funding to support medical marijuana and endocannabinoid system research (Seshata 2014).

Key Takeaway

As marijuana use continues, state and federal governments must work to promote and protect the public health by continuously supporting and funding scientific research that seeks to discover both the beneficial and adverse effects of marijuana on the human body via the endocannabinoid system, and appropriately support affordable drug commercialization of Δ^9-THC.

References

AIDSinfo. 2016. "Dronabinol." AIDSinfo Drug Database. June 3, 2016. https://aidsinfo.nih.gov/drugs/138/dronabinol/0/professional. Accessed June 03, 2016.

Alger, Bradley E. 2013. "Getting High on the Endocannabinoid System." *Cerebrum: The Dana Forum on Brain Science*. Dana Foundation. http://www.ncbi.nlm.nih.gov/pmc/articles/PMC3997295/. Accessed on June 5, 2016.

Bellum, Sarah. 2012. "Medical Marijuana: It's Complicated." NIDA for Teens. March 27, 2012. https://teens.drugabuse .gov/blog/post/medical-marijuana-its-complicated. Accessed June 3, 2016.

ClinicalTrials.gov. 2012. "Efficacy and Safety of the Pain Relieving Effect of Dronabinol in Central Neuropathic Pain Related to Multiple Sclerosis." February 2, 2012. https://clinicaltrials.gov/ct2/show/NCT00959218. Accessed June 3, 2016.

ClinicalTrials.gov. 2014. "A Study of the Abuse Potential of Dronabinol in Recreational Cannabinoid Users." May 12, 2014. https://www.clinicaltrials.gov/ct2/show/ NCT02094599. Accessed June 3, 2016.

ClinicalTrials.gov. 2016. Safety and Efficacy Study of Dronabinol to Treat Obstructive Sleep Apnea (PACE). May 11, 2016. https://clinicaltrials.gov/ct2/show/ NCT01755091. Accessed June 3, 2016.

Henderson-Redmond, Angela Net, al. 2016. "Roles for the Endocannabinoid System in Ethanol-Motivated Behavior." *Progress in Neuro-Psychopharmacology and Biological Psychiatry*. 65: 330–339.

Hillard, Cecilia J. 2014. "Stress Regulates Endocannabinoid-cb1 Receptor Signaling." *Seminars in Immunology*. 26(5): 380–388.

Matsuda, Lisa A., et al. 1990. "Structure of a Cannabinoid Receptor and Functional Expression of the Cloned cDNA." *Nature*. 346(6284): 561–564.

Mazier, Wilfrid, et al. 2015. "The Endocannabinoid System: Pivotal Orchestrator of Obesity and Metabolic Disease." *Trends in Endocrinology & Metabolism*. 26(10): 524–537.

Munro, Sean, et al. 1993. "Molecular Characterization of a Peripheral Receptor for Cannabinoids." *Nature*. 365(6441): 61–65.

National Institute on Drug Abuse. 2016. "Marijuana."
   DrugFacts. March 2016. https://www.drugabuse.gov/
   publications/drugfacts/marijuana. Accessed June 3, 2016.

Pandey, Rupal, et al. 2009 "Endocannabinoids and Immune
   Regulation." *Pharmacological Research.* 60(2): 85–92.

Pate, David. W. 1994. "Chemical Ecology of Cannabis."
   Journal of the International Hemp Association. 2(29): 32–37.

Seshata. 2014. "Who Funds Cannabis Research in the USA?"
   Sensi Seeds. July 31, 2014. https://sensiseeds.com/en/blog/
   funds-cannabis-research-usa/. Accessed June 3, 2016.

Vaughn, Linda K., et al. 2010. "Endocannabinoid Signalling:
   Has It Got Rhythm?" *British Journal of Pharmacology.*
   160(3): 530–543.

Rachele Hendricks-Sturrup is a biomedical scientist, health policy analyst, and active member of the Association for Women in Science, American Medical Writers Association, and National Association of Science Writers. She is currently pursuing a Doctor of Health Science Degree at Nova Southeastern University. Her doctoral study focus involves exploring and describing how various forms of biotechnology can be used within the scope of precision medicine and value-based care.

Medical Marijuana: A Perspective
Arthur Livermore

During the 1970s, when I was a medical student, I was told that marijuana (cannabis) was only a drug of abuse. The knowledge of medical uses of cannabis had been lost. Thirty years earlier, doctors were knowledgeable about medical marijuana, but now it was a forbidden plant. It took me years of research to discover the medical uses of marijuana.

My search through the medical school library was not helpful. I found some information in used book stores. There was a copy of a 1921 *Therapeutic Handbook* with medications made with cannabis. When I found Dr. Lester Grinspoon's book, *Marihuana Reconsidered* (Grinspoon 1971), it became clear that marijuana is medicine. How it works was still unknown. Many young people were using it in the 70s and some soldiers returning from Vietnam found that it helped them emotionally. My own experience showed that it is effective in treating bipolar mood disorder.

When I was learning how to control my emotional body, the psychiatric community didn't think that marijuana was helpful. I was given the most powerful prescription medicines available, but my episodic mania continued. I discovered that marijuana helped me avoid these episodes, and I began using it instead of the standard medications.

When I discussed using marijuana with my psychiatrist, she was not able to prescribe cannabis because the law said it wasn't medicine. She saw that it was effective treatment for my symptoms and did not object to my use of marijuana.

During the 1980s, marijuana was demonized in the "Just Say No" campaign. At the same time the U.S. government was running an Investigational New Drug (IND) program that allows patients to use medical marijuana. Robert Randall was the first patient in this program after he sued the Food and Drug Administration (FDA), the Drug Enforcement Administration (DEA), the National Institute on Drug Abuse (NIDA), the Department of Justice (DOJ), and the Department of Health, Education and Welfare (now the Department of Health and Human Services, HHS). He won this suit in November 1976 based on the medical necessity of marijuana in the treatment of his glaucoma.

The FDA's Compassionate IND program was expanded to include AIDS patients during the 1980s. When the George H. W. Bush administration closed the program in 1992, there were 30 patients receiving marijuana from the government. Twenty-four years later, four of these patients are still receiving marijuana from the federal government.

After the government stopped adding people to the legal medical marijuana list, patients who responded to cannabis therapy worked with political activists to pass medical marijuana laws in the United States. In 1996, California passed the first medical marijuana law. As of June, 2016, 24 states and the District of Columbia have made marijuana legal for medical use.

In spite of this support for recognizing marijuana as medicine, the DEA has refused to place marijuana in the medical use category. Repeated petitions to remove marijuana from the "no medical use" category have been denied. In 1988, the court reviewed the science of medical marijuana and the Administrative Law Judge, Francis Young, found that "Marijuana, in its natural form, is one of the safest therapeutically active substances known to man. By any measure of rational analysis marijuana can be safely used within a supervised routine of medical care. . . . To conclude otherwise, on this record, would be unreasonable, arbitrary and capricious" (In the Matter of Marijuana Rescheduling Petition 1988). Why does the DEA ignore the evidence that cannabis is a medicine? Quite simply, it is paid to say that all use of marijuana is abuse of marijuana (The DEA Position on Marijuana 2011).

The discovery of Δ^9-tetrahydrocannabinol (THC) as the active ingredient in marijuana by Ralph Mechoulam and Yechiel Gaoni (Gaoni and Mechoulam 1964) in 1964 led to the identification of the endocannabinoid receptor system in 1988 (Devane et al. 1988). In 1992, this previously unknown transmitter system was found to be activated by the endogenous neurotransmitter, anandamide (Devane et al. 1992). Exercise stimulates the release of anandamide so the "runner's high" associated with jogging is the result of elevated levels of endocannabinoids. Cannabinoid receptors are found in higher concentrations than any other receptor in the brain. They are in areas associated with pain reduction, coordination of movement, memory, emotions, reward systems, and reproduction (Pertwee 2008; Pizzorno 2012; Raichlen et al. 2011).

Clinical uses of marijuana are not limited to pain reduction, appetite enhancement, and controlling chemotherapy-induced vomiting. Cannabis protects nerve cells from damage and is also effective in reducing tumor growth. Multiple sclerosis patients use cannabis to treat peripheral neuropathy. It is effective in the treatment of movement disorders, glaucoma, asthma, bipolar disorder, depression, epilepsy, post-traumatic stress disorder (PTSD), arthritis, Parkinson's disease, Alzheimer's disease, amyotrophic lateral sclerosis, alcohol abuse, insomnia, digestive diseases, gliomas, skin tumors, sleep apnea, and anorexia nervosa (Cannabis and Cannabinoids 2016; Common Medical Uses for Cannabis 2012; Mikuriya 2004).

After four years of review by multiple agencies, in March 2014, Dr. Sue Sisley's research proposal on treating PTSD with cannabis gained federal approval (Kovaleski 2014). But the effort to begin this project faced another hurdle when Dr. Sisley was fired by the University of Arizona. Dr. Sisley is convinced that her outspoken support for marijuana research was the reason (Scutti 2014). Fear of association with marijuana research is an irrational product of our "War on Drugs." Two years later, she is still waiting for the National Institute on Drug Abuse (NIDA) to supply the marijuana she needs for the study. In May 2016 the Phoenix Veterans Affairs hospital blocked her from giving a lecture about marijuana's effect on veterans with PTSD (VA Hospital in Phoenix Blocks Presentation on Cannabis [PTSD] 2016).

A 2015 study found that treating epilepsy with a cannabis extract that is high in cannabidiol (CBD) was effective for patients who did not respond to other treatments (American Academy of Neurology 2015). Many of the patients in this study are children, and their stories have been seen on the television news. Cannabis has been used to treat epilepsy for centuries (Devinsky 2014). Only now are researchers beginning clinical trials to figure out how cannabinoids reduce or stop seizures.

Cannabinoids are emerging as treatments for psychiatric symptoms. CBD has antipsychotic effects and improves cognitive function in patients with schizophrenia (Celia 2010; Devinsky 2014).

Cannabis is a very safe medicine (In the Matter of Marijuana Rescheduling Petition 1988; Pizzorno 2012). The side effect of euphoria is one reason patients don't want to use marijuana, but most people like the feeling of well-being that cannabis provides. When patients get too high a dose, they may feel paranoid for a while and then fall asleep. Knowledgeable use of marijuana prevents these negative side effects.

The irrational marijuana policy of the last 75 years needs to end. Fear of addiction has led to common misconceptions about marijuana. Marijuana laws that are based on the discredited "gateway theory" and "reefer madness" propaganda fail because the truth is hidden. We now know a great deal about brain chemistry. The endocannabinoid system is an important part of our body's regulatory mechanisms.

Marijuana is not going to go away. We must create legal channels for the sale of marijuana so that people can use this valuable medicinal herb without the threat of legal consequences.

References

American Academy of Neurology (AAN). 2015. "Medical Marijuana Liquid Extract May Bring Hope for Children with Severe Epilepsy." *Science Daily*. Available online at www.sciencedaily.com/releases/2015/04/150413183743 .htm. Accessed on June 3, 2016.

"Cannabis and Cannabinoids." 2016. National Cancer Institute. http://www.cancer.gov/cancertopics/pdq/cam/ cannabis/healthprofessional/page4. Accessed on July 31, 2012.

Celia J. A., et al. 2010. "Impact of Cannabidiol on the Acute Memory and Psychotomimetic Effects of Smoked Cannabis: Naturalistic Study." *British Journal of Psychiatry* 197(4): 285–290.

"Common Medical Uses for Cannabis." 2016. American Alliance for Medical Cannabis. http://www .letfreedomgrow.com/cmu/. Accessed on July 31, 2012.

"The DEA Position on Marijuana." January 2011. http://www.justice.gov/dea/marijuana_position.pdf Accessed on July 31, 2012.

Devane, W. A., et al. 1988. "Determination and Characterization of a Cannabinoid Receptor in Rat Brain." *Molecular Pharmacology.* 34: 605–613.

Devane W. A., et al. 1992. "Isolation and Structure of a Brain Constituent That Binds to the Cannabinoid Receptor." *Science* 258: 1946–1949.

Devinsky, Orrin, et al. 2014. "Cannabidiol: Pharmacology and Potential Therapeutic Role in Epilepsy and Other Neuropsychiatric Disorders." *Epilepsia.* 55(6): 791–802.

Gaoni, Y., and R. Mechoulam, 1964. "Isolation, Structure and Partial Synthesis of an Active Constituent of Hashish." *Journal of the American Chemical Society.* 86: 1646–1647.

Grinspoon, Lester. 1971. *Marihuana Reconsidered.* Cambridge, MA: Harvard University Press.

Kovaleski, Serge F. 2014. "Medical Marijuana Research Hits Wall of U.S. Law." *New York Times.* Available online at http://www.nytimes.com/2014/08/10/us/politics/medical-marijuana-research-hits-the-wall-of-federal-law.html?_r=1.

Mikuriya, Tod H. 2004. "Chronic Conditions Treated with Cannabis." American Alliance for Medical Cannabis. http://www.letfreedomgrow.com/cmu/DrTodHMikuriya_list.htm. Accessed on July 31, 2012.

Pertwee, R.G. 2008. "The Diverse CB1 and CB2 Receptor Pharmacology of Three Plant Cannabinoids: Δ^9-tetrahydrocannabinol, Cannabidiol and Δ^9-tetrahydrocannabivarin." *British Journal of Pharmacology.* 153(2): 199–215.

Pizzorno, Lara, 2012 "New Developments in Cannabinoid-Based Medicine: An Interview with Dr. Raphael Mechoulam." *Longevity Medicine Review.* Available online at http://www.lmreview.com/articles/print/new-developments-in-cannabinoid-based-medicine-an-interview-with-dr-raphael-mechoulam/. Accessed on July 31, 2012.

Raichlen, David A., et al. 2011. "Wired to Run: Exercise-Induced Endocannabinoid Signaling in Humans and Cursorial Mammals with Implications for the 'Runner's High.'" *Journal of Experimental Biology.* 215: 1331–1336. Available online at http://jeb.biologists.org/content/215/8/1331.abstract. Accessed on July 31, 2012.

Scutti, Susan. 2014. "Medical Marijuana Researcher, Dr. Sue Sisley, Says She Was Fired for Political Reasons Despite Gaining Federal Approval." *Medical Daily.* Available online at http://www.medicaldaily.com/medical-marijuana-researcher-dr-sue-sisley-says-she-was-fired-political-reasons-despite-gaining.

"VA Hospital in Phoenix Blocks Presentation on Cannabis, PTSD." 2016. Available online at http://www.thecannabist.co/2016/05/26/phoenix-va-hospital-blocks-medical-marijuana-presentation/55052/.

Arthur Livermore has a B.A. in biology from Reed College. He studied medicine at the University of Oregon medical school before going into neurology and psychiatry research. He wrote software for the DEC PDP-12 computer to analyze neurophysiological data from schizophrenic patients. Software development projects include data collection and analysis for the Woodcock-Johnson cognitive abilities tests and the Gardenware plant labeling system. Arthur has been educating people about the medical use of cannabis for many years. He is a founding member of the American Alliance for Medical Cannabis and is its current national director.

Lies and Deception: The Origins of Today's Federal Marijuana Policy
Duane Ludwig

The past two years of marijuana legalization in Washington and Colorado have revealed many fascinating things to the rest of America. First and foremost is the realization that despite what the opponents of legalization have been claiming for years, a liberalization of marijuana policy has not been a catastrophe by any objective analysis. Statistics regarding usage rates and marijuana dependence are nearly unchanged. Driving accidents are no more frequent, and even though federal rules still require all marijuana-based commerce to be conducted entirely in cash, robberies have not spiked in any noticeable way (Reed 2016). What is undeniable is the significant economic boost to these states from marijuana industry jobs and tax revenues.

The fact that the sky has not fallen after legalization shows that the Chicken Littles of marijuana prohibition have been misleading or deceiving us for decades. What is not as well known is that an even more nefarious level of deception is what led to marijuana (cannabis) prohibition in the first place, and then upped the ante later as part of the so-called War on Drugs. Today's legalization proponents and opponents alike are generally unaware of the propaganda and outright lies that brought the United States to where it is today.

The 1937 Marihuana Tax Act marks the beginning of prohibition. Before that, cannabis was mainly used as an ingredient in medicinal tinctures and salves, and for a multitude of industrial purposes. Being four times more efficient than wood as a paper source, but also an easily grown, fantastic natural fiber for textiles, the hemp plant became a target for elimination from the market by powerful industrialists such as William Randolph Hearst and the DuPont Corporation. Thus began decades of "yellow journalism" that introduced the obscure Mexican slang term "marijuana" to the American public and inaccurately demonized its consumption as the motivating force behind car accidents, rapes, and murders. This was compounded by associating cannabis use with Mexicans and blacks, who were also victims of propaganda inciting fear and hated in this era (Herer 1993).

Historians universally point to Harry J. Anslinger, the first chief of the Federal Bureau of Narcotics, as the person most responsible for generating support for the prohibition legislation. For example, in congressional testimony, he remarked, "Marijuana is the most violence-causing drug in the history of mankind" (Gerber 2004, 7). The now-infamous 1936 film *Reefer Madness* portrayed marijuana causing users to become either promiscuous or homicidal. While it is now a laughable cult classic, this type of virtually unopposed propaganda stoked public unease with the recreational drug "marihuana." Relying on secrecy and legislative sleight of hand, bill sponsors never connected marijuana to the economically significant and biologically identical hemp plant or the cannabis used in many medicines and supported by the American Medical Association. As a result, there was virtually no debate when Congress overwhelmingly voted to outlaw it via a prohibitive tax (Sloman 1979).

Over 30 years later, the Nixon administration developed the Controlled Substances Act, and placed marijuana in Schedule I, the category reserved for substances with no medical use and high potential for abuse. What is most telling about this decision is the findings of the Shafer Commission, a group that Nixon specifically charged to closely examine the issue and produce a recommendation for marijuana. In 1972, the commission's report stated,

> [T]he criminal law is too harsh a tool to apply to personal possession even in the effort to discourage use. It implies an overwhelming indictment of the behavior which we believe is not appropriate. The actual and potential harm of use of the drug is not great enough to justify intrusion by the criminal law into private behavior, a step which our

society takes only with the greatest reluctance. . . . Therefore, the Commission recommends . . . [that the] possession of marijuana for personal use no longer be an offense, [and that the] casual distribution of small amounts of marihuana for no remuneration, or insignificant remuneration, no longer be an offense. (Commission on Marihuana and Drug Abuse, 1972, 176)

The commission was prescient in also concluding that the risks of drug use are the result of drug policy, rather than the drugs themselves, noting, "The Commission believes that the contemporary American drug problem has emerged in part from our institutional response to drug use. . . . We have failed to weave policy into the fabric of social institutions" (Commission on Marihuana and Drug Abuse, 1973, 37).

While the decision to label marijuana as addictive and nonmedical could be attributed to one of Nixon's many idiosyncrasies, an admission by his chief domestic policy advisor, John Ehrlichman, clarifies his action. In 1994, Ehrlichman candidly told a reporter for *Harper's Magazine*, "The Nixon campaign in 1968, and the Nixon White House after that, had two enemies: the antiwar left and black people. We knew we couldn't make it illegal to be either against the war or black, but by getting the public to associate the hippies with marijuana and blacks with heroin, and then criminalizing both heavily, we could disrupt those communities. We could arrest their leaders, raid their homes, break up their meetings, and vilify them night after night on the evening news. Did we know we were lying about the drugs? Of course we did" (Baum 2016). Thus began the "War on Drugs" that escalated further in the 1980s, has now cost taxpayers over $1 trillion, and has utterly failed to reduce the use of marijuana or control the Mexican drug cartel–dominated black market.

In recent decades, researchers have discovered and explored the body's endocannabinoid system. This explains why consumed cannabis is so readily converted into endogenous substances that provide relief for such a wide array of human health conditions. Cannabis medicine is now a promising field of study, and one that requires the laws relating to access to be relaxed in even more states, as well as federally.

Of course, neither Anslinger nor Nixon was privy to this knowledge, but one might reasonably wonder if such knowledge could have overcome the dark influences of racism, greed, and political power that drove them to demonize cannabis and its consumers. Going forward, society must endeavor to ensure that every argument either for or against cannabis is based only in scientific knowledge and sound reasoning. There is no place in public policy for the kind of deception and propaganda that effectively delayed recent medical cannabis breakthroughs for nearly 80 years.

References

Baum, Dan. 2016. "Legalize It All." *Harper's Magazine.* https://harpers.org/archive/2016/04/legalize-it-all/. Accessed on June 15, 2016.

Commission on Marihuana and Drug Abuse. 1972. *Marihuana: A Signal of Misunderstanding.* Washington, DC: Government Printing Office. Available online at https://babel.hathitrust.org/cgi/pt?id=mdp.390150156475 58;view=1up;seq=198. Accessed on June 15, 2016.

Commission on Marihuana and Drug Abuse. 1973. *Drug Use in America: Problem in Perspective.* Washington, DC: Government Printing Office.

Gerber, Rudolph J. 2004. *Legalizing Marijuana: Drug Policy Reform and Prohibition Politics.* Westport, CT: Praeger.

Herer, Jack. 1993. "The Emperor Wears No Clothes." Van Nuys, CA: Hemp Publishing. Available online at http://www.hampapartiet.se/25.pdf. Accessed on June 15, 2016.

Reed, Jack K. 2016., "Marijuana Legalization in Colorado: Early Findings." Colorado Department of

Public Safety. http://cdpsdocs.state.co.us/ors/docs/
reports/2016-SB13-283-Rpt.pdf. Accessed on June 15,
2016.

Sloman, Larry. 1979. *Reefer Madness: The History of
Marijuana in America.* Indianapolis, IN: Bobbs Merrill.

*Duane Ludwig is an aerospace engineer and advocate for com-
mon sense drug policy. He is on the Board of Directors of Virginia
NORML (National Organization for the Reform of Marijuana
Laws) and has served as its communications director. In the course
of fighting to end the criminalization of Virginia's cannabis patients
and recreational consumers, he has come to realize that smart regulation and careful expansion of the marijuana and industrial
hemp industries holds phenomenal promise for the economy and
ecology of the nation, and the planet.*

The Threat of Big Marijuana
Clara MacCarald

In 2015, legal sales of marijuana in the United States totaled
$5.4 billion. This lucrative market has grown enormously
despite the fact that only half of U.S. states have legalized marijuana sales in any form, and the four allowing recreational use
have only done so in the last few years. Other states are considering their own recreational laws, which could drive the growth
of the industry even faster (Huddleson 2016).

We've seen this before: a multibillion-dollar industry based on
a potentially addictive substance with uncertain health effects.
Without careful regulation, Big Marijuana will become the
next Big Tobacco.

Pot is less addictive than tobacco—for now. Only 9% of
marijuana users qualify as dependent on marijuana at some
point in their life, compared to 32% of tobacco users. But
some researchers point out that tobacco was once far less addictive than it is today. In the early 1900s, tobacco companies
deliberately blended tobacco types and additives to make more

appealing cigarettes. These changes increased both the toxins in cigarettes and their ability to addict more users, or, as they say in retail, customers (Richter and Levy 2014, 400).

The same folks behind deadlier cigarettes may soon be directly involved in engineering joints. Internal documents show that tobacco companies have been interested in marijuana for decades. In the past, they've denied that interest to preserve their reputation. But now, public acceptance of marijuana is climbing, while the stigma around tobacco use has grown (Barry et al. 2014).

The new marijuana markets have so far kept tobacco companies out with rules such as license limits and residency requirements for investors. But the industry is hungry for investment. In 2016, Washington and Oregon eliminated their residency requirements, and Colorado might follow suit (Anderson 2016).

If tobacco companies can get a foot in the door, they will bring more than just a knowledge of addictive chemistry. Big Tobacco has the money and the influence to roll out big advertising campaigns and to manipulate regulation (Barry et al. 2014). Despite the well-publicized dangers of smoking, and widespread social disapproval, around one in five American adults still smoked in 2014 (Richter and Levy 2014, 400).

Even if states succeed in keeping Big Tobacco out, marijuana companies themselves may prove to be fast learners. One study found increases in marijuana potency related to medical marijuana laws, particularly in states that allowed commercial cannabis dispensaries (Hall and Weier 2015, 610–611).

This may be just the beginning. Taxes on marijuana have been based on weight rather than tetrahydrocannabinol (THC) content. That gives growers an incentive to increase potency (Hall and Weier 2015, 611). THC content relates to pleasure as well as addiction and psychosis. The potential to attract and addict users gives growers a second incentive (Richter and Levy 2014, 400).

Marijuana companies are also working on new delivery systems. Vaporizing increases the THC inhaled by users (Richter and Levy 2014, 400). The National Organization for the Reform of Marijuana Laws (NORML) has assisted efforts to exclude e-cigarettes from clean indoor air laws (Barry et al. 2014).

Marijuana interests have fought other regulations. They fought to keep smoking restrictions from applying to marijuana clubs in Colorado (Barry et al. 2014). They originally lobbied both Colorado and Washington State to avoid heavy regulation of edible marijuana products (MacCoun and Mello 2015, 990).

Edibles may pose one of the biggest health threats to the public. Familiar forms, often similar to other candies and desserts, make edibles attractive to children. Consumed marijuana acts differently in the body than smoked or vaporized pot. Adding to this, their high potency makes an overdose more likely (MacCoun and Mello 2015, 989–990). But edibles are big money makers for the industry (Huddleson 2016).

So how do we protect the public from Big Pot? We need to set up controls around marijuana now, similar to those around alcohol and tobacco, before marijuana interests become more powerful. Since federal law still prohibits marijuana, federal agencies which normally try to the public from unsafe products cannot become involved (MacCoun and Mello 2015, 990). Either this must change, or states must take their responsibility more seriously.

Public education can help. As a result of public concern over overdoses and accidental ingestion by children, Colorado passed new regulations on edibles that are scheduled to go into effect on October 1, 2016 (Borchardt 2016). We need to do more. More research should investigate marijuana risks to personal and public health. Products should be labeled with known health risks, such as respiratory damage from smoking and impaired cognitive development (Richter and Levy 2014, 400).

Without a strong push to protect public health, marijuana interests, with or without the involvement of the tobacco industry, will work to maximize profits regardless of the cost to society.

References

Anderson, Rick. 2016. "How New Rules in Two States Could Give Birth to Big Marijuana." *Los Angeles Times.* http://www.latimes.com/nation/la-na-corporate-mari juana-20160324-story.html. Accessed on May 25, 2016.

Barry, Rachel Ann, et al. 2014. "Waiting for the Opportune Moment: The Tobacco Industry and Marijuana Legalization." *Millbank Quarterly.* 92: 207–242. http:// www.ncbi.nlm.nih.gov/pmc/articles/PMC4089369/. Accessed on June 3, 2016.

Borchardt, Debra. 2016. "Edible Marijuana Company Ready for New Colorado Rules." *Forbes.* http://www .forbes.com/sites/debraborchardt/2016/06/06/edible-marijuana-company-ready-for-new-rules/#32f20ecd 6987. Accessed on June 7, 2016.

Hall, W., and M. Weier. 2015. "Assessing the Public Health Impacts or Legalizing Recreational Cannabis Use in the USA." *Clinical Pharmacology and Therapeutics.* 97: 607–615. http://www.medicinalgenomics.com/ wp-content/uploads/2011/12/Assessing-the-pub-health-impacts-of-legalizing-recreational-cannabis-use-in-the-USA.pdf. Accessed on May 27, 2016.

Huddleson, Tom. 2016. "Legal Marijuana Sales Could Hit $6.7 Billion in 2016." *Fortune.* http://fortune.com/2016/ 02/01/marijuana-sales-legal/. Accessed on June 7, 2016.

MacCoun, Robert, and Michelle M. Mello. 2015. "Half-Baked—The Retail Promotion of Marijuana Edibles." *New England Journal of Medicine.* 372: 989–991. http://healthpolicy.fsi.stanford.edu/sites/default/files/ maccoun_mello_2015_nejmp1416014_0.pdf. Accessed on June 3, 2016.

Richter, Kimber, and Sharon Levy. 2014. "Big Marijuana-Lessons from Big Tobacco." *New England*

Journal of Medicine. 371: 399–401. http://dev.north starbehavioral.com/wp-content/uploads/2015/06/big marijuanaindustrynejm.pdf. Accessed on June 3, 2016.

Clara MacCarald is a freelance writer with an M.S. in biology who lives in Central New York. She is currently writing several educational books for children.

Is Marijuana Medicine? The Answer Is Yes, No, and Maybe
Kevin A. Sabet

Modern science has synthesized the marijuana plant's primary psychoactive ingredient—THC—into pill form. This pill, dronabinol (or Marinol, its trade name) is sometimes prescribed for nausea and appetite stimulation. Another drug, Cesamet, mimics chemical structures that occur naturally in the plant.

But when most people think of medical marijuana, they don't think of a pill with an isolated component of marijuana, but rather the entire smoked, vaporized, or edible version of the whole marijuana plant. Rather than isolate active ingredients in the plant—as we do with the opium plant when we create morphine, for example—many legalization proponents advocate strongly for smoked marijuana to be used as a medicine. But the science on smoking any drug is clear: smoking marijuana, especially highly potent whole marijuana, is not a proper delivery method, nor do other delivery methods ensure a reliable dose. And while parts of the marijuana plant have medical value, the Institute of Medicine said in its landmark 1999 report: "Scientific data indicate the potential therapeutic value of cannabinoid drugs . . . smoked marijuana, however, is a crude THC delivery system that also delivers harmful substances . . . and should not be generally recommended" (Joy et al. 1999, 10).

It is not so unimaginable to think about other marijuana-based medications that might come to market very soon. Sativex, an oral mouth spray developed from a blend of two marijuana extracts (one strain is high in THC and the other in CBD, which counteracts THC's psychoactive effect), has already been approved in 10 countries and is in late stages of approval in the United States. It is clear to anyone following this story that it is possible to develop marijuana-based medications in accordance with modern scientific standards, and many more such legitimate medications are just around the corner.

How Does Medical Marijuana Currently Work in the Various States?

At present in California, and in several other states, it is widely recognized that the reality of the "medical use" of marijuana is highly questionable. For payment of a small cash sum, almost anyone can obtain a physician's "recommendation" to purchase, possess, and use marijuana for alleged medical purposes. Indeed, numerous studies have shown that most customers of these dispensaries do not suffer from chronic, debilitating conditions such as HIV/AIDS or cancer (O'Connell and Bou-Matar 2007). Both sides of the argument agree that this system has essentially legalized marijuana for recreational use, at least among those individuals able and willing to buy a recommendation.

To date many pot dispensaries are mom-and-pop operations, although some act as multimillion dollar, professional companies. A recent documentary on the Discovery Channel, which examined the practices of Harborside Health Center in Oakland, California—by its own admission, the largest marijuana dispensary "on the planet"—the buds (which are distributed directly to member-patients) are merely examined visually and with a microscope. The buds are also handled by employees who do not use gloves or face masks. Steve DeAngelo, Harborside's co-founder, states that they must "take it as it comes." The documentary noted that some plant material is tested by Steep Hill Laboratory, but there was no evidence that Steep Hill's instrumentation and techniques are "validated," that its operators are properly trained and educated, that its reference standards are accurate, and that its results are replicable by other laboratories ("Weed Wars Now Streaming on Netflix" 2013).

What if We Rescheduled Marijuana?

Thanks to legalization advocates, an issue mostly confined to scholarly and legal debates—that of the scheduling of drugs as laid out in the Controlled Substances Act (CSA)—has recently gained prominence.

In short, the reason marijuana hasn't been rescheduled is because no product of whole, raw marijuana has a "currently accepted medical use" in the United States, which is part of the legal definition of Schedule I drugs defined by the Controlled Substances Act.

By contrast, Schedule II substances have a currently accepted medical use in the United States or a currently accepted medical use with severe restrictions (and, like Schedule I drugs, a high potential for abuse).

More importantly, regardless of the schedule, any substance may be prescribed by physicians and dispensed by pharmacists only when incorporated into specific FDA-approved products. That is why Schedule II opioid products can be obtained in pharmacies by prescription, but raw opium, despite being in Schedule II, cannot be prescribed.

This fact is sometimes articulated as follows: "Schedule II substances may be prescribed." This abbreviated description, however, is incomplete and has caused significant confusion. "An approved product comprised of a Schedule II substance may be prescribed" or even "An approved product based on ingredients found in Schedule I substances can be prescribed" would be accurate statements.

So why doesn't whole marijuana have a "currently accepted medical use"? Well, there have not been scientific studies, of adequate size and duration, showing that a product comprised of raw, whole marijuana (smoked or vaporized or otherwise ingested) has medicinal value. FDA has never approved crude plant materials as a prescription medicine, partly because there is no way to administer it in defined doses and without any toxic by-products. However, there have been studies showing that components or constituents within marijuana have medical value. This is where many people get confused. That is why both statements "marijuana has no medical value" and "marijuana is a medicine" are both untrue.

Which Components within Marijuana Have Accepted Medicinal Value?

At least one, and maybe even more than that. Right now, a capsule, Marinol, containing laboratory-made THC, the active ingredient in marijuana (e.g., what gets you high) is in Schedule III and widely available (though not often prescribed) at pharmacies. Marinol was approved first for nausea/vomiting from cancer chemotherapy and again during the height of the AIDS epidemic, specifically for people who could not eat (scientists have long known that THC boosts appetite). THC has also been tested (but not yet approved) as an analgesic—meaning it helps lessen severe pain (like the pain associated with cancer).

But we know that THC isn't the only interesting component in marijuana. Recently scientists have discovered that CBD (cannabidiol) has powerful anti-seizure and other therapeutic properties. CBD does not get you high and barely exists in the modern marijuana found on the street today. Some U.S. state-sanctioned medical dispensaries do contain expensive, specially grown strains of smoked/ingested/extracted (in an oil, for example) marijuana with very high levels of CBD (and low levels of THC—not enough to get you high). These products have not been properly tested and standardized, however.

Medical marijuana should really only be about bringing relief to the sick and dying, and it should be done in a responsible manner that formulates the active components of the drug in a nonsmoked form that delivers a defined dose. However, in most states with medical marijuana laws, it has primarily become a

license for the state-sanctioned use of a drug by almost anyone who desires it. Developing marijuana-based medications
through the FDA process is more likely to ensure that seriously
ill patients, who are being supervised by their actual treating
physicians, have access to safe and reliable products.

References

Joy, Janet E., et al. 1999. *Marijuana and Medicine: Assessing
the Science Base.* Institute of Medicine. Washington, DC:
National Academy Press.

O'Connell, T. and C. B. Bou-Matar. 2007. "Long Term
Marijuana Users Seeking Medical Cannabis in California
(2001–2007): Demographics, Social Characteristics,
Patterns of Cannabis and Other Drug Use of 4117
Applicants." *Harm Reduction Journal.* http://www
.harmreductionjournal.com/content/4/1/1. Accessed
on June 9, 2016.

"Weed Wars Now Streaming on Netflix." 2013. Harborside
Health Center. https://www.harborsidehealthcenter.com/
news/press-100713.html. Accessed on June 9, 2016.

*Kevin A. Sabet, Ph.D., is assistant professor in the Division of
Addiction Studies and chief of the Drug Policy Institute at the
University of Florida and president of Smart Approaches to
Marijuana.*

Common Sense Marijuana Policy Revisited
Douglas McVay

Should marijuana be legalized for adult social use? That question has been asked at least since the Nixon administration.
Now that eight states and the District of Columbia have legalized personal use, possession, and cultivation of marijuana,
and are regulating marijuana commerce, many more people
are asking that question.

There are really two policy questions here: Should there be any criminal penalties associated with possession of marijuana? And, should production and distribution of marijuana be legally regulated rather than left in the hands of criminals?

If the purpose of marijuana prohibition is to prevent marijuana use, then it has failed, but how badly? In 1937, when Congress passed the Marihuana Tax Act, the market for social-use marijuana—the so-called recreational market, as opposed to medicinal cannabis, or hemp—was small and limited. Today, marijuana is a multi-billion dollar industry, both legal and illegal.

Currently, marijuana is used by millions of people every day. Many major American politicians and other leaders have admitted to using marijuana. They were fortunate to have avoided an arrest that could have destroyed their future careers—though looking at the numbers perhaps that's not surprising.

According to the FBI, since 1997 in the United States there have been more than 680,000 arrests every year for various marijuana offenses, the vast majority of which were simple possession charges (Uniform Crime Reports 2002–2015).

More than 35 million people aged 12 and over in the United States have used marijuana at some point in the past year. In 2014, an estimated 22.2 million people aged 12 and over in the United States were so-called current, or monthly, users of marijuana, and of that number, at least 9.2 million used marijuana on 20 days or more days during the previous month (Center for Behavioral Health Statistics and Quality 2014). It's worth bearing in mind that the NSDUH estimate is based on the number of people willing to admit to illegal activity on a government survey.

The more than 1.5 million property crime arrests made in the United States in 2014 resulted in a clearance rate for overall property crime of 20.2%. The nearly half a million arrests for violent crimes in the United States in 2014 resulted in a clearance rate for overall violent crime of 47.4% (Uniform Crime Reports, 2015).

The cost of this enforcement can be measured by more than just dollars. Researchers in 2013 found that in New York City, a marijuana possession arrest takes from two to three hours of police time (Levine, Siegel, and Sayegh, 2013). Jurisdictions will vary, but for the sake of argument, say a marijuana possession arrest takes 2.5 hours of an officer's time. In that case, in 2014, police spent more than 1.5 million hours just arresting marijuana users, and that assumes only one officer was involved in the arrest rather than two partners.

Laws don't exist in a vacuum, so a comparison with other legal drugs is in order. There are two primary legal controlled substances that are used as social drugs, or recreationally, in the United States: alcohol and tobacco. Though some might argue it's not fair to make such comparisons, a de facto level of acceptable risk for controlled substances that are legally available for social use by adults has been established by society.

There is no question that marijuana use is well within acceptable levels of risk since alcohol is one of the yardsticks owing to one simple fact: it is relatively easy for a person to overdose fatally on alcohol. The CDC reported that in 2013 there were 29,001 alcohol-induced deaths (Deaths: Final Data for 2013, 2016). On the other hand, it is practically impossible to achieve a fatal overdose of marijuana (Iversen, 2002).

Leaving aside the question of lethality, alcohol is still more dangerous than marijuana. The UK's Advisory Council on the Misuse of Drugs performed an objective review of the health data regarding alcohol, marijuana, and other drugs. Ruth Weissenborn and David Nutt wrote about the ACMD's conclusions in the *Journal of Psychopharmacology* in 2011, noting that "Alcohol was confirmed as the most harmful drug to others and the most harmful drug overall. A direct comparison of alcohol and cannabis showed that alcohol was considered to be more than twice as harmful as cannabis to users, and five times as harmful as cannabis to others." They noted further that "as there are few areas of harm that each drug can produce where cannabis scores more highly than alcohol, we suggest that even if there were no legal impediment to cannabis use it would be unlikely to be more harmful than alcohol" (Weissenborn and Nutt, 2011).

Nearly 80 years of a failed and unjustified policy is long enough. Marijuana prohibition must come to an end.

References

Center for Behavioral Health Statistics and Quality. 2014 National Survey on Drug Use and Health: Detailed Tables. Substance Abuse and Mental Health Services Administration, Rockville, Maryland, 2015.

"Deaths: Final Data for 2013." 2016. Centers for Disease Control. National Vital Statistics Reports, Volume 64, Number 2. http://www.cdc.gov/nchs/data/nvsr/nvsr64/nvsr64_02.pdf, last accessed June 16, 2016.

Iversen, Leslie L. 2002. "The Science of Marijuana." https://global.oup.com/academic/product/the-science-of-marijuana-9780195328240?cc=us&lang=en&. Accessed on June 16, 2016.

Levine, Harry, Loren Siegel, and Gabriel Sayegh. 2013. "One Million Police Hours: Making 440,000 Marijuana Possession Arrests in New York City, 2002–2012." https://www.drugpolicy.org/sites/default/files/One_Million_Police_Hours.pdf. Accessed on June 16, 2016.

"Uniform Crime Reports." 2002–2015. Federal Bureau of Investigation. http://www.fbi.gov/ucr/ucr.htm. Accessed on June 16, 2016.

Weissenborn, Ruth, and David J. Nutt. 2011. "Popular Intoxicants: What Lessons Can Be Learned from the Last 40 Years of Alcohol and Cannabis Regulation?" *Journal of Psychopharmacology*. 2011, DOI: 10.1177/02

69881111414751. http://jop.sagepub.com/content/26/
2/213. Accessed on June 16, 2016.

*Douglas McVay is a journalist, policy analyst, and longtime advo-
cate for progressive social justice reform. He is the editor of Drug-
WarFacts.org, and serves on the board of directors of Common
Sense for Drug Policy and on the advisory council of Students for
Sensible Drug Policy.*

Introduction

This chapter contains brief sketches of individuals and organizations who are important in understanding the history of marijuana laws and policies in the United States and around the world. The number of such individuals and organizations is legion, and only some especially significant organizations and individuals, or those typical of other organizations and individuals, are included.

Americans for Safe Access

Americans for Safe Access (ASA) was founded in 2002 by Steph Sherer, a woman with torticollis, a neurological movement disorder that causes a person's head to tilt to one side. The disorder is sometimes known colloquially as "wry neck." It is accompanied by pain, inflammation, and muscle spasms that may be relieved by the use of marijuana. Sherer founded ASA for the purpose of educating the general public about the medical uses of cannabis and combating efforts by the U.S. Drug Enforcement Administration (DEA) to prevent the use of marijuana for medical purposes in places where state law permits such

A marijuana reform advocate with the group NORML holds a clipboard while waiting for passersby to sign a petition to get a pot club initiative on the ballot in the next election in Denver. Legal marijuana is giving Colorado a conundrum. Visitors can buy the drug, but they can't use it in public. Or in a rental car. Or in most hotel rooms. Some legalization advocates believe they have a solution—pot clubs. (AP Photo/Brennan Linsley) use. ASA claims to be "the largest national member-based organization of patients, medical professionals, scientists and concerned citizens promoting safe and legal access to cannabis for therapeutic use and research." At the time that Sherer founded ASA, there were only 11 marijuana dispensaries in the United States, all of which were operating illegally because no state had yet legalized the use of marijuana for therapeutic purposes. As of 2016, there are more than 1,000 marijuana dispensaries in California alone, and there may be more than 120,000 dispensaries and other facilities where medical marijuana is distributed throughout the nation.

ASA has developed a multifaceted program to achieve its objective of ensuring safe and legal access to anyone who needs the substance for therapeutic or research purposes. Some elements of that program are:

- The Medical Cannabis Advocate's Training Center, in which individuals are trained about the history and science of marijuana as a therapeutic agent and are taught the skills needed to work effectively within the political system to accomplish ASA goals.
- The Medical Cannabis Policy Shop, which studies current political and legislative developments with regard to therapeutic marijuana and offer information and advice to policymakers and legislators on relevant topics.
- The Federal Advocacy Project, run out of the Washington office of ASA, attempts to influence policymakers and legislators at all levels about the objectives of the "safe marijuana" movement.
- The California Campaign for Safe Access, which focuses specifically on the largest state in which medical marijuana has been legalized, dealing with patient's rights, education about the medical marijuana law in the state, and efforts to ensure that the law is implemented properly.
- The Raid Center, which is a carefully organized, very specific program designed to help individuals and organizations

whose activities have been subjected to raids by the DEA or other law enforcement agencies.

- The Patient's Rights Project, which deals directly with individuals who use marijuana therapeutically, explaining to them on a one-to-one basis what their rights are with regard to medical cannabis.
- The Community Support Project, an ambitious effort to provide all stakeholders in the medical marijuana community with the information and guidance they need to function effectively in their specific roles, with special programs for patients, clinicians, and medical advocates.
- State Campaigns, in which the resources and skills available among ASA staff are made available to medical marijuana efforts in individual states across the nation.
- Peace for Patients Campaign is the most recent program, adopted to convince the U.S. Congress to adopt legislation to end harassment of and attacks on individuals who use marijuana for medical purposes and their caregivers.

An important insight into the work that ASA does is its annual listing of "major accomplishments." For 2015, that listed included such items as:

- The organization was instrumental in the passage of the Rohrabacher-Farr Amendment in the U.S. Congress, an act designed to reduce federal interference with the use of medical marijuana in states where it is legal.
- It promoted adoption of the Compassionate Access, Research Expansion, and Respect States Act (CARERS) Act of 2015, designed to remedy the state-federal conflict over medical cannabis law.
- It contributed to a significant reduction in actions against the legal use of medical marijuana by all federal agencies except for the Food and Drug Administration.
- It promoted efforts to guarantee the safety and efficacy of marijuana products used for medical purposes in the United States.

- It promoted the adoption of improved medical marijuana legislation at the state level throughout the nation.
- It worked on an international level to change United Nations treaties on drugs that tend to limit or restrict the use of marijuana for medical purposes.

ASA annually publishes a wide variety of position statements, reports, background papers, and other documents on various aspects of the medical marijuana issue. Among the publications currently available are the policy statements, "Cannabis as Medicine," "Patients' Bill of Rights," "Reclassifying Medical Cannabis," "President Obama's Policy on Medical Cannabis," "Who Should Qualify as a Patient?" "Medical Cannabis Research," "Patient Cultivation," "Medical Cannabis and Genetic Engineering," and "Recognition and Regulation of Distribution Centers."

Harry J. Anslinger (1892–1975)

Anslinger was appointed the first commissioner of the Federal Bureau of Narcotics when it was established in 1930. He held that office for 32 years, one of the longest tenures of any federal officials in modern history. He was consistently a strong advocate for severe penalties against the manufacture, distribution, sale, and use of certain drugs, especially marijuana.

Harry Jacob Anslinger was born in Altoona, Pennsylvania, on May 20, 1892, to Robert J. and Rosa Christiana Fladt Anslinger, immigrants from Switzerland and Germany, respectively. Without completing high school, Anslinger attended the Altoona Business College before taking a job with the Pennsylvania Railroad. He received a leave of absence from the railway that allowed him to matriculate at Pennsylvania State College (now Pennsylvania State University), where he received his two-year associate degree in engineering and business management. He then returned to a full-time job at the railroad.

When World War I broke out, Anslinger was rejected for active service because of a childhood accident that had left him blind in one eye. Instead, he was accepted for volunteer service at the War Department in Washington, D.C., where he was made assistant to the Chief of Inspection of Equipment. He remained at the War Department for only a year before being transferred to the State Department, where his fluency in German was a greater asset. His first overseas assignment at State was to the U.S. mission in The Hague, The Netherlands, in 1918, where he was made special liaison to the deposed king of Germany, Wilhelm II. Three years later, Anslinger was transferred to the U.S. mission in Hamburg, Germany, and then, three years later, he was transferred again, this time to the U.S. mission in La Guaira, Venezuela.

In 1926, Anslinger received yet another assignment, this time to Nassau, in the British Bahamas. His job in Nassau was to try to reduce the flow of liquor from the Bahamas to the United States, following the adoption of the Prohibition Amendment to the U.S. Constitution in 1920. At the time, the Bahamas were one of the major venues for the shipment of illegal alcohol to the United States. Anslinger's work in this post was so impressive that the U.S. Treasury asked the State Department to transfer him to its own offices in Washington, D.C. His first job at Treasury was as chief of the Division of Foreign Control. That post allowed him to become active in the international war against illegal drugs, a war of major concern to the United States, but of relatively little concern to most other countries in the world. As official representative of the United States, Anslinger attended the Conference on Suppression of Smuggling in London in 1926; the Conference on Suppression of Smuggling in Paris in 1927; and the International Congress against Alcoholism in Antwerp in 1928. In all of these settings, Anslinger worked aggressively to promote an American agenda for much stronger legislative and regulatory controls over the production, transport, and use of narcotics, including marijuana.

In 1929, Anslinger was promoted to assistant commissioner in the U.S. Bureau of Prohibition. He held that position only briefly before being selected as the first commissioner of the newly created Federal Bureau of Narcotics in 1930. He began his assignment at the bureau at a time when state and federal officials were debating the need (or lack of need) for regulations of hemp and marijuana. Both hemp and marijuana are obtained from plants in the genus Cannabis, the former with many important industrial applications, and the latter used almost exclusively as a recreational drug. Historians have discussed the motivations that may have driven Anslinger's attitudes about the subject, but his actions eventually demonstrated a very strong opposition to the growing, processing, distribution, and use of all products of the cannabis plant. He was instrumental in formulating federal policies and laws against such use that developed during the 1930s. Throughout his career, he also continued his efforts to influence the direction of international drug policies, always working for more severe penalties in drug trafficking and drug use. In this effort, he served as co-observer at the League of Nation's Opium Advisory Commission between 1932 and 1939, as a delegate to the International Conference for Suppression of Illicit Traffic in Narcotic Drugs of the League of Nations in 1936, and as U.S. representative to the Commission on Narcotic Drugs of the United Nations in 1952.

Anslinger has long been criticized for the extremes with which he pursued his campaign against drugs and his use of racist and sexist themes in that campaign. At one time or another, for example, he wrote that:

- There are 100,000 total marijuana smokers in the US, and most are Negroes, Hispanics, Filipinos and entertainers. Their Satanic music, jazz and swing, result from marijuana usage. This marijuana causes white women to seek sexual relations with Negroes, entertainers and any others.

- Marihuana influences Negroes to look at white people in the eye, step on white men's shadows and look at a white woman twice.
- Reefer makes darkies think they're as good as white men.

Anslinger remained in his post until 1970, staying on even after his 70th birthday until a replacement was found. He then served two more years as U.S. representative to the United Nations Narcotic Convention. By the end of his tenure with the convention, he was blind and suffered from both angina and an enlarged prostate. He died in Hollidaysburg, Pennsylvania, on November 14, 1975, of heart failure.

Although little definitive information is available, Anslinger apparently earned his LL.B. from the Washington College of Law in 1930 and was later awarded an honorary LL.D. degree from the University of Maryland (date unknown). Among his many awards were the Proctor Gold Medal, Alumni Recognition Award of American University, distinguished alumnus award of Pennsylvania State University, Remington Medal, and the Alexander Hamilton Medal. He was the author or co-author of three major books, *The Traffic in Narcotics* (1953), *The Murderers: The Story of the Narcotic Gangs* (1961), and *The Protectors: The Heroic Story of the Narcotics Agents, Citizens, and Officials in Their Unending, Unsung Battles against Organized Crime in America and Abroad* (1964).

Steve DeAngelo (1958–)

As his official biography claims, DeAngelo "has spent his entire career at the intersection of cannabis activism and entrepreneurship." He is currently CEO of Harborside Health Center, in Oakland, California, a company he cofounded with Troy Dayton in 2006. Harborside Center is currently California's largest medical marijuana facility and, by some accounts, the most respected such facility in the state, if not in the country.

Steve DeAngelo was born in Philadelphia, Pennsylvania, on June 12, 1958. At an early age, he moved with his family to Washington, D.C., where his father worked in the administration of President John Kennedy. The DeAngelo family was active in the civil rights movement at the time, and Steve's father served with the Peace Corps from 1967 to 1969. The family's relatively liberal views did not extend to the use of marijuana, however. When his parents learned that Steve, at the age of 13, had begun smoking the drug, they confiscated his stash and grounded him for a period of time. In response, Steve ran away from home for "a few weeks." When he returned, he had not abandoned his interest in marijuana, and was later suspended from school twice for smoking the drug. By the time he was 16, DeAngelo decided that school was not an important part of his life, and he dropped out.

That act only gave DeAngelo more time for the political activism in which he had been involved for many years. One of his first acts was to join the Yippies, more formally the Youth International Party, founded by activists Abbie Hoffman and Jerry Rubin in 1968 to carry out actions in opposition to the Vietnam War and other national policies to which they objected. Although still only 16 years old, DeAngelo was one of the key organizers of a marijuana "smoke-in" on July 4, 1970, an event that is still celebrated on that date every year. He also became active in other venues, primarily the music industry, where he became a record producer, nightclub manager, and concert promoter, as well as renovated a number of concert sites in which to produce events. Along the way, DeAngelo returned to formal schooling at the University of Maryland, from which he earned his law degree in 1984.

After completing his studies at Maryland, DeAngelo opened a home in Washington, D.C., called The Nuthouse, to serve as a refuge for individuals interested in the movement to legalize marijuana. It was there that he later met Jack Herer, author of one of the most famous books on cannabis in history, *The Emperor Wears No Clothes*. Very much impressed by the message of the book, DeAngelo decided to join with Herer on a cross-country tour to make known the message of the book, namely that cannabis was not the entirely evil drug that it had come to be viewed, but that it had a number of valuable applications in everyday life.

When the tour was completed, DeAngelo returned to Washington, where he worked on the city's Initiative 59, calling for approval of marijuana for medical uses. Although the proposition won by a large margin, the U.S. Congress exerted its authority to invalidate the vote, which it did, much to DeAngelo's consternation. He decided that California was a more receptive region for the work he wanted to accomplish in the field of marijuana legalization, and he returned to the state in 2000, where he has spent essentially all of his professional efforts in that campaign. One of his first acts in California was to join with other interested individuals in the formation of Americans for Safe Access, an organization designed to educate the general public about the beneficial effects of marijuana for a variety of medical conditions. He also wrote and produced a film called *For Medical Use Only*, also touting the medical benefits of cannabis products.

In 2006, DeAngelo applied (along with many other individuals) for a license being offered by the city of Oakland for the creation of a dispensary for medical marijuana. He was awarded the license, which he used to found Harborside Health Center, a facility designed to provide medical marijuana that had been tested and certified for individuals of all income levels by a staff of highly trained medical professionals.

Lyster Hoxie Dewey (1865–1944)

Dewey is probably best known for his lifetime commitment to the study of useful fiber plants and weeds, including cotton, flax, sisal, henequén, manila, and hemp. The significance of his work to modern life came to light in 2010 when a cache of his never-published personal diaries was discovered at a yard sale in

Amherst, New York. The diaries contained a meticulous record of his research on a variety of hemp plants between 1896 and 1944 on a plot of land now occupied by the Pentagon. The diaries were later purchased by the Hemp Industries Association to illustrate the critical role of hemp, later to fall into disrepute because of its association with marijuana, in an earlier period of American history.

Lyster Hoxie Dewey was born in Cambridge, Michigan, on March 14, 1865. He graduated from Tecumseh (Michigan) High School in 1885 and then matriculated at Michigan Agricultural College (now Michigan State University). He then stayed on at the college as an instructor in botany for two years before accepting a position as assistant botanist with the U.S. Department of Agriculture. He remained at the USDA until his retirement in 1935, at which point he had become director of research on all fiber plants with the exception of cotton. After his retirement, he published a group of papers summarizing much of his work at the USDA including a special section on taxonomy of fiber plants in the department's Standardized Plant Names publication and two publications on fiber plants, "Fibras Vegetales y su Produccion en America," for the Pan American Union, and "Fiber Production in the Western Hemisphere" for the Department of Agriculture.

Dewey died at his home in Kenmore, New York, on November 27, 1944.

Drug Free America Foundation, Inc.

Drug Free American Foundation, Inc. (DFAF) is a 501(c)(3) nonprofit organization that, according to its mission statement, is "committed to developing, promoting and sustaining global strategies, policies and laws that will reduce illegal drug use, drug addiction, drug-related injury and death." The organization was founded by Mr. and Mrs. Mel Sembler in 1995. Mr. Sembler was chairman of the board of the Sembler Company, a developer and manager of shopping centers. He also served as U.S. ambassador to Italy and to Australia and Nauru. In the DFAF 2010 annual report, Mrs. Sembler is listed as founder and chair of the organization.

Mr. and Mrs. Sembler originally founded the organization known as Straight, Inc., in 1976, as a nonprofit drug treatment program that claims to have treated more than 12,000 young people with substance abuse problems in eight cities in the United States. Straight was long the subject of intense scrutiny for alleged abusive practices used in its drug treatment programs. It later changed its name to Straight Foundation, Inc., and spun off a number of drug treatment programs, such as The Seed, Kids Helping Kids, Pathway Family Center, Life, Growing Together, KIDS (of various cities and regions), SAFE, and Alberta Adolescent Recovery Center (AARC). Drug Free America Foundation is reputed to be one of the Straight spinoffs. The DFAF website makes little or no mention of this alleged connection.

Most of DFAF's work is carried out through six divisions:

- The Institute on Global Drug Policy is an alliance of physicians, scientists, attorneys, and drug specialists who advocate for the adoption of public policies that curtail the use of illicit and misuse of licit drugs and alcohol. A major activity of the institute is co-sponsorship of the *Journal of Global Drug Policy and Practice* with another division of DFAF, the International Scientific and Medical Forum on Drug Abuse. Relatively little information is available online about the organization, membership, or activities of the institute. In a statement announcing formation of the division, its mission was described as "creating and strengthening international laws that hold drug users and dealers criminally accountable for their actions. It will vigorously promote treaties and agreements that provide clear penalties to individuals who buy, sell or use harmful drugs. It will push for a uniform legal requirement that marijuana and other addictive drugs must meet the same scientific standards as other drugs to be deemed therapeutic for medical conditions."

- The International Scientific and Medical Forum on Drug Abuse is described by DFAF as a "brain trust" of researchers and physicians concerned about substance abuse who have an interest in dispelling incorrect depictions of the consequences of drug use among the general public. The division is a co-sponsor of the *Journal of Global Drug Policy and Practice* with The Institute on Global Drug Policy.

- The International Task Force on Strategic Drug Policy is a network of professionals in the field of substance abuse and community leaders who work together to develop and implement drug reduction principles around the world. The task force convenes meetings in cooperation with other divisions of the DFAF to train individuals in methods of drug reduction principles. The task force reports having held eight such conferences of about 60 to 130 individuals since 2001 in locations such as London, Buenos Aires, Tampa, and Guayaquil, Ecuador.

    The Drug Prevention Network of the Americas (DPNA) is a cooperative effort of nongovernmental agencies in North, South, and Central America working to reduce demand for illegal substances through conferences, training seminars, and Internet communications.

- Students Taking Action Not Drugs (STAND) is a student-based organization whose goal it is to distribute on campuses accurate scientific information about the effects of taking illegal drugs.

- National Drug-Free Workplace Alliance (NDWA) is a division attempting to develop drug free work environments in the state of Florida and, working with other agencies and organizations, throughout the United States.

The organization's website provides its views on a broad array of drug topics, including marijuana, overcoming addiction, prescription drug abuse, drug policy, drug testing, prevention of substance abuse, and international drug policy. Associated with each topic is a PDF file or other attachment that provides more detail on the subject such as on federal and state laws dealing with medical marijuana, "the truth" about marijuana, and how to get rich by suing a doctor who prescribes marijuana for medical purposes. The organization's website also contains the Otto and Connie Moulton Library for Drug Prevention, which contains more than 2,100 books and other media dealing with substance abuse issues. In addition to three position statements on substance abuse (on harm reduction, student drug testing, and medical marijuana), DFAF offers a small number of DVDs dealing with substance abuse issues, including "True Compassion: About Marijuana," "Real View Mirror: Looking at Your Future, Leaving the Drug Culture Behind," "In Focus: A Clear Message about Drugs," and "Deadly Indifference: The Price of Ignoring the Youth Drug Epidemic."

Drug Policy Alliance

The Drug Policy Alliance (DPA) was created in July 2000 as a result of the merger of the Lindesmith Center (TLC) and the Drug Policy Foundation (DPF). The Lindesmith Center, in turn, had been formed in 1994 as a think-tank for the consideration of alternatives to existing policies and practices for dealing with drug issues, while the Drug Policy Foundation had been established in 1987 as an organization established to work for drug reform, largely through the provision of grants to advance further studies on drug policies. The DPA now claims to be "the world's leading drug policy reform organization of people who believe the war on drugs is doing more harm than good." The organization currently claims to have nearly 35,000 members, with more than 300,000 individuals receiving its one-line e-newsletter and action alerts.

DPA organizes its work under the rubric of about a half-dozen major issues: reforming marijuana laws, harm reduction, fighting injustice, protecting youth, defending liberty, making economic sense, and global reform. Each of these general topics is further divided into more specific issues. The reforming marijuana laws topic, for example, covers issues such as developing a legal regulatory market for marijuana, helping individuals who have been arrested for marijuana possession, and providing information about the potential health and social effects of marijuana use. The topic of protecting youth is further divided into efforts to deal with drug testing in schools and zero-tolerance policies in some school districts, as well as provides information and materials on "reality-based" drug education. The making economic sense topic deals in more detail with subjects such as problems of supply and demand for marijuana, the problem of drug prohibition and violence, and the economic benefits of legalizing and taxing the sale of marijuana.

An important part of the DPA efforts on behalf of marijuana issue is a series of action alerts, through which members and friends of the association are encouraged to contact legislators, administrative officials, and other stakeholders about specific issues of concern to the organization. During 2016, for example, DPA sponsored action alerts (1) directed to members of the U.S. Senate encouraging them to roll back harsh minimum sentences for drug offenses, (2) to members of Congress asking for a stop to seizure of personal property from individuals suspected of violating drug laws, (3) to President Barack Obama to overhaul the operation of the Drug Enforcement Administration, (4) to the U.S. Senate to legalize medical marijuana nationwide, and (5) to President Obama to free prisoners who have been convicted of minor drug offenses.

The Drug Policy Alliance publishes a number of reports, fact sheets, and other print and electronic materials on the topic of marijuana legalization. Members receive the tri-annual newsletter the *Ally*, which provides information on the organization's current activities and successes. Other publications include

"Safety First: A Reality-Based Approach to Teens and Drugs," a tool designed to help parents evaluate and discuss strategies for protecting teenagers from drug abuse; "Crime and Punishment in New Jersey: The Criminal Code and Public Opinion on Sentencing," a report on the legal status of marijuana in that state; "Drug Courts Are Not the Answer: Toward a Health-Centered Approach to Drug Use," an analysis of existing laws on marijuana possession; "Overdose: A National Crisis Taking Root in Texas," a report on the growing number of overdose deaths in that state and the United States; "Arresting Latinos for Marijuana in California: Possession Arrests in 33 Cities, 2006–08," a report on the special risk faced by Latinos in California for marijuana offenses; and "Healing a Broken System: Veterans Battling Addiction and Incarceration," which deals with the special problems of marijuana use faced by veterans returning from service in Iraq and Afghanistan.

On its website, DPA also provides an excellent resource dealing with drug facts. Some of the topics covered on this page include fundamental facts about marijuana and other drugs, some new solutions for dealing with the nation's drug problems, the relevance of federal and state drug laws for individuals, a summary of individual rights in connection with existing drug laws, statistical information about the nation's war on drugs, and drug laws around the world.

European Monitoring Centre for Drugs and Drug Addiction

The concept of an all-European agency to deal with the growing problem of substance abuse on the continent was first proposed by French president Georges Pompidou in the late 1960s. That idea languished for about two decades before it was raised once more in 1989 by French president François Mitterrand in 1989. Mitterrand suggested a seven-step program that would involve establishing a common method for analyzing drug addiction in the European states: harmonizing national policies for substance abuse; strengthening controls and improving cooperation among states; finding ways of implementing the 1988 UN Convention against Illicit Traffic in Narcotic Drugs and Psychotropic Substances; coordinating policies and practices between producing and consuming countries; developing a common policy dealing with drug-related money laundering; and designating a single individual in each country responsible for antidrug actions within that country.

Mitterrand's suggestion led to a series of actions within the European community that eventually resulted, in 1993, in the creation of the European Monitoring Centre for Drugs and Drug Addiction (EMCDDA) under Council Regulation (EEC) number 302/93. The general administrative structure was established the following year, consisting of an executive director, a management board, and a scientific committee. The management board is the primary decision-making body for EMCDDA. It meets at least once a year and is composed of one representative from each member state of the European Union (EU), two representatives from the European Commission, and two representatives from the European Parliament. The board adopts an annual work program and a three-year work program that guides the organization's day-to-day operations. The three-year program is developed with input from a wide variety of sources, including the general public (through the organization's website). The 2016–2018 program focused on six strategic action areas, communicating evidence and knowledge exchange; early warning and threat assessment; situation, responses, and trend analysis; information collection and management; quality assurance; and cooperation with partners.

The scientific committee consists of 15 members appointed by the management board for the purpose of advising the board on scientific issues related to substance abuse. The first meeting of the management board was held in April 1994 at its Lisbon headquarters, where its administrative offices remain until today. Much of the work of EMCDDA takes place within seven units of the scientific committee. The seven units focus on prevalence, data management and content coordination; consequences, responses, and best practices; supply reduction and new drugs; Reitox and external partners; communication; information and communication technology; and administration. Reitox is the name given to a network of human and computer links among the 27 nations that make up the EMCDDA operation.

The EMCDDA website is one of the richest resources available on nearly every aspect of substance abuse issues in the world. It contains information on a wide variety of topics, such as health consequences (deaths and mortality, infectious diseases, treatment demand, and viral hepatitis); prevalence and epidemiology (general population surveys, drug trends in youth, problem drug use, key indicators, and wastewater analysis); best practice (prevention, treatment, harm reduction, standards and guidelines, Exchange on Drug Demand Reduction Action (EDDRA), and Evaluation Instruments Bank (EIB)); drug profiles (amphetamine, barbiturates, benzodiazepines, BZP and other piperazines, cannabis, cocaine, and crack, fentanyl, hallucinogenic mushrooms, heroin, khat, LSD, MDMA, methamphetamine, *Salvia divinorum*, synthetic cannabinoids and "Spice," synthetic cathinones, synthetic cocaine derivatives, and volatile substances); health and social interventions (harm reduction, prevention of drug use, social reintegration, and treatment of drug use); policy and law (EU policy and law, laws, and public expenditure); new drugs and trends (action on new drugs); supply and supply reduction (interventions against drug supply, interventions against diversion of chemical precursors, interventions against money laundering activities, supply reduction, markets, and crime and supply reduction indicators); resources by drug (cannabis thematic page, cocaine and crack thematic page, and opioids and heroin thematic page); drugs and society (crime, driving, social exclusion, women and gender issues, and young people); and science and research (addiction medicine, neuroscience, and research in Europe).

Barney Frank (1940–)

Frank is a long-serving (1981–2013) member of the U.S. House of Representatives from the Fourth Congressional District of Massachusetts. He is widely regarded as having been one of the most liberal members of both the House and of the Democratic Party. He is perhaps best remembered for his legislative efforts during the economic downturn that ran from 2006 into the middle of the 2010s. He spearheaded the passage of legislation that led to the creation of the Troubled Asset Relief Program (TARP) in 2008, which allowed the U.S. Treasury to buy up bad mortgage securities. In 2010, he was one of the two major co-sponsors (with Senator Christopher Dodd, D-CT) of a bill enacting regulatory reform of the nation's financial structure. Frank was also a lead sponsor of a number of bills to reform the nation's marijuana laws, essentially aimed at reducing or eliminating fines and penalties for the use of marijuana for personal purposes. During his tenure, Frank sponsored and co-sponsored a number of bills designed to decriminalize marijuana and to authorize the use of marijuana for medical purposes. Among these bills were the States' Rights to Medical Marijuana Act of 2001 (H.R. 2592), the Personal Use of Marijuana by Responsible Adults Act of 2008 (HR 5843; reintroduced in 2009 as H.R. 2943), the States' Medical Marijuana Patient Protection Act of 2011 (H.R. 1983), and the Ending Federal Marijuana Prohibition Act of 2011 (H.R. 2306).

Barney Frank was born Barnett Frank on March 31, 1940, in Bayonne, New Jersey, to Samuel and Elsie (née Golush) Frank. Samuel Frank operated a truck stop in Jersey City, which reputedly had connections to crime that led to his incarceration in prison for a year. After graduating from Bayonne High School in 1957, Frank matriculated at Harvard College, from which he graduated in 1962. (He had taken a year off to deal with family affairs upon his father's death, a period during which his father's Mafia friends were "very helpful.") Frank then enrolled in the Ph.D. program in government at Harvard, but left the program in 1968 to become chief assistant to Boston mayor Kevin White. Although Frank eventually earned his law degree from Harvard in 1977, he had set his path on a role in politics by joining White's staff. After three years with the mayor, he joined the staff of Congressman Michael J. Harrington, Democratic representative from the Massachusetts's Sixth District, as administrative assistant.

After a year with Representative Harrington, Frank ran for and won a seat in the Massachusetts House of Representatives from Boston's Back Bay District. He also immediately made a name for himself crusading for liberal approaches to solving social problems in Boston. He was easily elected to three more terms in the Massachusetts House. In addition to his position in the Massachusetts legislature, Frank taught part time at the Harvard University John F. Kennedy School of Government, at the University of Massachusetts at Boston, and at Boston University.

A somewhat unusual opportunity presented itself to Frank in 1979 when Pope John Paul II decreed that members of the Roman Catholic clergy were not allowed to hold political office, thereby making it impossible for the sitting member of the U.S. House of Representatives for Massachusetts's Fourth District, Father Robert Drinan, from continuing in office. Frank ran for the office and won by a vote of 52% to 48%. Two years later, Frank anticipated an even more difficult challenge when he was paired with sitting Congresswoman Margaret Heckler in the newly drawn Fourth District. Frank won the election going away, however, by 20 percentage points. It was the closest election he was to experience during the remainder of his career.

Jon Gettman (1957–)

Gettman has long been active in the campaign to have marijuana rescheduled under provisions of the Controlled Substances Act of 1970 (CSA) from its current listing as a Schedule I substance to a less restrictive status. A Schedule I substance is so listed because (1) it has a high potential for abuse, (2) the substance has no currently accepted medical use in treatment in the United States, and (3) there is a lack of accepted safety for use of the substance under medical supervision. The act makes it illegal for any person, except with special authorization, (1) to manufacture, distribute, dispense, or possess with intent to manufacture, distribute, or dispense the substance, or (2) to create, distribute, or dispense, or possess with intent to distribute or dispense, a counterfeit of the scheduled substance. Gettman was a leader of the Coalition for Rescheduling Cannabis, a group of organizations and individuals formed in about 2002 seeking to have marijuana listed under a less restrictive CSA schedule. Members of the Coalition included the American Alliance for Medical Cannabis, Americans for Safe Access, California National Organization for the Reform of Marijuana Laws (NORML), the Drug Policy Forum of Texas, *High Times* magazine, the Los Angeles Cannabis Resource Center, the National Organization for the Reform of Marijuana Laws (NORML), the Oakland Cannabis Buyers Cooperative, and Patients Out of Time. Ten years later, in 2012, the District of Columbia Court of Appeals announced that it would finally hear oral arguments in the case.

Jon Gettman was born on August 20, 1957. He attended the Catholic University of America, from which he received his B.A. in anthropology in 1985; the American University (Washington, D.C.), which awarded him his M.S. in justice (with a specialization in drug policy) in 1992; and George Mason University, where he received his Ph.D. in public policy (specialization: regional economic development) in 2000. While still a young man, from 1973 to 1980, Gettman worked for the Stone Age Trading Company in wholesale and retail management. He then became involved in the effort to have marijuana use legalized in the United States, serving as policy analyst, business manager, director of communications, president, and national director of NORML from 1981 to 1993. In 1994 he left NORML to work on his own. He has been research analyst, program manager, expert witness, and writer and columnist for public policy, business, legal, and editorial clients. In these roles, he has testified in important cannabis-related cases, including *United States v. Phillip Schmoll, Commonwealth of Pennsylvania v. Ryan Free, United States v. Timothy Perry, Commonwealth of Virginia v. Michael Firth, Commonwealth of Pennsylvania v. James Almquist, Commonwealth of Virginia v. David May,* and *Commonwealth of Virginia v. Brad Gillies.* Gettman has also appeared before a number of state and federal legislative bodies, including the House/Senate Special Subcommittee of Agriculture, and the House Committee of Agriculture of the Virginia legislature, and the Senate Judiciary Committee of the Alaska legislature. In addition to his freelance work as a consultant, Gettman has held other work positions, such as program developer, research analyst, and project manager for Mouncey & Company, Waterford, Virginia; instructor at the College of Southern Maryland, La Plata, Maryland; and volunteer resource person for the Loudoun County, Virginia, Task Force to Propose a Rural Economic Development Plan. Gettman has also served as adjunct assistant professor in the Graduate School of Management and Technology at the University of Maryland University College (2008 to present); adjunct professor in public administration at Shepherd University (2007 to present); and senior research fellow at the School of Public Policy of George Mason University (2003 to 2005 and 2008 to present).

Gettman has written and spoken extensively about the reclassification of cannabis in the United States. Among his print articles are "Marijuana Arrests in Massachusetts," "Marijuana Treatment Admissions," "Marijuana Use in the

United States," "Lost Taxes and Other Costs of Marijuana Laws," "Marijuana Production in the United States," (all *Bulletin of Cannabis Reform*); "Marijuana and the Controlled Substances Act" (*Journal of Cannabis Therapeutics*); and "Decriminalizing Marijuana" (*American Behavioral Scientist*). Among his conference presentations are "Medical Cannabis and the Public Policy Process," "Medical Cannabis and the Public Policy Process," "Dynamic Portfolio Variance Analysis and the Study of Regional Economic Instability," "Crimes of Indiscretion: Marijuana Arrests in the United States," "Personal Use v. Distribution of Cannabis," and "Science and the End of Marijuana Prohibition."

Hemp Industries Association

The Hemp Industries Association (HIA) is a federally chartered 501(c)(6) nonprofit organization representing the hemp industry in the United States, Canada, and a number of other countries, including Australia, China, Mexico, the Netherlands, New Zealand, and the United Kingdom. The organization was formed in 1992 to work for fair and equitable treatment of hemp, a material produced from the cannabis plant with a very low (usually less than 1%) concentration of Δ^9-tetrahydrocannabinol (THC), the compound responsible for the psychoactive effects associated with the ingestion of marijuana. The mission statement of the organization lists the following goals:

- Educate the general public about the qualities of hemp that make it useful for a variety of consumer products.
- Facilitate the exchange of information and technology between hemp agriculturists, processors, manufacturers, distributors, and retailers.
- Maintain and defend the integrity of hemp products.
- Advocate and support socially responsible and environmentally sound business practices.

As of 2016, the organization had more than 320 members representing virtually every conceivable phase of the hemp industry. Some examples of HIA members and the products and services they offer include:

- AZIDA: Body care products;
- Cannabis Basics: Producer of hempseed oil and cannabis flower topical therapy products;
- FarmMax Biomass Harvesting Equipment: Developers of specialized biomass harvesting equipment;
- Native Farms: Suppliers of hemp seed and raw hemp;
- Nature's Path Organic Foods: Food products;
- Dr. Bronner's Magic Soaps: Body care and food products;
- Hemp Traders: Textiles, fabric, and yarns;
- Nutiva: Books, periodicals, food products, seed oil, seeds, and grain;
- Satori Movement, Inc.: Apparel, accessories, and skateboards;
- Ultra Oil for Pets: Animal care products and seed oil;
- Concord Minutemen Solutions Group: Consulting, lobbying, promoting, and marketing.

One of HIA's most important accomplishments was defeat of a 2001 effort by the U.S. Drug Enforcement Administration (DEA) to include hemp under Schedule I of the Controlled Substances Act of 1970 (CSA), a category under which another cannabis product, marijuana, is currently listed. Substances listed under Schedule I are regarded as (1) having a high potential for abuse, (2) having no currently accepted medical use in treatment in the United States, and (3) lacking safe use under medical supervision. The DEA argued that it had the authority to list hemp as a Schedule I substance because in almost all cases, the fibers and oils made from hemp contain greater than zero concentrations of THC. Granted that those concentrations are very low, the DEA said, they are still measurable and, therefore, capable of being listed under Schedule I under the CSA. The HIA brought suit against the DEA, claiming that the agency had gone beyond the provisions laid down by the CSA. The association was funded and supported in this effort by one of its best-known and economically successful members, known at the time as ALL-ONE-GOD-FAITH, Inc., doing business as (and much better known to the public as) Dr. Bronner's Magic Soaps, and joined by a number of other hemp interests, including Atlas Corporation; Nature's Path Foods USA, Inc.; Hemp Oil Canada, Inc.; Hempzels, Inc.; Kenex Ltd.; Tierra Madre, LLC; Ruth's Hemp Foods, Inc.; and the Organic Consumers Association. Plaintiffs were eventually successful in their complaint, with the Ninth Circuit Court of Appeals ruling in 2003 that the DEA had overstepped its authority in listing hemp as a Schedule I substances. The material is, therefore, still legal to grow and sell in the United States, provided that its THC level is less than 0.3%.

HIA achieved another important breakthrough in 2010 when it purchased the diaries of Lyster Dewey, a project once again financed by Dr. Bronner's Magic Soap. (David Bronner, current president of Bronner's Magic Soaps, is past president of HIA and a current member of the organization's board of advisors.) Lyster Dewey has been described by hemp authority, David P. West, as "unarguably the most significant individual in US hemp history." West makes that assessment because of Dewey's role in the study of hemp at the U.S. Department of Agriculture (USDA) from 1890 to 1935. Dewey joined the department as "assistant to the botanist" in 1890 and remained with the department for all but the last two years of his life. In 1912, he began a hemp breeding program that, by 1917, was beginning to produce healthier, more productive varieties of the cannabis plant. The interesting point that connects Dewey with HIA was the discovery of Dewey's notebooks at a yard sale in Amherst, New York, in 2010. The notebooks not only tell about Dewey's work with the cannabis plant, but provide photograph evidence of the success of his research.

Perhaps most interesting of all, at least from a public relations standpoint, was the discovery that Dewey conducted much of his cannabis research on the present site of the Pentagon, the home of the U.S. military. HIA took advantage of this discovery by announcing the First Annual Hemp History Week in May 2010, celebrating, among other things, the discovery of Dewey's notebooks. Reports of that event told of nearly 200 events in 32 states, including programs in support of House Bill 1866, the Industrial Hemp Farming Act of 2009, introduced by Representative Ron Paul (R-TX).

Among its activities, the HIA has developed (in conjunction with Vote Hemp) Test Pledge, a voluntary testing program through which hemp growers pledge that the level of THC contained within their products is less than can be detected by any marijuana test. The association has also developed standards for hemp fibers indicating whether such fibers are pure hemp (Pure Hemp), more than half but less than pure hemp (Hemp Rich), or more than 20% but less than 50% hemp (Hemp Content). The HIA website also has a rich resources section that lists many books, periodicals, reports, scientific studies, websites, and other resources of information about hemp.

John W. Huffman (1932–)

Huffman is best known for having developed a group of synthetic compounds that produce physiological effects similar to those caused by Δ^9-tetrahydrocannabinol (THC), the principal psychoactive component of marijuana. These synthetic cannabinoids are chemical analogs of THC; that is, they have the same basic structure as THC, but differ in groups that have been substituted on the basic molecule. The compounds are known by abbreviations such as JWH-007, JWH-081, and JWH-398, where the "JWH" part of the name are Huffman's own initials. Huffman spent a significant portion of his academic career working on the development of these compounds, which are used primarily for two research purposes.

First, they can be used to obtain additional information about cannabinoid receptors in the endocannabinoid system. (The endocannabinoid system is a collection of fatty acid derivatives that occur in animal bodies and the receptor sites to which they bond. The endocannabinoid system is implicated in a number of fundamental physiological responses, such as appetite, pain-sensation, mood, and memory.) Scientists now know that cannabinoids produce their psychoactive effects by attaching to receptor sites in the brain and peripheral nervous system, setting off a chain of chemical reactions. What they know relatively little about is the chemical structure of those receptors. The chemical structure of Huffman's synthetic cannabinoids can be used to solve that problem by finding out which compounds (and therefore which structures) activate receptor sites, thereby elucidating the three-dimensional structure of the receptor sites. The second purpose of the research, arising out of these discoveries, is the development of new pharmaceuticals that can produce cannabis-like physical effects, such as increasing one's appetite, reducing nausea, and treating glaucoma.

Huffman's research has been enormously useful in providing researchers with a better understanding of the way the endocannabinoid system works. But that research has also gained a level of notoriety among the general public because of its use in developing new types of psychoactive drugs used for recreational purposes. These drugs are incorrectly known as synthetic cannabis when, in fact, they often consist of a mixture of traditional herbs with mild mood-altering properties (such as *Canavalia maritima, Nymphaea caerulea,* and *Scutellaria nana*) coated with one or more of Huffman's synthetic cannabinoids. The resulting product may have psychoactive effects more than a hundred times greater than that of THC. They are sold under a variety of names, including Spice, K2, Chronic Spice, Spice Gold, Spice Silver, Stinger, Yucatan Fire, Skunk, Pulse, and Black Mamba. When they first became available to the general public, they were legal because they contained no THC or other banned substance. Over time, however, a number of states in the United States and countries around the world have banned products of this kind.

Huffman himself has spoken out strongly about the risks involved in using synthetic cannabinoids as recreational drugs. The compounds were prepared, he points out, for research purpose, and little is known about their general effects on the body. Indeed, public health officials have reported emergency room visits as a result of using Spice, K2, and its analogs, a fact responsible for most of the bans now being adopted. The problem is that most of the now-illegal compounds are still generally available on the Internet.

John William Huffman was born in Evanston, Illinois, on July 21, 1932. He attended Northwestern University, which granted his B.S. in chemistry in 1954. He then continued his studies at Harvard University, where he earned his A.M. and his Ph.D. in chemistry in 1956 and 1957, respectively. At Harvard, he studied under probably the century's greatest synthetic organic chemist, Robert B. Woodward. Huffman's first job was as assistant professor of chemistry at the Georgia Institute of Technology. He left Georgia Tech in 1960 to take a position at Clemson University as assistant professor of chemistry. Over time, he rose to the position of associate professor and then, in 1967, full professor at Clemson. He remained at Clemson until his retirement in 2005. He then continued to work at the university as research professor until he took full retirement in 2011. He also spent one year as visiting professor of chemistry at Colorado State University in 1982. During his career, Huffman published more than 100 papers in peer-reviewed journals.

Among the honors and awards granted Huffman have been a National Institutes of Health (NIH) Career Development Award for 1965–1970, a Senior Scientist Award from the National Institute on Drug Abuse, Clemson University Alumni Association Award for Outstanding Research

Accomplishments, and Raphael Mechoulam Annual Award in Cannabinoid Research.

In June 2011, Huffman talked with ABC News about the dangers of synthetic cannabinoids as recreational drugs. It would make more sense, he said, to legalize the use of marijuana, which has been thoroughly studied and whose effects are now well known. "The scientific evidence is," he explained, "that it's not a particularly dangerous drug," and, in any case, it is much less dangerous than the poorly understood and potentially highly risky synthetic cannabinoids.

International Association for Cannabinoid Medicines

The International Association for Cannabinoid Medicines (IACM) was founded in March 2000 for the purpose of advancing knowledge about cannabis, cannabinoids, and the endocannabinoid system and related topics. A major mission of the organization is to discover and distribute information related to how information about cannabinoids can be used for therapeutic purposes. In 2009, the organization changed its original name, International Association for Cannabis as Medicine to its current name. The change in name reflected a recognition by the organization that research has found a number of substances that affect cannabinoid receptors beyond cannabis itself and that a wider range of researchers should be attracted to the services that the association offers. The IACM statement of mission identifies five primary areas of concern:

- Support for research on cannabinoid products and the endocannabinoid system;
- Promotion of the exchange of information about cannabinoids and the endocannabinoid system among researchers, healthcare practitioners, patients, and the general public;
- Preparation and distribution of information about the pharmacology, toxicology, and therapeutic applications of cannabinoids and modulators of the endocannabinoid system;

- Monitoring international and national developments related to therapeutic applications of the cannabinoids;
- Cooperation with other organizations whose goals and mission are similar to those of the International Association for Cannabinoid Medicines.

The three most important functions of the association are its website, its two major publications, and its annual conference. The IACM website is a treasure chest trove of information on the medicine, science, and law related to cannabinoids and the endocannabinoid system. For example, the section on medicine includes reports on medical uses of the cannabinoids, reported side effects of the use of cannabinoids, and a large selection of studies and case reports. The section on science provides definitions of important terms used in discussing cannabinoids and the endocannabinoid system, a list of clinical studies with descriptions of their general findings, an interactive database of clinical studies, and a comprehensive review and commentary of studies on cannabinoids and the endocannabinoid system between 2005 and 2014. The law and politics section provides a general summary of the legal status of cannabinoid therapeutics in about a dozen countries, including Canada, Finland, France, Germany, Israel, New Zealand, Spain, Sweden, the Netherlands, the United Kingdom, and the United States. Each of these summaries discusses laws dealing with the therapeutic uses of cannabinoids, court rulings, and a review of the legal and political "realities" in each country.

IACM makes available two essential publications in the field of cannabinoid therapeutics. One is *Cannabinoids*, a peer-reviewed journal published electronically on an irregular, as-needed basis. It consists of mini reviews of recent medical and scientific research, ideas, and issues; commentaries on other articles in the field of cannabinoid therapeutics; and letters about relevant topics in the field. Another publication of IACM was the short-lived *Journal of Cannabis Therapeutics*, which produced 10 issues between 2001 and 2004, at which time it discontinued publication. *IACM Bulletin* is a free, bi-weekly, online publication that covers every aspect of cannabinoid therapeutics. All past copies of the *IACM Bulletin* are available in the archives section of the organization's website.

The IACM's other major activity is a biannual conference, held in odd-numbered years at various locations. The 2017 conference will be held in Cologne, Germany, on September 29–30, 2017.

Marijuana Policy Project

The Marijuana Policy Project (MPP) was founded in 1995 by Rob Kampia, Chuck Thomas, and Mike Kirshner, former members of the National Organization for the Reform of Marijuana Laws (NORML), after an internal disagreement about proposed changes in the parent organization. MPP was chartered in the District of Columbia as a nonprofit association lobbying for changes in the legal status of marijuana. The organization continues as a lobbying organization, while also maintaining a 501(c)(4) tax-free educational foundation, the MPP Foundation, to which charitable contributions can be made. MPP's mission statement consists of four major objectives: "(1) increase public support for non-punitive, non-coercive marijuana policies; (2) identify and activate supporters of non-punitive, non-coercive marijuana policies; (3) change state laws to reduce or eliminate penalties for the medical and non-medical use of marijuana; and (4) gain influence in Congress." Its corresponding vision statement calls for a nation in which marijuana is regulated in much the same way that alcohol currently is regulated, in which education about marijuana use is "honest and realistic," and in which treatment for those who abuse marijuana is provided in a non-coercive way aimed at reduced harm to the individual.

The work of the Marijuana Policy Project is divided into a half-dozen major areas. In the field of legislation, it promotes the filing, consideration, and adoption of laws at the federal and state levels designed to reduce harsh legal penalties for the use of marijuana. It has also developed a model state medical marijuana law for legislators' consideration. MPP also works at both federal and state levels to influence legislative action on all phases of marijuana laws, including medical marijuana policies and laws in particular. The Marijuana Policy Project also organizes and conducts a number of marijuana-related campaigns that deal with a changing set of themes, such as (in 2016) Consume Responsibly, Minnesotans for Compassionate Care, Marijuana Policy Coalition of Maryland, Regulate Rhode Island, Vermont Coalition to Regulate Marijuana, Texans for Responsible Marijuana Policy, and Mandatory Madness.

Another area of focus for MPP is its Patients campaign, which collects and distributes stories of specific individuals who require and/or have used marijuana for medical purposes. The organization's website carries these stories on its "Patients" page. Finally, the organization's Victims campaign tells the stories of individuals who have become enmeshed in the legal system because of their possession and/or use of marijuana.

MPP also organizes its work into a number of "issues" areas that deal with specific aspects of the marijuana legalization effort. In 2016, those issues included medical marijuana laws and public safety; Colorado: the economy after legalization and regulation; medical marijuana protection in 50 states; summary of MPP's model medical cannabis bill; and racial justice.

The Marijuana Policy Project is a rich source of written and electronic articles and reports on many aspects of the legalization of marijuana. They include items such as PDF files on "Know the Facts," "Marijuana Prohibition Facts," "Marijuana Policy Map," "Tax & Regulate: Effective Arguments," "Top Ten Reasons to Tax & Regulate Marijuana," "Dollars and Common Sense: Summary and Arguments for MPP's Decriminalization

Bill," "MPP's Model Decriminalization Bill," "State Polling," "Federal Obstruction of Medical Marijuana Research Memo," and "Federal Enforcement Policy De-Prioritizing Medical Marijuana." Other articles and reports available from MPP include "Overview and Explanation of MPP's Model State Medical Marijuana Bill," "Marijuana and DUI Laws: How Can We Best Guard against Impaired Driving,?" "Marijuana: Myths vs. Reality," "Implications of U.S. Supreme Court Medical Marijuana Ruling," "Common Questions about Marijuana," "Treatment for Marijuana Problems: Separating Fact from Fiction," "Medical Marijuana Overview," "Model State Medical Marijuana Bill," and "Questions and Answers about SATIVEX® Liquid Medical Marijuana."

Raphael Mechoulam (1930–)

Mechoulam is professor of medicinal chemistry and natural products at the Hebrew University of Jerusalem, Israel. He is best known for having isolated, determined the chemical structure of, and synthesized Δ^9-tetrahydrocannabinol, best known as THC, the primary psychoactive ingredient in cannabis.

Raphael Mechoulam was born in Sofia, Bulgaria, on November 5, 1930. His father was a physician and head of a local hospital. His mother was not employed, but, as he later told an interviewer with the Endocannabinoid System Network (ESN), "enjoyed the life of a well-to-do Jewish family." Mechoulam attended the American Grade School in Sofia, "the only regular schooling" he could remember, as he told the ESN interviewer. As World War II approached, life for the Mechoulams became much more difficult because of the anti-Semitic laws adopted by the Nazi-leaning Bulgarian government. The family was forced to move from village to village seeking enough work to survive. Eventually, Raphael's father was sent to a concentration camp, an experience he survived. Mechoulam was able to obtain only one year of secondary education, at Sofia's First Male Gymnasium, where he had his first exposure to chemical engineering, an experience that he later said he did not enjoy.

As circumstances in Bulgaria became ever more difficult for Jewish families, the Mechoulams finally decided to emigrate to Israel in 1949. There Raphael enrolled at the Hebrew University at Jerusalem, from which he received his M.Sc. in biochemistry in 1952. It was not until he began his military service a year later, however, did that he really become interested in scientific research. His assignment in the military involved a research project on insecticides. It was as a result of that experience, he later told an ESN interviewer, that he "found the independence of research to be an addiction from which I do not want to be cured."

Upon completing his military service in 1956, Mechoulam decided to return to academia, beginning his doctoral studies at the Weizmann Institute in Rehovot, Israel. He completed his studies and was granted his Ph.D. in steroid studies in 1958. After a two-year postdoctoral program at the Rockefeller Institute in New York, Mechoulam returned to Israel, where he served first as junior scientist, and later as senior scientist, at the Weizmann Institute from 1960 to 1965. His research assignments at Weizmann involved the study of natural products, such as alkaloids, terpenes, and cannabinoids. It was during his tenure at Weizmann that Mechoulam and his colleagues first identified THC as the primary psychoactive compound in cannabis and then were able to synthesize the substance in the laboratory. The accomplishment was significant because cannabis was at the time one of the most poorly understood of all psychoactive compounds. Laws against its possession made research difficult and without access to the pure substance, learning more about its chemical structure and properties was difficult. Mechoulam's research changed that scenario and made it possible for researchers to mount an aggressive campaign to understand more about the compound and the mechanisms by which it acts in animal bodies.

Mechoulam's discoveries about THC marked only the beginning of a lifelong study of the whole cannabinoid family. He eventually isolated and identified a large number of naturally occurring members of the family. In 1992, Mechoulam's research took a somewhat different direction when his research team identified the first endocannabinoid, which they named anandamide (which means "bliss" in Sanskrit). Endocannabinoids are substances produced by animal bodies that activate cannabinoid receptors in the body and, thus, have psychoactive effects similar to those of natural cannabinoids like THC. In 1995, Mechoulam's research team discovered a second endocannabinoid, arachidonoyl glycerol (2-AG), which occurs in the intestines. Today, Mechoulam remains a major figure in research on cannabinoids and endocannabinoids.

In 1966, Mechoulam accepted an appointment at Hebrew University, where he was later promoted to associate professor in 1968 and full professor in 1972. In 1975, he was named Lionel Jacobson Professor of Medicinal Chemistry, a post he continues to hold. From 1979 to 1982, he was named rector (academic head) of Hebrew University; and from 1983 to 1985, he served as prorector of the university. From 1993 to 1994, Mechoulam was also visiting professor in the Department of Pharmacology at the Medical College of Richmond, in Richmond, Virginia.

During his career, Mechoulam has received a number of honors and awards, including the Somach Sachs Prize for the best research by a scientist under the age of 35 at the Weizmann Institute (1964); the Kolthof Prize in Chemistry from The Technion, Haifa, Israel (1994); elected as a member of the Israel Academy of Sciences (1994); the Hanus Medal of the Czech Chemical Society (1998); the David R. Bloom Prize of the Center for Pharmacy at Hebrew University (1998); the Israel Prize in Exact Sciences (2000); the Heinrich Wieland Prize, endowed by Boehringer-Ingelheim (2004); the Henrietta Szold Prize for achievements in medical research, awarded by the city of Tel-Aviv (2005); the Lifetime Achievement

Award of the European College of Neuropsychopharmacology (2006); a Special Award of the International Association for Cannabinoids in Medicine (2007); the Israel Chemical Society Prize for Excellence in Research (2009); Lifetime Achievement Awards from Hebrew University (2010) and the Eicosanoid Research Society (2011); and the NIDA [National Institute on Drug Abuse] Discovery Award (2011). In 1999, in Mechoulam's honor, the International Cannabinoid Research Society established an annual award to be named The R. Mechoulam Annual Award in Cannabinoid Research. Mechoulam has also received honorary doctorates from Ohio State University and Complutense University, Madrid. In addition to numerous peer-reviewed scientific papers, Mechoulam has edited four books, has published numerous book chapters, and has been awarded 25 patents for his new discoveries.

Tod Hiro Mikuriya (1933–2007)

Mikuriya was possibly the best-known medical professional working for the legalization of marijuana for medical purposes. He first became interested in the topic during the 1960s, during which time he was briefly director of non-classified marijuana research at the National Institute of Mental Health Center for Narcotics and Drug Abuse Studies (1967). He came to the conclusion that government officials and many medical researchers were largely ignoring a vast body of research on the medical benefits of marijuana and were focusing instead on any and all research reporting the harmful effects of the plant. In 1972, he self-published the book for which he is perhaps best known, *Marijuana Medical Papers, 1839–1972*. The book contained about two dozen studies dealing with the medical effects of marijuana, personal experiences with the drug, discussions of the therapeutic value of marijuana, recent clinical studies, chemical and pharmacological research, and a social history of the origin of marijuana laws. Among the papers included in the book are an early (1839) scientific paper on the medical effects of marijuana by W. B. O'Shaughnessy, a report on the medical effects of *Cannabis indica* by the Ohio State Medical Committee on Cannabis Indica in 1860, a review of the LaGuardia Committee report on marijuana of 1944, a section from the Dispensatory of the United States for 1918 that contains a description of the medical uses of marijuana, a paper on the relative effects of alcohol and marijuana on driving ability (1969), and an analysis of the 1937 Marihuana Tax Act as a commentary on the social origins of marijuana laws.

Tod Hiro Mikuriya was born on September 20, 1933, in Bucks County, Pennsylvania, to Tadafumi Mikuriya, a former Japanese samurai who had converted to Christianity and become a civil engineer who specialized in bridge design, and Anna Schwenk Mikuriya, a German immigrant who taught special education. Tod received his secondary education at George School in Newtown, Pennsylvania (1948–1951), and then matriculated at Haverford College, in Haverford, Pennsylvania, both Quaker institutions. In 1954, Mikuriya was expelled from Haverford for allegedly being involved in panty raids at nearby Bryn Mawr College (an act to which he later admitted his guilt), and he transferred to yet another Quaker institution, Guilford College in Greensboro, North Carolina. He remained at Guilford for only one semester before changing institutions once more, this time to Reed College, in Portland, Oregon, from which he finally received his bachelor's degree in psychology in 1956. He is reported to have earned his way through college by writing and singing folk songs, an interest he retained throughout his life. After graduating from Reed, Mikuriya was drafted into the U.S. Army, where he served as a neuropsychiatric technician until he was discharged in 1958. He then continued his studies at Temple University, from which he received his M.D. in 1962. He later reported that his lifelong interest in marijuana was triggered by an article about the medical uses of marijuana that he read at Temple. Mikuriya completed his internship at Southern Pacific Hospital (later Harkness Community Hospital and now closed) and his psychiatric residencies at the Oregon State Hospital, in Salem, and the Mendocino State Hospital, in Talmage, California.

In October 1966, Mikuriya was appointed director of the Drug Addiction Treatment Center at the New Jersey Neuro-Psychiatric Institute in Princeton, New Jersey, a post he held for 10 months. He then accepted a job as director of marijuana research at the Center for Narcotics and Drug Abuse Studies of the National Institute of Mental Health. He left that post after only three months because he had become convinced that his superiors were interested only in marijuana research with negative connotations. Mikuriya then moved to the West Coast, where he served as consulting psychiatrist at the Alameda County Alcoholism Clinic and the county Health Department Drug Abuse Program in 1968 and 1969. In 1970, he went into private practice in Berkeley while also acting as attending staff psychiatrist at the Gladman Hospital in Oakland, California. He remained active until a few weeks before his death on May 20, 2007, in Berkeley.

In addition to his private practice, Mikuriya was active in organizations that were interested in the use of marijuana for medical purposes, as well as a number of professional organizations, including the Drug Use and Abuse Committee of the Northern California Psychiatric Society, the National Commission on Marihuana and Drug Abuse, the Biofeedback Society of California, and the Society of Cannabis Clinicians, of which he was founder. For a major part of his life, Mikuriya was essentially the only physician who advocated publicly and enthusiastically for the use of marijuana to treat a variety of medical conditions. In 1996, he helped draft California Proposition 215, which legalized the use of marijuana for medical conditions.

As part of the campaign in support of Proposition 215, Mikuriya distributed a list of medical conditions for which marijuana could be used in treatment, a list compiled from the historic medical literature. After the proposition passed, U.S. Drug Czar Barry McCaffrey held a press conference threatening to prosecute any California doctor who wrote prescriptions for marijuana under the recently adopted California law. At that conference, where he was joined by Secretary of Health, Education, and Welfare Donna Shalala and Alan Lesher of the National Institute on Drug Abuse, McCaffrey said of Mikuriya's list of medical conditions, "This isn't medicine. This is a Cheech and Chong Show." (Cheech and Chong were two stand-up comedians from the 1970s and 1980s who supposedly typified the strange behavior of marijuana-addicted hippies.)

In 2000, the California Medical Board investigated Mikuriya for using marijuana in the treatment of some of his patients. The complaint was brought not by the patients, but by law enforcement officers. The board fined him $75,000 and placed him on probation, but he continued to practice under supervision. He announced that he would continue to appeal the board's decision, and did follow that path until his health made it impossible for him to pursue the issue further. Mikuriya had announced plan for an updated and expanded version of Marijuana Medical Papers, a project he was unable to complete before his death.

Ethan Nadelmann (1957–)

Nadelmann is widely considered to be one of the most influential individuals in the campaign to legalize the use of marijuana for medical and recreational purposes in the United States. For more than two decades, he has argued that the so-called war on drugs, especially in the case of marijuana, has been a social, political, economic, and personal failure. It has cost the nation untold billions of dollars, sent far too many otherwise harmless individuals to prison for extended periods of time, and created a host of other crime-related problems. To put his beliefs into action, Nadelmann founded the Drug Policy Alliance in 2000. He remains executive director of the organization today.

Ethan Nadelmann was born in New York City on March 13, 1957. His father was a rabbi, and he grew up in a strict Jewish setting. He attended Harvard College and Harvard University, from which he received his B.A. degree (1979), J.D. degree (1984) and Ph.D. degree (1987). He also spent a year at the London School of Economics, from which he earned an M.S. degree in 1980. In 1987 Nadelmann accepted an offer to teach politics and public affairs at Princeton University, where he remained until 1994. He then left Princeton to found the Lindemith Center, a drug policy instituted founded by philanthropist George Soros. Six years later, the Lindemith Center merged with the Drug Policy Foundation to form the Drug Policy Alliance.

Rolling Stone magazine has called Nadelmann "the driving force for the legalization of marijuana in America." He has spoken and written about issues relating to the legalization of marijuana for most of his professional life, arguing primarily from the standpoint of marijuana's legalization being an issue of compassionate concern for individuals and sound public health policy rather than a matter of criminal justice and law enforcement. He has recommended that marijuana be approved for appropriate medical use and that the recreational use of the drug be legalized and regulated as with other psychoactive substances such as alcohol and tobacco.

Nadelmann is the author of two books, *Cops across Borders: The Internationalization of U.S. Criminal Law Enforcement* (Pennsylvania State University Press, 1993) and *Policing the Globe: Criminalization and Crime Control in International Relations* (with Peter Andreas; Oxford University Press, 2006). He has also developed a popular TED talk on marijuana issues, "Why We Need to End the War on Drugs."

National Institute on Drug Abuse

The origins of the federal government's interest in drug abuse issues can be traced to 1935 with the establishment of a research facility at the U.S. Public Health Service (USPHS) hospital in Lexington, Kentucky. Originally called the U.S. Narcotics Farm, the facility was a joint project of the USPHA and the U.S. Bureau of Prisons. It eventually underwent a number of name changes. In 1948, the facility became the Addiction Research Center and in 1967, the National Institute of Mental Health Clinical Research Center. The National Institute on Drug Abuse (NIDA) was created in 1972 by Public Law 92-255, the Drug Abuse Office and Treatment Act of 1972, to become operational in 1974 as a division within the National Institute of Mental Health (NIMH). NIDA's mission was to be responsible for developing a national community-based treatment system and a program for treatment of narcotic addicts. A year later, a reorganization act created the Alcohol, Drug Abuse, and Mental Health Administration (ADAMHA), an umbrella organization of NIDA, NIMH, and the National Institute on Alcohol Abuse and Alcoholism. In 1992, another reorganization act moved the NIDA from ADAMHA to the National Institutes of Health, where it resides today.

The primary responsibility of the NIDA is to sponsor and conduct research on all aspects of substance use and abuse. This charge includes research on topics such as the genetic, neurobiological, behavioral, and social mechanisms underlying drug abuse and addiction; the causes and consequences of substance abuse, including issues of concern to special populations such as ethnic minorities, youth, and women; the relationship of substance abuse to other forms of mental illness and to related issues such as unemployment, low socioeconomic status, and violence; effective methods of prevention and treatment, including new medications and behavioral therapies for drug addiction; the relationship of substance abuse to cultural and ethical issues such as health disparities; and the relationship of substance abuse to the acquisition, transmission, and clinical course of diseases such as HIV/ AIDS, tuberculosis, and other diseases.

NIDA's work is carried out through nine divisions and offices concerned with specific aspects of the organization's mission. For example, the Division of Epidemiology, Services, and Prevention Research is responsible for a broad extramural research program on topics such as the nature, patterns, and consequences of drug use among general, special, and community-based populations; prevention of substance abuse and addiction; behavioral and social science research among communities and specialized populations; and economic modeling and structuring of treatment systems. The Division of Basic Neuroscience and Behavioral Research focuses on studies of the neurobiological and behavioral actions of legal and illegal drugs. The Division of Clinical Neuroscience and Behavioral Research deals with applications of neurobiological research to real-life substance abuse issues. The Division of Pharmacotherapies and Medical Consequences of Drug Abuse is responsible for the design, development, FDA approval, and marketing of new medications for the treatment of drug-related disorders and addictions.

One of NIDA's signature programs is its Monitoring the Future survey, conducted annually since 1975 by the Institute for Social Research at the University of Michigan. The survey is designed to provide an overview of drug use by high school students and their attitudes toward drug abuse. Originally aimed at 12th graders throughout the United States, in 1991, the survey was extended to include 8th and 10th graders in 1991. Another important NIDA function, its Research Monographs Series, was also initiated in 1975. The series is designed to make available to specialists in the field the most recent information about scientific research on substance abuse and related issues. A third important NIDA program, the Drug Abuse Information and Treatment Referral Hotline,

was initiated in 1986 and continues to be an essential feature
of the agency's services.

National Organization for the Reform
of Marijuana Laws (NORML)

NORML (the name by which the organization is almost universally known today) was founded in 1970 by attorney Keith
Stroup with a $5,000 grant from the Playboy Foundation. Ac-
cording to NORML's Policy on Personal Use, the organization
"supports the removal of all penalties for the private possession
of marijuana by adults, cultivation for personal use, and the
casual nonprofit transfers of small amounts. NORML also supports the development of a legally controlled market for marijuana." Although NORML is not a tax-deductible organization,
its sister association, the NORML Foundation, is a 501(c)(3)
tax-deductible organization. The NORML Foundation was
established in 1997 with the goal of educating the American
public about the costs associated with prohibiting marijuana
use and the benefits of pursuing alternative policies. The foundation also provides legal support and assistance to individuals
who have been or are being persecuted under existing laws.

NORML has its main headquarters in Washington, D.C.,
with more than 100 chapters in every state of the union,
plus international chapters in Australia, Colombia, England,
France, Ireland, Norway, Spain, South Africa, and New Zealand
(five chapters). Depending on the geographic region served,
chapters are designated as regional chapters, chapters, or
subchapters.

NORML's work focuses on four major areas: research on
marijuana use, the use of marijuana for medical purposes, legal
assistance for individuals arrested for marijuana-related crimes,
and public education. In the area of research, the organization
has been collecting information on the personal, medical, and
industrial uses of cannabis products for more than 40 years.
A collection of that information is now available on the

organization's website at http://norml.org/library. The website also contains detailed information about laws dealing with marijuana production, transport, and use. The area of the site for doctors and patients deals with all aspects of the medical marijuana issue, including a general overview of the topic, reports on the use of marijuana for medical purposes, health reports, and a detailed review of the legal availability of medical marijuana in various parts of the country. A guide to marijuana dispensaries is also available on the website through an external source at http://legalmarijuanadispensary.com/.

The organization's "Legal" page provides a list of lawyers with special interest and expertise in the field of marijuana issues, including the field of medical marijuana. It also has a "Legal Brief Bank" page with special resources on topics such as constitutional challenges to marijuana laws, medical marijuana issues, search and seizure, challenges to marijuana laws based on religious arguments, state laws on marijuana, drug testing, drug scheduling laws and regulations, and a variety of miscellaneous issues. NORML's page on "Busted?" provides practical information for individuals who have been arrested for a marijuana-related crime. In addition to providing suggestions for attorneys and legal defenses, the page suggests immediate actions that one can take in response to a recent arrest. Historical data on arrests are also provided.

Another section of the organization's website deals with drug testing issues, including a general overview of the philosophy behind drug testing and the methodologies used in the procedure. It also provides detailed information about the process involved in carrying out a drug test, along with advice for individuals who may be required to undergo drug testing for marijuana.

Office of National Drug Control Policy

The Office of National Drug Control Policy (ONDCP) was established in 1989 as a provision of the Anti-Drug Abuse Act of 1988. Attached to the director's office are administrative units that include the offices of the Legal Counsel, Research and Data Analysis, Legislative Affairs, Management and Administration, Public Affairs, Performance and Budget, and Intergovernmental Public Liaison. The three programmatic offices attached to the director's office deal with demand reduction; supply reduction; and state, local, and tribal affairs. The office's mission is to advise the president on drug-control issues, coordinate drug-control activities and related funding across the federal government, and produce the annual National Drug Control Strategy. This document outlines efforts by the federal government to reduce illicit drug use, manufacturing and trafficking, drug-related crime and violence, and drug-related health consequences.

Under the administration of President Barack Obama, ONDCP took a somewhat different approach to the nation's drug control problem than that of earlier administrations. It announced on its website that it would be focusing on "community-based prevention programs, early intervention programs in healthcare settings, aligning criminal justice policies and public health systems to divert non-violent drug offenders into treatment instead of jail, funding scientific research on drug use, and, through the Affordable Care Act, expanding access to substance abuse treatment."

Much of the office's work is organized under one of about a half-dozen initiatives and key policies areas: prescription drug abuse, drugged driving, community-based drug prevention, healthcare, marijuana, methamphetamine, and public lands. The office takes among the strongest and most aggressive stands on the use of marijuana of any American organization. It warns that marijuana is "addictive and unsafe," especially for adolescents. Cannabis contains, the office warns, chemicals that "can change the way the brain works," and is associated with a host of mental and physical disorders, including "addiction, respiratory and mental illness, poor motor performance, and cognitive impairment." The office also campaigns strongly against the use of smoked marijuana for medicinal purposes.

It acknowledges that, although some orally administered components of cannabis may have medicinal value, "smoking marijuana is an inefficient and harmful method for delivering the constituent elements that have or may have medicinal value." It also reiterates the fact that, while a number of states have legalized the use of marijuana for medicinal purposes, possession and use of the drug are illegal under federal law, and anyone who uses marijuana for medicinal purposes in any part of the nation is liable for arrest and prosecution under the Controlled Substances Act of 1970.

ONDCP has also developed a number of programs for populations that it regards as being at special risk for drug abuse: military, veterans, and their families; women, children, and families; college\s and university students; and Native Americans and Alaskan Natives. The office argues, for example, that men and women who have served in the military are at special risk for drug abuse both while they are in active service and after they have been discharged. They point to the high proportion of veterans who are currently serving prison terms (60% of 140,000 men and women) and who are "struggling with substance abuse." The office reminds members of the military and veterans of the host of services available for assistance with substance abuse, such as the U.S. Department of Veterans Affairs; the Veterans Suicide Prevention Hotline of SAMHSA; the "Dealing with Effects of Trauma" self-help guide provided by SAMHSA; and the federal government's Veterans Employment Website of the Office of Personnel Management.

President Obama's emphasis on prevention and treatment has been reflected in a number of well-developed programs for the general public. The major focus of the ONDCP National Youth Anti-Drug Media Campaign, for example, is a program called Above the Influence, which includes both national-level advertising and targeted efforts at the local community level. A similar program is the ONDCP Drug-Free Communities Support Program, which provides federal grants to community-based coalitions working to prevent and reduce youth substance abuse. The other prong of President Obama's approach to substance abuse is treatment, with an emphasis on getting young substance abusers into treatment programs rather than prison systems. Existing federal and state services, as well as new programs, are available to achieve this objective.

The two primary components of supply reduction efforts by the office are international agreements and a strong enforcement program. The international programs involve agreements with Afghanistan, the Andean region, Canada, the Caribbean, Central America, Europe, Mexico, and Russia to reduce the production, processing, and distribution of illegal substances within and through these areas. The enforcement aspect of ONDCP's work focuses on the range of activities through which illegal substances are distributed in the United States. One of the major programs in this area is the High Intensity Drug Trafficking Area (HIDTA) Program, which targets regions where the transport and distribution of illegal substances is especially high.

William B. O'Shaughnessy (1809–1889)

O'Shaughnessy was an Irish-born physician who introduced the use of cannabis products to Western medicine. Although he is probably best known for this accomplishment, he made other important contributions in a variety of fields, including laying the first telegraph system in Asia, developing a treatment for cholera, and inventing a system for laying telegraphic systems under water. (Although he was trained as a physician and made important contributions to the field of medicine, he also developed an interest in electric telegraphy. At first only a hobby, that interest eventually led to important discoveries and inventions in that field also.)

William Brooke O'Shaughnessy was born in Limerick, Ireland, in 1809 to Daniel O'Shaughnessy and his wife (whose first name is not recorded, although her maiden name was Boswell). Little is known about his early life, but it is known that he was admitted to the University of Edinburgh in 1827, where he studied medicine, chemistry, anatomy, and forensic science. He received his medical degree from Edinburgh in 1829 but was unable to obtain a medical practice in London, where he had hoped to practice. Instead, he established his own forensic toxicology laboratory, where he carried out chemical analyses of blood, feces, urine, and tissue for doctors, hospitals, and the courts. In 1831, O'Shaughnessy made an important discovery concerning cholera. Cholera was (and still is) one of the most devastating of all diseases, in which death occurs because of persistent diarrhea and vomiting. O'Shaughnessy made what in retrospect appears to be a relatively simple suggestion, but one that had not yet been employed by the medical profession. Supplying a cholera victim with water and salts to replace those lost by vomiting and diarrhea, he said, could sustain their bodies and perhaps save their lives. In fact, when the practice was introduced in the treatment of cholera, up to half of all patients survived the disease.

In 1833, O'Shaughnessy accepted an appointment as assistant surgeon in the East India Company, with an assignment in Calcutta (present-day Kolkata). His life in India was a busy one in which he not only served in his medical post, but also helped to found the Calcutta Medical College, where he also served as professor of chemistry and *materia medica*. He also became very interested in the use of native materials for the treatment of diseases. In 1839, he read a 40-page paper on the subject to the Medical and Physical Society of Calcutta; this is sometimes said to be the first modern paper on the medical uses of cannabis. That paper is now considered a classic in the field of medicine, and certainly in the field of medical applications of cannabis. It is available online at http://www.lycaeum.org/~sputnik/Ludlow/Texts/gunjah.html. In the paper, O'Shaughnessy discusses the botanical and chemical characteristics of the plant, its popular uses, something of its known history, and six experiments he conducted to test its physical and medical effects on animals and humans. He concludes the paper with a review of the use of cannabis in the treatment of rheumatism, hydrophobia, cholera, infantile convulsions, and tetanus, the last of these perhaps the most influential portion of the paper for medical observers. In a short section at the end of the paper, he also reviews a type of delirium that results from overuse of the drug which, he says, is "easily treated."

During this period, O'Shaughnessy also became interested in the recently invented telegraph and pushed his superiors for permission to construct a telegraph system in India. At the time, he received no encouragement from the governor general, Lord Ellenborough. Instead, exhausted by his many endeavors in the country, O'Shaughnessy requested and received a furlough that allowed him to return to England. During his visit home, he brought with him samples of cannabis used for medicinal purposes and began to write and speak about the potential applications of the drug. His work swept through the medical profession, and more than a hundred scientific papers on the medical applications of cannabis were written between 1839 and 1900. In recognition of his work, Queen Victoria (who had taken cannabis for menstrual cramps) eventually knighted O'Shaughnessy (in 1856), and he was elected a member of the Royal Society in 1843.

In 1844, O'Shaughnessy returned to India and threw his energies into a new endeavor: working on a national telegraph system for India. By this time, a new governor general had been installed in India, Lord Dalhousie, who was much more receptive to O'Shaughnessy's plans for the telegraph. Dalhousie appointed O'Shaughnessy superintendent of telegraphy, and the cannabis proponent began work on the project. The challenges he faced were profound as he sought to lay down wires across inhospitable land using untrained laborers working with primitive equipment. Yet he was successful in his efforts, opening the first 27-mile segment of the system from Alipore to

Diamond Harbor in 1852. At the time, the longest telegraph line in England was only two-thirds as long, 18 miles. Eventually, O'Shaughnessy oversaw the completion of more than 4,000 lines of the telegraph system before he returned to England in 1855.

O'Shaughnessy's furlough in England was interrupted in 1857 when he returned once more to India in order to deal with the restoration and rebuilding of much of the telegraph system that had been destroyed during the Sepoy Mutiny of 1857. He ended his last tour of duty in India in 1861, when he retired from the East India Company and settled in the south of England. Almost nothing is known about the last 28 years of his life. He died in Southsea, England, on January 10, 1889.

Raymond P. Shafer (1917–2006)

Shafer was appointed in 1970 by then president Richard M. Nixon to chair a commission studying the legal status of marijuana and drug abuse, the National Commission on Marihuana and Drug Abuse, a committee established by the U.S. Congress in October 1970. Nixon selected Shafer because he had a solid reputation as a strong antidrug person who was very likely to produce a report that pointed out the harmful effects of marijuana and to call for severe restrictions on the drug's production, transport, and use. As it turned out, events did not develop in just that way as committee members from a wide variety of backgrounds—health experts, judges, probation officers, and clinicians—took seriously the charge of Public Law 91-513 and assembled an impressive collection of research, reports, and expert opinions on the topic. In the end, the commission produced a recommendation precisely the opposite of that expected by Nixon, calling for the legalization of marijuana. Whatever Shafer's own personal views on marijuana were, the commission's report ultimately represented the majority view of the best scientific information on the dangers (or lack of dangers) posed by legalization of marijuana.

Raymond Philip Shafer was born on March 5, 1917, in New Castle, Pennsylvania, to the Reverend David P. and Mina Belle Shafer. The family moved to Meadville, Pennsylvania, in 1933 when Rev. Shafer was offered a position at the First Christian Church there. Raymond graduated from Meadville High School in 1934, where he was valedictorian of his class and active in a variety of sports. He then matriculated at Allegheny College, where he served as class president for four years and president of the Allegheny Undergraduate Council. Shafer then went on to Yale Law School, where he was a member of an illustrious class that included future president Gerald Ford and Supreme Court justices Potter Stewart and Byron White. He was granted his LL.B by Yale in 1941. During World War II, Shafer served in Naval Intelligence and as captain of a PT boat in the South Pacific. For his role in the war effort, he was awarded the Bronze Star and Purple Heart.

After the war, Shafer returned to Meadville, where he set up a law practice. In 1948, he made his first attempt at elected office, and won the post of Crawford County District Attorney, a post in which he served until 1956. He then decided to run for statewide office and was elected a senator from the Fiftieth District in 1958. He served in that post until 1962, beginning to establish himself as a moderate Republican on most issues. In March 1962, William M. Scranton, candidate for governor of the state, asked Shafer to join him on the ticket as candidate for lieutenant governor, an offer that Shafer accepted. The Scranton-Shafer ticket won the general election by almost a half million votes. Four years later, with Scranton prevented from serving a second term by the state constitution, Shafer became the Republican candidate for governor. He won that election also, this time by an even larger margin than in 1962. Shafer also served the one term permitted by the constitution, leaving office in 1971. Shafer's record as governor features his two special areas of interest: reform of the state constitution and development of the state's highway system, especially construction of the state's portion of the National System of Interstate and Defense Highways (the Interstate Highway System). Today, the portion of Interstate 79 that runs through Pennsylvania is known as the Raymond P. Shafer Highway.

After leaving the governor's office, Shafer remained active in the Republican Party, a stalwart member of its moderate wing. In 1968, he gave the nominating speech for the presidential candidacy of Governor Nelson Rockefeller of New York, thereby earning the enmity of the eventual nominee, Richard Nixon. When searching for a chair of the marijuana commission, however, Nixon apparently overlooked his earlier concerns about Shafer, certain that the commission would produce the result that he wanted and anticipated, which, as it turns out, was not the case.

After a brief foray into the private sector as chief executive officer (CEO) of the TelePrompter corporation, Shafer returned to federal service in 1974, when he served as special council to newly appointed Vice President Nelson Rockefeller. At the end of that tenure, he returned to private business permanently, serving as partner in the accounting firm of Coopers & Lybrand from 1977 to 1988. Shafer also served briefly as president of his alma mater, Allegheny College, from 1985 to 1986.

Shafer died in Meadville on December 12, 2006. In a somewhat ironic tribute to his work on marijuana, a 2011 bill dealing with medical marijuana use in Pennsylvania, House Bill 1652, was named "The Governor Raymond P. Shafer Compassionate Use Medical Marijuana Act." The bill did not pass the legislature.

Keith Stroup (1943–)

Stroup is founder of the National Organization for the Reform of Marijuana Laws (NORML). He is an attorney and has spent most of his adult life on efforts to legalize the use of marijuana in the United States. He served as president of NORML from its founding in 1970 to 1979 and then returned to the organization as executive director from 1995 to 2004 and as legal counsel from 2005 to the present.

Keith Stroup was born in Dix, Illinois, on December 27, 1943. His parents were Russell Stroup, who had come from a farming family, and was then a successful building contractor and unofficial head of the regional Republican Party, and Vera Stroup, whose father was a miner who died of black lung disease. Keith's childhood has been described by his biographer Patrick Anderson in his book *High in America: The True Story behind NORML and the Politics of Marijuana* as "as American as apple pie." Keith and his older brother Larry were brought up in a strict Southern Baptist tradition in which all types of immoral behavior, such as smoking, drinking, and dancing, were prohibited. As the boys grew older, according to Anderson, Larry developed into the a successful conservative businessman who married his high school sweetheart and remained loyal to the Pleasant Hill Baptist Church, while Keith began to rebel against the strictures of his parent's beliefs.

The turning point for Keith, according to Anderson, came when he entered high school in nearby Mount Vernon. Although he was very successful academically and socially at Mount Vernon, Keith gradually grew further and further apart from his family. The final break seemed to come just after graduation when his parents angrily expelled a group of Keith's friends from the family home for playing poker and drinking beer. Outraged at this turn of events, Keith left for Yellowstone National Park without telling his family, and returned to Illinois only to enter the University of Illinois in the fall of 1961. Only a short time into his college years at Illinois, he was expelled for violating university regulations at an off-campus party. The following year was one of uncertainty and confusion, spent as a furniture repossessor at a Portland (Oregon) loan company, a short-lived candidate for the Peace Corps, and a student for one term at a small college in Kentucky. He was finally readmitted to Illinois, from which he graduated with a B.A. in political science and sociology in 1965. He then continued his studies at the Georgetown University Law Center, from which he received his law degree in 1968. While at Georgetown, Stroup had a part-time job working for Senator Everett Dirkson (R-IL), earning $50 a week and gaining invaluable experience in the wheelings and dealings of Washington politics. Ironically, it is said that he got the job because of the influence of his father, who had remained a powerful voice in southern Illinois politics.

In the last few months before graduating from Georgetown, Stroup noticed an advertisement on a bulletin board for positions at the federal Consumer Product Safety Commission (CPSC). He applied for and received a job with the CPSC, where he came into contact with activist Ralph Nader. This experience provided Stroup with the opportunity to learn more about political activism and encouraged him to form a new organization devoted to the legalization of marijuana. Based on that background and with a grant of $5,000 from the Playboy Foundation, Stroup and a group of friends founded NORML in 1970. He continued to serve as executive director of the organization until 1979, when he was asked to leave by the organization's board of directors. The explanation for Stroup's removal from his post was that he had "outed" Dr. Peter Bourne, special advisor for health to President Jimmy Carter and de factor "drug czar" in the Carter administration, for using cocaine at a 1977 party they had both attended. Stroup, in turn, had been relieved of his NORML job apparently because the board of directors did not approve of "snitches" in its organization. Many years later, Stroup was to tell a *Washington Post* reporter that this episode was "probably the stupidest thing I ever did." By involving Bourne in a drug-related incident (which Bourne has always denied), Stroup lost a valuable contact with a presidential administration that was, in fact, open to the possibility of changing federal regulations concerned with marijuana possession.

In any case, Stroup then cofounded his own law firm, Stroup, Goldstein, Jacobs, Jenkins, Pritzker, and Ware, which specialized in the defense of citizens charged with drug-related crimes. He left that firm in 1983 to become a lobbyist for the American Agriculture Movement, an organization that represents farmers and ranchers in rural areas of the United States. In that capacity, he also represented James Nichols, then secretary of agriculture for the state of Minnesota. After working for four years as a lobbyist, Stroup then took a position as executive director of the National Association of Criminal Defense Lawyers (NACDL), a bar association for criminal defense attorneys in the United States, where he remained until 1993. For the next two years, he was employed in Alexandria, Virginia, as staff counsel for the National Center on Institutions and Alternatives (NCIA), an organization that works to keep nonviolent offenders (such as individuals arrested for marijuana possession) out of prison. In 1995, Stroup returned once more to NORML, where he resumed his post as executive director before leaving that post in 2005 to become legal counsel for the organization, a post he still holds today.

UN Office on Drugs and Crime

The UN Office on Drugs and Crime (UNODC) was created in 1997 as the Office for Drug Control and Crime Prevention by the merger of two preexisting United Nations (UN) organizations, the United Nations International Drug Control Programme and the Crime Prevention and Criminal Justice Division of the United Nations office at Vienna, Austria. The organization's name was changed to its present name in 2002.

UNODC is one of 32 funds, programs, agencies, departments, and offices that make up the United Nations Development Group (UNDG) and whose goal it is to provide more effective and more efficient support to nations attempting to achieve certain internationally agreed-upon development goals. A few other members of the UNDG are the United Nations Children's Fund, United Nations Population Fund, World Food Programme, Office of the High Commissioner for Human Rights, Joint United Nations Programme on HIV/AIDS, and the World Health Organization.

UNODC has adopted a wide ranging list of topics with a connection to drug production and consumption and/or crime, including alternative development (development of crops other than those for the production of illegal drugs); corruption; crime prevention and criminal justice; drug prevention, treatment, and care; drug trafficking; firearms; fraudulent medicines; HIV and AIDS; human trafficking and migrant smuggling; money laundering; organized crime; maritime crime and piracy; terrorism prevention; and wildlife and forest crime. The agency has developed comprehensive research, educational, and outreach programs in each of these areas.

UNODC also regularly sets out a strategic plan for its work on drugs and crime, usually on a three-year basis but, most recently, for only one year. The 2016–2017 strategic framework calls for a series of subprograms designed to help member states enhance their responses to the problems of drug use, illicit drug trafficking, trafficking in human beings and firearms and, transnational crime, corruption, and terrorism. The subprograms selected for 2016–2017 are countering illicit drug trafficking and transnational organized crime; prevention, treatment, and reintegration, and alternative development; countering corruption; terrorism prevention; justice; research and trend analysis and forensics; policy support; technical cooperation and field support; and provision of secretariat services and substantive support to the governing bodies and the International Narcotics Control Board.

The agency provides a host of resources for member states attempting to deal with specific drug and/or crime issues in their own territories. Among these resources are:

- Campaigns, designed to raise public awareness about specific issues in the field of drugs and crime, such as the annual International Day against Drug Abuse and Illicit Trafficking and the International Anti-Corruption Day;
- Commissions appointed to work on specific problems in the field of drugs and crime, such as the Commission on Narcotic Drugs and the Commission on Crime Prevention and Criminal Justice;
- An annual conference on Crime Prevention and Criminal Justice;
- Research programs on topics such as transnational organized crime, synthetic drugs, trafficking in persons, drug production and trafficking, and wildlife;
- Laboratory and forensic science services that are made available to member states for dealing with issues specific to those states;
- Legal tools for dealing with drug and crime problems, including a legal library, the SHERLOC knowledge management portal, a human trafficking case law database, and a model laws and treaties resource center; and
- A collection of international and regional treaties dealing with drugs and crime.

U.S. Drug Enforcement Administration

The U.S. government has had a succession of agencies designed to deal with substance abuse problems in general, and marijuana, in particular. The earliest of these agencies was the Narcotics Division, established within the Bureau of

Internal Revenue in 1921. The agency was created to carry out mandates of the Harrison Narcotic Act of 1914. A year later, a second agency was created, the Federal Narcotics Control Board, whose mandate it was to make and publish regulations concerning the import and export of narcotic substances. These two agencies were consolidated in 1930 to form the Bureau of Narcotics within the U.S. Department of the Treasury. In yet another reorganization act, the Bureau of Narcotics and the Bureau of Drug Abuse Control (created within the Food and Drug Administration in 1965) were combined to form the Bureau of Narcotics and Dangerous Drugs within the Department of Justice. The final step in this sequence of events occurred on July 28, 1973, when President Richard Nixon signed the Reorganization Plan No. 2 of 1973, bringing under one roof all agencies in the federal government with some responsibility for substance abuse, including the Bureau of Narcotics and Dangerous Drugs and a number of smaller agencies in a variety of cabinet departments. The new agency, which still exists today, was the Drug Enforcement Administration (DEA). The first administrator of the DEA was John R. Bartels, Jr., a former federal prosecutor. The current DEA administrator is Michele M. Leonhart, a career DEA agent.

As specified on its website, the mission of the DEA is

> to enforce the controlled substances laws and regulations of the United States and bring to the criminal and civil justice system of the United States, or any other competent jurisdiction, those organizations and principal members of organizations, involved in the growing, manufacture, or distribution of controlled substances appearing in or destined for illicit traffic in the United States; and to recommend and support non-enforcement programs aimed at reducing the availability of illicit controlled substances on the domestic and international markets.

DEA activities fall into one of about 20 major categories, including:

- Organized Crime Drug Enforcement Task Forces (OCDETF): This program involves the participation of a number of federal agencies to attack major drug trafficking and money laundering activities related to the importation and sale of illegal drugs to the United States.
- Demand reduction: In addition to apprehending and prosecuting substance abusers and their enablers, the agency works to reduce the use of illegal drugs by working with state, regional, and local agencies to help individuals understand the dangers posed by substance abuse and to find ways of avoiding involvement in drug activities.
- Asset forfeiture: Federal law provides that profits from drug-related activities collected by drug enforcement activities are forfeited to the government and may be used to support worthy causes through the Asset Forfeiture Fund.
- Aviation program: Since 1971, the DEA has provided air support for ground activities of the agency's agents, helping to detect, locate, identify, and assess narcotics-related trafficking activities.
- Diversion control: This program is aimed at monitoring and controlling the illegal use of prescription drugs, the fastest-growing substance abuse problem in the United States today. The program involves the arrest of physicians who sell prescriptions to drug dealers, pharmacists who falsify records and sell prescription drugs to dealers, employees who steal from inventories and/or falsify records, and individuals who obtain prescription drugs by illegal activities.
- Forensic sciences: The DEA forensic science laboratory provides assistance to prosecutors who need evidence for the conduct of criminal cases involving the use of illegal substances.

- Foreign cooperative investigations. Since almost all illegal substances (except for marijuana) are grown or produced outside the United States, cooperation with foreign government where drugs are produced is an essential feature of the U.S. drug control program.

The DEA Domestic Cannabis Eradication/Suppression Program (DCE/SP) is of special interest largely because marijuana is the only major Schedule I drug grown in the United States. One of the major goals of DCE/SP, then, is to eliminate the supply of marijuana in the United States by finding and destroying farms where the cannabis plant is being grown. In 2014, for example, DEA agents identified and eradicated a total of 6,796 outdoor marijuana growing sites with an estimated total of 3,904,213 individual plants. In addition, 2,283 indoor sites were identified and eradicated, with a loss of 396,620 plants. Total estimated value of all the destroyed plants was $27,342,950. In addition to plant destruction, DEA agents made 6,310 arrests of individuals associated with plant growth and collected 4,989 weapons.

Each year, the DEA schedules special operations to carry out the agency's mission. In 2011, for example, those operations included Operation Fire and Ice, a five-year investigation of an international drug trafficking organization called La Oficina de Envigado, based in Medellín, Colombia; Operation Pill Nation, which involved the arrest of 22 individuals and the seizure of more than $2.2 million in cash from rogue pain clinics in South Florida; and the 38th Street Gang Roundup, in which federal agents seized more than seven kilograms of cocaine, one pound of methamphetamine, and about $250,000 cash from a notorious gang located in south Los Angeles.

Introduction

This chapter provides some relevant data and documents dealing with cannabis and related products. The "Data" section provides basic information on current and historical trends in marijuana use as well as arrests in the United States. The "Documents" section, which follows, is arranged in chronological order and includes excerpts from important committee and commission reports; from bills, acts, and laws; and from important legal cases.

Data

Table 5.1   Marijuana Use by Persons Aged 12 Years and Older in the United States, 2002–2014, Past Month[1]

Year	Age Group			
	12 and older	12 to 17	18 to 25	26 and older
2002	8.3	11.6	20.2	5.8
2003	8.2	11.2	20.3	5.6
2004	7.9	10.6	19.4	5.5
2005	8.1	9.9	20.1	5.8
2006	8.3	9.8	19.8	6.1

(continued)

LivWell store manager Carlyssa Scanlon shows off some of the products available in the marijuana line marketed by rapper Snoop Dogg in one of the marijuana chain's outlets south of downtown Denver. LivWell grows the Snoop Dogg pot alongside many other strains on its menu. (AP Photo/ David Zalubowski)

Table 5.1   (*continued*)

Year	Age Group 12 and older	12 to 17	18 to 25	26 and older
2007	8.0	9.6	19.8	5.8
2008	8.1	9.3	19.7	5.9
2009	8.7	10.1	21.4	6.3
2010	8.9	10.1	21.6	6.6
2011	8.7	10.1	21.4	6.3
2012	9.2	9.5	21.3	7.0
2013	9.4	8.8	21.5	7.3
2014	10.2	9.4	22.0	8.3

[1]Percent of respondents

Source: Center for Behavioral Health Statistics and Quality. 2015. *Behavioral Health Trends in the United States: Results from the 2014 National Survey on Drug Use and Health*. HHS Publication No. SMA 15-4927, NSDUH Series H-50, Tables A.1B–A.4B, pages A-1–A-5. Available online at http://www.samhsa.gov/data/sites/default/files/NSDUH-FRR1-2014/NSDUH-FRR1-2014.pdf. Accessed on May 2, 2016.

Table 5.2   Marijuana Use by Persons Aged 12 Years and Older in the United States, 2002–2014, Past Year[1]

Year	Age Group 12 and older	12 to 17	18 to 25	26 and older
2002	1.8	4.3	6.0	0.8
2003	1.8	3.8	5.9	0.7
2004	1.9	3.9	6.0	0.8
2005	1.7	3.6	5.9	0.7
2006	1.7	3.4	5.7	0.8
2007	1.6	3.1	5.6	0.7
2008	1.7	3.4	5.6	0.8
2009	1.7	3.4	5.6	0.8
2010	1.8	3.6	5.7	0.9
2011	1.6	3.5	5.7	0.7

Year	Age Group 12 and older	12 to 17	18 to 25	26 and older
2012	1.7	3.2	5.5	0.8
2013	1.6	2.9	5.4	0.8
2014	1.6	2.7	4.9	0.9

[1]Percent of respondents

Source: Center for Behavioral Health Statistics and Quality. 2015. *Behavioral Health Trends in the United States: Results from the 2014 National Survey on Drug Use and Health*. HHS Publication No. SMA 15-4927, NSDUH Series H-50, Tables A.11B–A.14.B, pages A-9–A-12. Available online at http://www.samhsa.gov/data/sites/default/files/NSDUH-FRR1-2014/NSDUH-FRR1-2014.pdf. Accessed on May 2, 2016.

Table 5.3   Marijuana Arrests 1980–2014

Year	Trafficking	Possession	Percentage of All Drug Arrests All Marijuana	Trafficking	Possession
1980	63,318	338,664	—	—	—
1990	66,460	260,390	—	—	—
1995	85,614	503,356	39.9	5.8	34.1
1996	94,891	546,751	42.6	6.3	36.3
1997	88,682	606,591	43.9	5.6	38.3
1998	84,191	598,694	43.8	5.4	38.4
1999	85,641	630,626	46.0	5.5	40.5
2000	88,455	646,042	46.5	5.6	40.9
2001	82,519	641,109	45.6	5.2	40.4
2002	83,096	613,896	45.3	5.4	39.9
2003	92,300	662,886	45.0	5.5	39.5
2004	87,329	686,402	42.6	4.9	37.7
2005	90,471	696,074	42.6	4.9	37.7
2006	90,711	738,916	43.9	4.8	39.1
2007	97,583	775,137	47.4	5.3	42.1
2008	93,640	754,224	49.8	5.5	44.3

(continued)

Table 5.3   (*continued*)

Year	Trafficking	Possession	Percentage of All Drug Arrests		
			All Marijuana	Trafficking	Possession
2009	99,815	758,593	51.6	6.0	45.6
2010	103,247	750,591	52.1	6.3	45.8
2011	94,937	663,032	49.5	6.2	43.3
2012	91,593	658,231	48.3	5.9	42.4
2013	84,058	609,423	46.2	5.6	40.6
2014	81,184	619,809	44.9	5.2	39.7

Source: "Get the Facts." 2016. DrugWars.org. Table information calculated from Federal Bureau of Investigations. *Crime in the United States*, annual publication, 1989–2010. http://www.drugwarfacts.org/cms/Marijuana#Prevalence. Accessed on May 3, 2016.

Table 5.4   Marijuana Use by U.S. High School Students by Gender, Ethnicity, and Grade Level, 2013

Category	Ever Used Marijuana			Current Marijuana Use[1]		
	Female	Male	Total	Female	Male	Total
Race/ethnicity						
White	34.8	38.6	36.7	18.0	22.8	20.4
Black	45.4	48.2	46.8	27.1	30.6	28.9
Hispanic	47.6	50.0	48.8	27.4	27.7	27.6
Grade						
9	29.0	31.1	30.1	17.6	17.7	17.7
10	37.4	40.7	39.1	22.7	24.3	23.5
11	45.1	47.8	46.4	22.8	28.4	25.5
12	46.4	50.9	48.6	24.6	30.9	27.7
Total	39.2	42.1	40.7	21.9	25.0	23.4

[1]Use within 30 days prior to survey.

Source: "Youth Risk Behavior Surveillance—United States 2013. 2014. MMWR 63(4): whole, Table 49, page 98, and Table 51, page 100. http://www.cdc.gov/mmwr/pdf/ss/ss6304.pdf. Accessed on May 3, 2016.

Table 5.5   2014 Domestic U.S. Cannabis Eradication/Suppression Program Statistical Report, 10 Largest States[1]

State	Outdoor Sites	Plants	Indoor Sites	Plants	Arrests	Value
California	2,013	2,405,49	682	279,145	2,442	$10,174,103
Kentucky	986	458,133	76	3,410	564	$1,036,903
Texas	37	255,201	31	6,562	53	$191,714
West Virginia	302	195,548	34	1,025	152	$349,524
Tennessee	296	110,496	12	865	53	$119,513
Indiana	370	70,726	159	13,802	279	$657,944
Arkansas	11	75,988	2	45	10	$269,526
Michigan	355	64,234	212	11,193	307	$2,015,146
Washington	50	49,027	38	8,236	37	$1,465,076
Florida	217	10,642	382	20,762	520	$245,506
National total	6,796	3,904,213	2,283	396,620	6,310	$27,342,950

[1]By number of plants destroyed.

Source: "2014 Domestic Cannabis Eradication/Suppression Program Statistical Report." Drug Enforcement Administration. http://www.dea.gov/ops/cannabis_2014.pdf. Accessed on May 3, 2016.

Table 5.6   Attitudes and Practices Concerning Marijuana among U.S. 12th Graders, 1975–2015

Year	Percentage of "Disapproving"[1] Trying Marijuana Once or Twice	Smoking Marijuana Occasionally	Smoking Marijuana Regularly	Used Marijuana within the Past 30 Days
1975	47.0	54.8	71.9	27.1
1976	38.4	47.8	69.5	32.2
1977	33.4	44.3	65.5	35.4
1978	33.4	43.5	67.5	37.1
1979	34.2	45.3	69.2	36.5
1980	39.0	49.7	74.6	33.7
1981	40.0	52.6	77.4	31.6

(continued)

Table 5.6   (*continued*)

Year	Percentage of "Disapproving"[1]			
	Trying Marijuana Once or Twice	Smoking Marijuana Occasionally	Smoking Marijuana Regularly	Used Marijuana within the Past 30 Days
1982	45.5	59.1	80.6	28.5
1983	46.3	60.7	82.5	27.0
1984	49.3	63.5	84.7	25.2
1985	51.4	65.8	85.5	25.7
1986	54.6	69.0	86.6	23.4
1987	56.6	71.6	89.2	21.0
1988	60.8	74.0	89.3	18.0
1989	64.6	77.2	89.8	16.7
1990	67.8	80.5	91.0	14.0
1991	68.7	79.4	89.3	13.8
1992	69.9	79.7	90.1	11.9
1993	63.3	75.5	87.6	15.5
1994	57.6	68.9	82.3	19.0
1995	56.7	66.7	81.9	21.2
1996	52.5	62.9	80.0	21.9
1997	51.0	63.2	78.8	23.7
1998	51.6	64.4	81.2	22.8
1999	48.8	62.5	78.6	23.1
2000	52.5	65.8	79.7	21.6
2001	49.1	63.2	79.3	22.4
2002	51.6	63.4	78.3	21.5
2003	53.4	64.2	78.7	21.2
2004	52.7	65.4	80.7	19.9
2005	55.0	67.8	82.0	19.8
2006	55.6	69.3	82.2	18.3
2007	58.6	70.2	83.3	18.8
2008	55.5	67.3	79.6	19.4
2009	54.8	65.6	80.3	20.6
2010	51.6	62.0	77.7	21.4

Year	Percentage of "Disapproving"[1]			
	Trying Marijuana Once or Twice	Smoking Marijuana Occasionally	Smoking Marijuana Regularly	Used Marijuana within the Past 30 Days
2011	51.3	60.9	77.5	22.6
2012	48.8	59.1	77.8	22.9
2013	49.1	58.9	74.5	22.7
2014	48.0	56.7	73.4	21.2
2015	45.5	52.9	70.7	21.3

[1]Answer alternatives were: (1) Don't disapprove, (2) Disapprove, and (3) Strongly disapprove. Percentages are shown for categories (2) and (3) combined.

Source: Johnston, L. D., et al. 2016. *Monitoring the Future National Survey Results on Drug Use, 1975–2015: Overview, Key Findings on Adolescent Drug Use.* Ann Arbor: Institute for Social Research, The University of Michigan, Table 7, page 72 and Table 14, pages 92–93. Available online at http://www.monitoringthefuture .org/pubs/monographs/mtf-overview2015.pdf. Accessed on May 4, 2016.

Documents

Indian Hemp Drugs Commission (1895)

In 1893, the British House of Commons, concerned about reported harmful effects of the use of marijuana by Indian natives, commissioned a study of the use of marijuana in India. The report of the commission, completed in 1894 and issued in 1895, was 3,281 pages long and contained the views of more than 1,200 witnesses from every level of society. The main conclusions reached by the commission were as follows (typographical errors in the cited source have been corrected at †):

552. The Commission have now examined all the evidence before them regarding the effects attributed to hemp drugs. It will be well to summarize briefly the conclusions to which they come. It has been clearly established that the occasional use of hemp in moderate doses may be beneficial; but this use may be regarded as medicinal in character. It is rather to the popular

and common use of the drugs that the Commission will now confine their attention. It is convenient to consider the effects separately as affecting the physical, mental, or moral nature. In regard to the physical effects, the Commission have come to the conclusion that the moderate use of hemp drugs is practically attended by no evil results at all. There may be exceptional cases in which, owing to idiosyncracies of constitution, the drugs in even moderate use may be injurious. There is probably nothing the use of which may not possibly be injurious in cases of exceptional intolerance. There are also many cases where in tracts with a specially malarious climate, or in circumstances of hard work and exposure, the people attribute beneficial effects to the habitual moderate use of these drugs; and there is evidence to show that the popular impression may have some basis in fact. Speaking generally, the Commission are of opinion that the moderate use of hemp drugs appears to cause no appreciable physical injury of any kind. The excessive use does cause injury. As in the case of other intoxicants, excessive use tends to weaken the constitution and to render the consumer more susceptible to disease. In respect to [†] particular diseases which according to a [†] considerable number of witnesses should be associated directly with hemp drugs, it appears to be reasonably established that the excessive use of these drugs does not cause asthma; that it may indirectly cause dysentery by weakening the constitution as above indicated; and that it may cause bronchitis mainly through the action of the inhaled smoke on the bronchial tubes.

In respect to the alleged mental effects of the drugs, the Commission have come to the conclusion that the moderate use of hemp drugs produces no injurious effects on the mind. It may indeed be accepted that in the case of specially marked neurotic diathesis, even the moderate use may produce mental injury. For the slightest mental stimulation or excitement may have that effect in such cases. But putting aside these quite exceptional cases, the moderate use of these drugs produces no mental injury. It is otherwise with the excessive use. Excessive use indicates and intensifies mental instability. It tends to weaken the mind. It may even lead to insanity. It has been said by Dr. Blanford that "two factors only are necessary for the causation of insanity, which are complementary, heredity, and stress. Both enter into every case: the stronger the influence of one factor, the less of the other factor is requisite to produce the result. Insanity, therefore, needs for its production a certain instability of nerve tissue and the incidence of a certain disturbance." It appears that the excessive use of hemp drugs may, especially in cases where there is any weakness or hereditary predisposition, induce insanity. It has been shown that the effect of hemp drugs in this respect has hitherto been greatly exaggerated, but that they do sometimes produce insanity seems beyond question.

In regard to the moral effects of the drugs, the Commission are of opinion that their moderate use produces no moral injury whatever. There is no adequate ground for believing that it injuriously affects the character of the consumer. Excessive consumption, on the other hand, both indicates and intensifies moral weakness or depravity. Manifest excess leads directly to loss of self-respect, and thus to moral degradation. In respect to his relations with society, however, even the excessive consumer of hemp drugs is ordinarily inoffensive. His excesses may indeed bring him to degraded poverty which may lead him to dishonest practices; and occasionally, but apparently very rarely indeed, excessive indulgence in hemp drugs may lead to violent [†] crime. But for all practical purposes it may be laid down that there is little or no connection between the use of hemp drugs and crime.

Source: Young, W. Mackworth, et al. *Report of the Indian Hemp Drugs Commission, 1893–94.* [n.p.]: Government Central Printing Office, 1894, vol. 1, 263–264. Also available online at http://www.druglibrary.org/schaffer/library/effects.htm. Accessed on May 4, 2016.

Marihuana Tax Act (1937)

This act was the first effort by the U.S. government to regulate the use of marijuana, hemp, and other forms of cannabis. It did not actually make such use illegal, but it did assess a tax on the use of such materials. The tax was modest—about $1 for each type of use—but the penalties for not paying the tax were severe. The Congress hoped, apparently, to "tax out of existence" the use of cannabis products in the United States.

Section 1 of the act consists of definitions of terms used in the act. The two most important sections of the act are Section 2, which defines the individuals who are required to pay a tax and the amount of the tax, and Section 12, which defines the penalties for nonpayment of the tax.

SEC. 2. (a) Every person who imports, manufactures, produces, compounds, sells, deals in, dispenses, prescribes, administers, or gives away marihuana shall (1) within fifteen days after the effective date of this Act, or (2) before engaging after the expiration of such fifteen-day period in any of the above mentioned activities, and (3) thereafter, on or before July 1 of each year, pay the following special taxes respectively:

(1) Importers, manufacturers, and compounders of marihuana, $24 per year.

(2) Producers of marihuana (except those included within subdivision (4) of this subsection), $1 per year, or fraction thereof, during which they engage in such activity.

(3) Physicians, dentists, veterinary surgeons, and other practitioners who distribute, dispense, give away, administer, or prescribe marihuana to patients upon whom they in the course of their professional practice are in attendance, $1 per year or fraction thereof during which they engage in any of such activities.

(4) Any person not registered as an importer, manufacturer, producer, or compounder who obtains and uses marihuana

in a laboratory for the purpose of research, instruction, or analysis, or who produces marihuana for any such purpose, $1 per year, or fraction thereof, during which he engages in such activities.

(5) Any person who is not a physician, dentist, veterinary surgeon, or other practitioner and who deals in, dispenses, or gives away marihuana, $3 per year: Provided, That any person who has registered and paid the special tax as an importer, manufacturer, compounder, or producer, as required by subdivisions (1) and (2) of this subsection, may deal in, dispense, or give away marihuana imported, manufactured, compounded, or produced by him without further payment of the tax imposed by this section.

. . .

SEC. 12. Any person who is convicted of a violation of any provision of this Act shall be fined not more than $2,000 or imprisoned not more than five years, or both, in the discretion of the court.

Source: The Marihuana Tax Act of 1937. Pub. 238, 75th Congress, 50 Stat. 551 (August 2, 1937).

The Marihuana Problem in the City of New York (1944)

In 1939, Mayor Fiorello LaGuardia appointed a committee from the New York Academy of Medicine to study "the marihuana problem in the city of New York." The committee's final report dealt with the sociological, medical, psychological, and pharmacological consequences of marijuana use. The committee's major conclusions were as follows:

1. Under the influence of marihuana the basic personality structure of the individual does not change but some of the more superficial aspects of his behavior show alteration.

2. With the use of marihuana the individual experiences increased feelings of relaxation, disinhibition and self-confidence.

3. The new feeling of self-confidence induced by the drug expresses itself primarily through oral rather than through physical activity. There is some indication of a diminution in physical activity.

4. The disinhibition which results from the use of marihuana releases what is latent in the individual's thoughts and emotions but does not evoke responses which would be totally alien to him in his undrugged state.

5. Marihuana not only releases pleasant reactions but also feelings of anxiety.

6. Individuals with a limited capacity for effective experience and who have difficulty in making social contacts are more likely to resort to marihuana than those more capable of outgoing responses.

Source: The LaGuardia Committee Report on Marihuana. Summary and discussion. Available online at http://www.drug library.org/schaffer/library/studies/lag/sumdis.htm. Accessed on May 4, 2016.

Leary v. United States, 395 U.S. 6 (1969)

This case is important because it was the first successful test, at the highest level, of the constitutionality of the Marihuana Tax Act of 1937. The syllabus for the case provided here describes the circumstances of the case and the major decisions held unanimously by the Supreme Court. Shortly after the decision was issued, the U.S. Congress repealed the 1937 act and replaced it with the Controlled Substances Act of 1970.

Petitioner, accompanied by his daughter, son, and two others, on an automobile trip from New York to Mexico, after apparent denial of entry into Mexico, drove back across the International Bridge into Texas, where a customs officer, through a search, discovered some marihuana in the car and on petitioner's daughter's person. Petitioner was indicted under 26 U.S.C. § 4744(a)(2), a subsection of the Marihuana Tax Act, and under 21 U.S.C. § 176a. At petitioner's trial, which resulted in his conviction, petitioner admitted acquiring the marihuana in New York (but said he did not know where it had been grown) and driving with it to Laredo, Texas, thence to the Mexican customs station, and back to the United States. The Marihuana Tax Act levies an occupational tax upon all those who "deal in" the drug, and provides that the taxpayer must register his name and place of business with the Internal Revenue Service. The Act imposes a transfer tax "upon all transfers of marihuana" required to be effected with a written order form, and all except a limited number of clearly lawful transfers must be effected with such a form. The Act further imposes a transfer tax of $1 per ounce on a registered transferee and $100 per ounce on an unregistered transferee. The forms, executed by the transferee, must show the transferor's name and address and the amount of marihuana involved. A copy of the form is "preserved" by the Internal Revenue Service, and the information contained in the form is made available to law enforcement officials. Possession of marihuana is a crime in Texas, where petitioner was arrested, in New York, where petitioner asserted the transfer occurred, and in all the other States. Section 4744(a)(2) prohibits transportation or concealment of marihuana by one who acquired it without having paid the transfer tax, which petitioner conceded that he had not done. Petitioner claimed in his motion for a new trial that his conviction under the Marihuana Tax Act violated his privilege against self-incrimination, and he argues that this Court's subsequent decisions in *Marchetti v. United States*, 390 U.S. 39, *Grosso v. United States*, 390 U.S. 62, and *Haynes v. United States*, 390 U.S. 85, require reversal. The Government contends that the Act's transfer tax provisions do not compel incriminatory disclosures because, as administratively construed and applied, they permit prepayment of the tax only by persons whose activities are otherwise lawful. Title 21 U.S.C. § 176a makes it a crime to transport or facilitate the transportation of illegally imported marihuana, with knowledge of its illegal importation, and provides that a defendant's possession of marihuana shall be deemed sufficient evidence that the marihuana was illegally imported or brought into the United States, and that the defendant knew of the illegal importation or bringing in, unless the defendant explains his possession to the satisfaction of the jury. The trial court instructed the jury that it might find petitioner guilty of violating § 176a (1) solely on petitioner's testimony that the marihuana had been brought back from Mexico into the United States and that, with knowledge of that fact, petitioner had continued to transport it, or (2) partly upon his testimony that he had transported the marihuana from New York to Texas and partly upon the § 176a presumption. Petitioner contends that application of that presumption denied him due process of law.

Held:

1. Petitioner's invocation of the privilege against self-incrimination under the Fifth Amendment provided a full defense to the charge under 26 U.S.C. § 4744(a)(2). Pp. 395 U.S. 12-29.

   [*The Court then provides five reasons for this decision, the first of which was as follows:*]

   (a) Since the effect of the Act's terms were such that legal possessors of marihuana were virtually certain to be registrants or exempt from the order form requirement, compliance with the transfer tax provisions would have required petitioner, as one not registered but obliged to obtain an order form, unmistakably to identify himself as a member of a "selective group inherently suspect of criminal activities," and thus those provisions created a "real and appreciable" hazard of incrimination within the meaning of *Marchetti, Grosso, and Haynes*. Pp. 395 U.S. 16–18.

. . . .

2. In the circumstances of this case, the application of that part of the presumption in 21 U.S.C. § 176a which provides that a possessor of marihuana is deemed to know of its unlawful importation denied petitioner due process of law in violation of the Fifth Amendment. Pp. 395 U.S. 29–53.

[*The Court provides four explanations for this part of the decision.*]

Source: *Leary v. United States*, 395 U.S. 6 (1969).

Controlled Substances Act (1970)

Leary v. United States *(discussed in the preceding section) essentially invalidated U.S. policy for the control of marijuana production, trade, and use. A replacement for the Marihuana Tax Act of 1937 was passed only a year after the Supreme Court's decision in* Leary v. United States. *The new act was the Controlled Substances Act of 1970, now a part of the U.S. Code, Title 21, Chapter 13. That act established the system of "schedules" for various categories of drugs that is still used by agencies of the U.S. government today. It also provides extensive background information about the domestic and international status of drug abuse efforts. Some of the most relevant sections for the domestic portion of the act are reprinted here.*

Section 801 of the act presents Congress's findings and declarations about controlled substances, with special mention in Section 801a of psychotropic drugs:

§ 801. Congressional findings and declarations: controlled substances

The Congress makes the following findings and declarations:

(1) Many of the drugs included within this subchapter have a useful and legitimate medical purpose and are necessary to maintain the health and general welfare of the American people.

(2) The illegal importation, manufacture, distribution, and possession and improper use of controlled substances have a substantial and detrimental effect on the health and general welfare of the American people.

    . . .

(7) The United States is a party to the Single Convention on Narcotic Drugs, 1961, and other international conventions designed to establish effective control over international and domestic traffic in controlled substances.

§ 801a. Congressional findings and declarations: psychotropic substances

The Congress makes the following findings and declarations:

(1) The Congress has long recognized the danger involved in the manufacture, distribution, and use of certain psychotropic substances for nonscientific and nonmedical purposes, and has provided strong and effective legislation to control illicit trafficking and to regulate legitimate uses of psychotropic substances in this country. Abuse of psychotropic substances has become a phenomenon common to many countries, however, and is not confined to national borders. It is, therefore, essential that the United States cooperate with other nations in establishing effective controls over international traffic in such substances.

(2) The United States has joined with other countries in executing an international treaty, entitled the Convention on

Psychotropic Substances and signed at Vienna, Austria, on February 21, 1971, which is designed to establish suitable controls over the manufacture, distribution, transfer, and use of certain psychotropic substances. The Convention is not self-executing, and the obligations of the United States thereunder may only be performed pursuant to appropriate legislation. It is the intent of the Congress that the amendments made by this Act, together with existing law, will enable the United States to meet all of its obligations under the Convention and that no further legislation will be necessary for that purpose.

. . .

[Section 802 deals with definitions used in the act, and section 803 deals with a minor housekeeping issue of financing for the act. Section 811 deals with the Attorney General's authority for classifying and declassifying drugs and the manner in which these steps are to be taken. In general:]

§ 811. Authority and criteria for classification of substances

(a) Rules and regulations of Attorney General; hearing

The Attorney General shall apply the provisions of this subchapter to the controlled substances listed in the schedules established by section 812 of this title and to any other drug or other substance added to such schedules under this subchapter. Except as provided in subsections (d) and (e) of this section, the Attorney General may by rule—

(1) add to such a schedule or transfer between such schedules any drug or other substance if he—

(A) finds that such drug or other substance has a potential for abuse, and

(B) makes with respect to such drug or other substance the findings prescribed by subsection (b) of section 812 of this title for the schedule in which such drug is to be placed; or

(2) remove any drug or other substance from the schedules if he finds that the drug or other substance does not meet the requirements for inclusion in any schedule.

. . .

[Section (b) provides guidelines for the evaluation of drugs and other substances. The next section, (c), is a key element of the act:]

(c) Factors determinative of control or removal from schedules

In making any finding under subsection (a) of this section or under subsection (b) of section 812 of this title, the Attorney General shall consider the following factors with respect to each drug or other substance proposed to be controlled or removed from the schedules:

(1) Its actual or relative potential for abuse.

(2) Scientific evidence of its pharmacological effect, if known.

(3) The state of current scientific knowledge regarding the drug or other substance.

(4) Its history and current pattern of abuse.

(5) The scope, duration, and significance of abuse.

(6) What, if any, risk there is to the public health.

(7) Its psychic or physiological dependence liability.

(8) Whether the substance is an immediate precursor of a substance already controlled under this subchapter.

[Section (d) is a lengthy discussion of international aspects of the nation's efforts to control substance abuse. Sections (e) through (h) deal with related, but less important, issues of the control of substance abuse. Section 812 is perhaps of greatest interest to the general reader in that it establishes the system of classifying drugs still used in the United States, along with the criteria for

classification and the original list of drugs to be included in each schedule (since greatly expanded):]

§ 812. Schedules of controlled substances

(a) Establishment

There are established five schedules of controlled substances, to be known as schedules I, II, III, IV, and V. Such schedules shall initially consist of the substances listed in this section. The schedules established by this section shall be updated and republished on a semiannual basis during the two-year period beginning one year after October 27, 1970, and shall be updated and republished on an annual basis thereafter.

(b) Placement on schedules; findings required

Except where control is required by United States obligations under an international treaty, convention, or protocol, in effect on October 27, 1970, and except in the case of an immediate precursor, a drug or other substance may not be placed in any schedule unless the findings required for such schedule are made with respect to such drug or other substance. The findings required for each of the schedules are as follows:

(1) Schedule I.—

  (A) The drug or other substance has a high potential for abuse.

  (B) The drug or other substance has no currently accepted medical use in treatment in the United States.

  (C) There is a lack of accepted safety for use of the drug or other substance under medical supervision.

(2) Schedule II.—

  (A) The drug or other substance has a high potential for abuse.

  (B) The drug or other substance has a currently accepted medical use in treatment in the United States or a currently accepted medical use with severe restrictions.

(C) Abuse of the drug or other substances may lead to severe psychological or physical dependence.

(3) Schedule III.—

(A) The drug or other substance has a potential for abuse less than the drugs or other substances in schedules I and II.

(B) The drug or other substance has a currently accepted medical use in treatment in the United States.

(C) Abuse of the drug or other substance may lead to moderate or low physical dependence or high psychological dependence.

(4) Schedule IV.—

(A) The drug or other substance has a low potential for abuse relative to the drugs or other substances in schedule III.

(B) The drug or other substance has a currently accepted medical use in treatment in the United States.

(C) Abuse of the drug or other substance may lead to limited physical dependence or psychological dependence relative to the drugs or other substances in schedule III.

(5) Schedule V.—

(A) The drug or other substance has a low potential for abuse relative to the drugs or other substances in schedule IV.

(B) The drug or other substance has a currently accepted medical use in treatment in the United States.

(C) Abuse of the drug or other substance may lead to limited physical dependence or psychological dependence relative to the drugs or other substances in schedule IV.

(c) Initial schedules of controlled substances

Schedules I, II, III, IV, and V shall, unless and until amended . . . pursuant to section 811 of this title, consist of the following drugs or other substances, by whatever official name, common or usual name, chemical name, or brand name designated: [*The initial list of drugs under each schedule follows.*]

Source: U.S. Code, Title 21, Chapter 13.

In the Matter of Marijuana Medical Rescheduling Petition (1988)

In 1972, NORML submitted a petition to the U.S. Drug Enforcement Administration (DEA) asking that marijuana be transferred from Schedule I to Schedule II under provisions of the Controlled Substances Act of 1970. Sixteen years later, DEA administrative judge Francis L. Young announced his decision on this request. Young reviewed and commented on the use of marijuana to treat certain specific medical conditions: cancer, glaucoma, multiple sclerosis, spasticity, and hyperparathyroidism. His general conclusions are as follows:

IX. Conclusion And Recommended Decision

Based upon the foregoing facts and reasoning, the administrative law judge concludes that the provisions of the Act permit and require the transfer of marijuana from Schedule I to Schedule II. The Judge realizes that strong emotions are aroused on both sides of any discussion concerning the use of marijuana. Nonetheless it is essential for this Agency, and its Administrator, calmly and dispassionately to review the evidence of record, correctly apply the law, and act accordingly.

Marijuana can be harmful. Marijuana is abused. But the same is true of dozens of drugs or substances which are listed in Schedule II so that they can be employed in treatment by physicians in proper cases, despite their abuse potential.

Transferring marijuana from Schedule I to Schedule II will not, of course, make it immediately available in pharmacies throughout the country for legitimate use in treatment. Other government authorities, Federal and State, will doubtless have to act before that might occur. But this Agency is not charged with responsibility, or given authority, over the myriad other regulatory decisions that may be required before marijuana can actually be legally available. This Agency is charged merely with determining the placement of marijuana pursuant to the provisions of the Act. Under our system of laws the responsibilities of other regulatory bodies are the concerns of those bodies, not of this Agency, [*sic*]

There are those who, in all sincerity, argue that the transfer of marijuana to Schedule II will "send a signal" that marijuana is "OK" generally for recreational use. This argument is specious. It presents no valid reason for refraining from taking an action required by law in light of the evidence. If marijuana should be placed in Schedule II, in obedience to the law, then that is where marijuana should be placed, regardless of misinterpretation of the placement by some. The reasons for the placement can, and should, be clearly explained at the time the action is taken. The fear of sending such a signal cannot be permitted to override the legitimate need, amply demonstrated in this record, of countless suffers for the relief marijuana can provide when prescribed by a physician in a legitimate case.

The evidence in this record clearly shows that marijuana has been accepted as capable of relieving the distress of great numbers of very ill people, and doing so with safety under medical supervision. It would be unreasonable, arbitrary and capricious for DEA to continue to stand between those sufferers and the benefits of this substance in light of the evidence in this record.

The administrative law judge recommends that the Administrator conclude that the marijuana plant considered as a whole has a currently accepted medical use in treatment in the United States, that there is no lack of accepted safety for use of it under medical supervision and that it may lawfully be transferred from Schedule I to Schedule II. The judge recommends that the Administrator transfer marijuana from Schedule I to Schedule II.

Drug Enforcement Administrator John Lawn declined to carry out Judge Young's recommendation, and marijuana was not rescheduled. In 1994, the District of Columbia Court of Appeals upheld Lawn's authority to act as he did.

Source: "In the Matter of Marijuana Rescheduling Petition." Docket No. 86-22. Available online at http://www.druglibrary .org/olsen/MEDICAL/YOUNG/young1.html. Accessed on May 5, 2016.

Interpretation of Listing of "Tetrahydrocannabinols" in Schedule I. 21 CFR Part 1308 [DEA-204] RIN 1117-AA55 (2001)

In 2001, the U.S. Drug Enforcement Administration (DEA) issued a group of three rules reinterpreting the regulation of any product containing THC. In essence, the new rules prohibited the growing, importation, or use of any cannabis product that contains any level of THC whatsoever. This regulation is considerably more severe than earlier interpretations of the Controlled Substances Act of 1970. The regulations were later overturned by a decision of the Ninth Circuit Court of Appeals (whose decision follows) in 2003.

SUMMARY: For the reasons provided herein, the Drug Enforcement Administration (DEA) interprets the Controlled Substances Act (CSA) and DEA regulations to declare any product that contains any amount of tetrahydrocannabinols (THC) to be a schedule I controlled substance, even if such product is made from portions of the cannabis plant that are excluded from the CSA definition of "marihuana."

[The DEA next provides a lengthy justification for the action it is taking in this rule, followed by this conclusion:]

Conclusion

By stating that "any material, compound, mixture, or preparation, which contains any quantity of . . . Tetrahydrocannabinols" is a schedule I controlled substance, the plain language of the CSA leads to the conclusion that all products containing any amount of THC are schedule I controlled substances. The legislative history supports this conclusion by revealing that Congress wrote the definition of marijuana intending to control all parts of the cannabis plant that were believed to contain THC. When the CSA was enacted, the implementing regulations did not simply adopt, verbatim, the prior regulations that were expressly limited to synthetic forms of THC. Rather, the word "Tetrahydrocannabinols" was inserted in the regulations at the top of the listing, thereby including all forms of THC (natural and synthetic). DEA therefore interprets the CSA and DEA regulations such that any product that contains any amount of THC is a schedule I controlled substance, even if such product is made from portions of the cannabis plant that are excluded from the definition of marijuana. DEA recognizes that this interpretive rule, standing alone, would effectively prohibit the use of an assortment of industrial products made from the cannabis plant (such as certain paper products, fiber, rope, and animal feed) that Congress intended to allow under the 1937 Marihuana Tax Act. Although the intent of the now-repealed 1937 Act is no longer controlling, DEA is issuing today, in a separate Federal Register document that accompanies this document, an interim rule that will except from CSA control the types of industrial products that were allowed under the 1937 Act, provided such products do not cause THC to enter the human body. See [insert Federal Register cite for interim rule]. *[The rule mentioned here is found at 21 CFR Part 1308, page 51539; http://frwebgate.access.gpo.gov/cgi-bin/get doc.cgi?dbname=2001_register&docid=01-25024-filed.pdf]* As explained further in the interim rule, all other products made from any of the excluded portions of the cannabis plant (such as edible "hemp" products) remain controlled substances if they cause THC to enter the human body.

Source: "Interpretation of Listing of 'Tetrahydrocannabinols' in Schedule I." *Federal Register*. Volume 66, Number 195. October 9, 2001. Rules and Regulations, 51530, 51533.

Hemp Industries Association, et al. v. Drug Enforcement Administration, 333 F.3d 1082 (2003)

The DEA's listing of new rules for the regulation of cannabis, outlined in the preceding document, was challenged by a group of companies, including Hemp Industries Association; All-One-God-Faith, Inc. (dba Dr. Bronner's Magic Soaps); Atlas Corporation; Nature's Path Foods USA, Inc.; Hemp Oil Canada, Inc.; Hempzels, Inc.; Kenex Ltd.; and Tierra Madre, LLC. The case was argued and decided in two parts, called Hemp I and Hemp II. The court's final decision about the DEA's action as outlined in Hemp II included the following conclusion. (Citations are omitted and indicated by ellipses.)

[7] Congress was aware of the presence of trace amounts of psychoactive agents (later identified as THC) in the resin of non-psychoactive hemp when it passed the 1937 "Marihuana Tax Act," and when it adopted the Tax Act marijuana definition in the CSA. As a result, when Congress excluded from the definition of marijuana "mature stalks of such plant, fiber . . . , [and] oil or cake made from the seeds," it also made an exception to the exception, and included "resin extracted from" the excepted parts of the plant in the definition of marijuana, despite the stalks and seeds exception. . . . Congress knew what it was doing, and its intent to exclude non-psychoactive hemp from regulation is entirely clear. The DEA's Final Rules are inconsistent with the unambiguous meaning of the CSA definitions of marijuana and THC, and the DEA did not use the appropriate scheduling procedures to add non-psychoactive hemp to the list of controlled substances.

[The court then notes that it has already determined in Hemp I that nonpsychoactive hemp is not banned under Schedule I.]

We find unambiguous Congress' intent with regard to the regulation of non-psychoactive hemp. Therefore, we reject the Final Rules at step one of the Chevron test and need not reach Chevron step two. *["Chevron" refers to a case whose precedent is cited in this decision.]*

IV. Conclusion

[9] The DEA's Final Rules purport to regulate foodstuffs containing "natural and synthetic THC." And so they can: in keeping with the definitions of drugs controlled under Schedule I of the CSA, the Final Rules can regulate foodstuffs containing natural THC if it is contained within marijuana, and can regulate synthetic THC of any kind. But they cannot regulate naturally-occurring THC not contained within or derived from marijuana—i.e., non-psychoactive hemp products—because non-psychoactive hemp is not included in Schedule I. The DEA has no authority to regulate drugs that are not scheduled, and it has not followed procedures required to schedule a substance.

[10] The DEA's definition of "THC" contravenes the unambiguously expressed intent of Congress in the CSA and cannot be upheld. DEA-205F and DEA-206F *[the two new rules proposed by the DEA]* are thus scheduling actions that would place non-psychoactive hemp in Schedule I for the first time. In promulgating the Final Rules, the DEA did not follow the procedures in §§ 811(a) and 812(b) of the CSA required for scheduling. The amendments to 21 C.F.R. § 1308.11(d)(27) that make THC applicable to all parts of the Cannabis plant are therefore void. We grant Appellants' petition and permanently enjoin enforcement of the Final Rules with respect to non-psychoactive hemp or products containing it.

Source: *Hemp Industries Association v. DEA.* 333 F.3d 1082 (2003).

Gonzales, Attorney General, et al. v. Raich et al., 545 U.S. 1 (2005)

In 1996, voters in California approved Proposition 215, permitting the use of marijuana for medical purposes. An obvious problem created by that action was possible conflict between the new permissive state law and federal law, which prohibits the use of marijuana for any purpose whatsoever. When two California women, Angel Raich and Diane Monson, had their marijuana stashes confiscated by federal officials in 2002, the two filed suit against the Attorney General of the United States, John Ashcroft. (Ashcroft was replaced by Alberto Gonzales as attorney general in 2005, thus accounting for the final title of the case.) The petitioners' case was that the seized marijuana had been grown in the state of California and was used only within the state; the federal government had, therefore, no basis for taking action in the matter. The federal government claimed that there was a possibility that the marijuana being grown in California might be sold or transported out of the state, and therefore the federal government had authority over the case because of the Commerce Clause of the U.S. Constitution. The Court ruled in favor of the government by a 6 to 3 vote. In their decision, the majority relied heavily on a 1942 case, Wickard v. Filburn *(317 U.S. 111), which established the right of the federal government to control wheat grown by a farmer in Ohio strictly for his own use. The main elements of the decision and the dissenting opinions are as follows (References are omitted, as indicated by ellipses.):*

For the majority:

Respondents in this case do not dispute that passage of the CSA [Controlled Substances Act of 1970], as part of the Comprehensive Drug Abuse Prevention and Control Act, was well within Congress' commerce power. . . . Nor do they contend that any provision or section of the CSA amounts to an unconstitutional exercise of congressional authority. Rather, respondents' challenge is actually quite limited; they argue that the CSA's categorical prohibition of the manufacture and possession of marijuana as applied to the intrastate manufacture and possession of marijuana for medical purposes pursuant to California law exceeds Congress' authority under the Commerce Clause.

[The court next shows how the issue in the present case is similar to the one posed in Wickard v. Filburn.]

Even respondents acknowledge the existence of an illicit market in marijuana; indeed, Raich has personally participated in that market, and Monson expresses a willingness to do so in the future. More concretely, one concern prompting inclusion of wheat grown for home consumption in the 1938 Act was that rising market prices could draw such wheat into the interstate market, resulting in lower market prices. . . . The parallel concern making it appropriate to include marijuana grown for home consumption in the CSA is the likelihood that the high demand in the interstate market will draw such marijuana into that market. While the diversion of homegrown wheat tended to frustrate the federal interest in stabilizing prices by regulating the volume of commercial transactions in the interstate market, the diversion of homegrown marijuana tends to frustrate the federal interest in eliminating commercial transactions in the interstate market in their entirety. In both cases, the regulation is squarely within Congress' commerce power because production of the commodity meant for home consumption, be it wheat or marijuana, has a substantial effect on supply and demand in the national market for that commodity.

[An important element in the dissents written by Justices O'Connor, Thomas, and Rehnquist leaned heavily on states' rights arguments. For example, Justice O'Connor writes:]

We enforce the "outer limits" of Congress' Commerce Clause authority not for their own sake, but to protect historic spheres of state sovereignty from excessive federal encroachment and thereby to maintain the distribution of power fundamental to our federalist system of government. . . . One of federalism's chief virtues, of course, is that it promotes innovation by allowing for the possibility that "a single courageous State may, if its citizens choose, serve as a laboratory; and try novel social and economic experiments without risk to the rest of the country." . . .

This case exemplifies the role of States as laboratories. The States' core police powers have always included authority to define criminal law and to protect the health, safety, and welfare of their citizens. . . . Exercising those powers, California (by ballot initiative and then by legislative codification) has come to its own conclusion about the difficult and sensitive question of whether marijuana should be available to relieve severe pain and suffering. Today the Court sanctions an application of the federal Controlled Substances Act that extinguishes that experiment, without any proof that the personal cultivation, possession, and use of marijuana for medicinal purposes, if economic activity in the first place, has a substantial effect on interstate commerce and is therefore an appropriate subject of federal regulation.

[*Justice Thomas offered an even more strongly worded dissent on the same basis*].

Respondents' local cultivation and consumption of marijuana is not "Commerce . . . among the several States." . . . By holding that Congress may regulate activity that is neither interstate nor commerce under the Interstate Commerce Clause, the Court abandons any attempt to enforce the Constitution's limits on federal power.

. . .

If the Federal Government can regulate growing a half-dozen cannabis plants for personal consumption (not because it is interstate commerce, but because it is inextricably bound up with interstate commerce), then Congress' Article I powers—as expanded by the Necessary and Proper Clause—have no meaningful limits.

. . .

If the majority is to be taken seriously, the Federal Government may now regulate quilting bees, clothes drives, and potluck suppers throughout the 50 States. This makes a mockery of Madison's assurance to the people of New York that the "powers delegated" to the Federal Government are "few and defined," while those of the States are "numerous and indefinite."

Source: *Gonzales v. Raich*, 545 U.S. 1 (2005).

Rohrabacher-Farr Amendment (2005)

The disconnect between federal prohibitions against the sale and use of marijuana expressed in the Controlled Substances Act of 1970 and the action by certain states permitting the use of marijuana for medical purposes has continued now for more than a decade. One expression of this disconnect has been a series of efforts by the U.S. Congress to prohibit federal authorities from carrying out punitive actions against individuals who sell or use medical marijuana in states where it has been approved. These actions in the U.S. House of Representatives go back to 2003, when Representative Barney Frank (D-MA) introduced the States' Rights to Medical Marijuana Act, which failed in a 273 to 152 floor vote. Similar bills and amendments were introduced again in 2004 through 2007, 2012, 2014, and 2015. The later versions of these bills were introduced by Representative Dana Rohrabacher (R-CA) and his colleagues Representative Maurice Hinchey (D-NY) and Representative Sam Farr (D-CA). The bill finally passed the House by a 219–189 vote in 2014 and again by a 242–186 vote in 2015. The relevant portion of the 2015 bill is reproduced here, followed by Representative Rohrabacher's comments about the purpose of the amendment. Following this section is an excerpt from a court case dealing with the interpretation of the amendment.

I have an amendment at the desk. . . .

At the end of the bill (before the short title), insert the following:

Sec. __. None of the funds made available in this Act to the Department of Justice may be used, with respect to any of the States of Alabama, Alaska, Arizona, California, Colorado, Connecticut, Delaware, Florida, Georgia, Hawaii, Illinois, Iowa, Kentucky, Louisiana, Maine, Maryland, Massachusetts, Michigan, Minnesota, Mississippi, Missouri, Montana, Nevada, New Hampshire, New Jersey, New Mexico, New York, North Carolina, Oklahoma, Oregon, Rhode Island, South Carolina, Tennessee, Texas, Utah, Vermont, Virginia, Washington, and Wisconsin, or with respect to either the District of Columbia or Guam, to prevent any of them from implementing their own laws that authorize the use, distribution, possession, or cultivation of medical marijuana.

. . .

Today, I ask my colleagues to make a practical as well as a principled vote. My amendment would prohibit any Federal funds from being used to supersede State law in those States that have legalized the use of medical marijuana.

Let's be clear. The intent of this amendment is to make it illegal for Federal employees to engage in efforts to enforce Federal law that makes the medical use or distribution of medical marijuana illegal in States where the use of marijuana for medical purposes has been made legal.

The practical aspect of this vote is based on the realization that, at a time of severely limited resources, it makes sense to target terrorists, criminals, and other threats to the American people rather than use Federal law enforcement resources to prevent suffering and sick people from using a weed that may or may not alleviate their suffering.

There are many examples—yes, anecdotal—in which the use of marijuana has helped end severe suffering.

Trying to prevent this use of marijuana once it has been legalized by a State government is a travesty, an inexcusable waste of our limited resources. That is the practical reason to vote for my amendment.

As for the principle, we Republicans claim to base our decisions on individual freedom, on states' rights as mandated by the 10th Amendment to the Constitution, and especially on the doctor-patient relationship.

Don't bother to use rhetoric about those principles on other issues if you vote for the Federal Government to supersede individual rights, states' rights, and the doctor-patient relationship when it comes to marijuana.

Source: H.Amdt.332 to H.R.2578. 2015. Congress.gov. https://www.congress.gov/amendment/114th-congress/house-amendment/332/text. Accessed on May 6, 2016.

FDA Statement on Health Effects of Marijuana (2006)

By the early 2000s, many claims were being made about the medical benefits of smoking marijuana. At that point, the U.S. Food and Drug Administration (FDA) apparently felt it necessary to issue a statement about these claims. On April 20, 2006, the agency issued the following news release on the medical benefits of marijuana.

Claims have been advanced asserting smoked marijuana has a value in treating various medical conditions. Some have argued that herbal marijuana is a safe and effective medication and that it should be made available to people who suffer from a number of ailments upon a doctor's recommendation, even though it is not an approved drug.

Marijuana is listed in schedule I of the Controlled Substances Act (CSA), the most restrictive schedule. The Drug Enforcement Administration (DEA), which administers the CSA, continues to support that placement and FDA concurred because marijuana met the three criteria for placement in Schedule I under 21 U.S.C. 812(b)(1) (e.g., marijuana has a high potential for abuse, has no currently accepted medical use in treatment in the United States, and has a lack of accepted safety for use under medical supervision). Furthermore, there is currently sound evidence that smoked marijuana is harmful. A past evaluation by several Department of Health and Human Services (HHS) agencies, including the Food and Drug Administration (FDA), Substance Abuse and Mental Health Services Administration (SAMHSA) and National Institute for Drug Abuse (NIDA), concluded that no sound scientific studies supported medical use of marijuana for treatment in the United States, and no animal or human data supported the safety or efficacy of marijuana for general medical use. There are alternative FDA-approved medications in existence for treatment of many of the proposed uses of smoked marijuana.

FDA is the sole Federal agency that approves drug products as safe and effective for intended indications. The Federal Food, Drug, and Cosmetic (FD&C) Act requires that new drugs be shown to be safe and effective for their intended use before being marketed in this country. FDA's drug approval process requires well-controlled clinical trials that provide the necessary scientific data upon which FDA makes its approval and labeling decisions. If a drug product is to be marketed, disciplined, systematic, scientifically conducted trials are the best means to obtain data to ensure that drug is safe and effective when used as indicated. Efforts that seek to bypass the FDA drug approval process would not serve the interests of public health because they might expose patients to unsafe and ineffective drug products. FDA has not approved smoked marijuana for any condition or disease indication.

A growing number of states have passed voter referenda (or legislative actions) making smoked marijuana available for a variety of medical conditions upon a doctor's recommendation. These measures are inconsistent with efforts to ensure that medications undergo the rigorous scientific scrutiny of the FDA approval process and are proven safe and effective under the standards of the FD&C Act. Accordingly, FDA, as the federal agency responsible for reviewing the safety and efficacy of drugs, DEA as the federal agency charged with enforcing the CSA, and the Office of National Drug Control Policy, as the federal coordinator of drug control policy, do not support the use of smoked marijuana for medical purposes.

Source: "Inter-Agency Advisory Regarding Claims That Smoked Marijuana Is a Medicine." Available online at http://www.fda.gov/NewsEvents/Newsroom/PressAnnouncements/2006/ucm108643.htm. Accessed on May 5, 2016.

Memorandum for All United States Attorneys (2013)

The decision by many states to approve the use of marijuana for medical purposes has created a problem for the federal government. Since marijuana is still a Schedule I drug under the Controlled Substances Act of 1970, should or must federal law enforcement agencies follow federal law or state law in dealing with individuals who use the drug in states where it has been approved for medical use? The administration of President Barack Obama made up its mind on this issue early on in his term of office, deciding essentially not to prosecute people who were using marijuana for medical purposes in states that had adopted laws permitting such use. Perhaps the most famous statement on the issue was announced to U.S. attorneys in a memorandum from Deputy Attorney General James M. Cole in August 2013, a portion of which is reprinted here.

As the Department noted in its previous guidance, Congress has determined that marijuana is a dangerous drug and that the illegal distribution and sale of marijuana is a serious crime that provides a significant source of revenue to large-scale criminal enterprises, gangs, and cartels. The Department of Justice is committed to enforcement of the CSA consistent with those determinations. The Department is also committed to using its limited investigative and prosecutorial resources to address the most significant threats in the most effective, consistent, and rational way. In furtherance of those objectives, as several states enacted laws relating to the use of marijuana for medical purposes, the Department in recent years has focused its efforts on certain enforcement priorities that are particularly important to the federal government:

• Preventing the distribution of marijuana to minors;
• Preventing revenue from the sale of marijuana from going to criminal enterprises, gangs, and cartels;
• Preventing the diversion of marijuana from states where it is legal under state law in some form to other states;
• Preventing state-authorized marijuana activity from being used as a cover or pretext for the trafficking of other illegal drugs or other illegal activity;
• Preventing violence and the use of firearms in the cultivation and distribution of marijuana;
• Preventing drugged driving and the exacerbation of other adverse public health consequences associated with marijuana use;
• Preventing the growing of marijuana on public lands and the attendant public safety and environmental dangers posed by marijuana production on public lands; and
• Preventing marijuana possession or use on federal property.

These priorities will continue to guide the Department's enforcement of the CSA against marijuana-related conduct. Thus, this memorandum serves as guidance to Department attorneys and law enforcement to focus their enforcement resources and efforts, including prosecution, on persons or organizations whose conduct interferes with any one or more of these priorities, regardless of state law. *[Footnote omitted here.]*

Outside of these enforcement priorities, the federal government has traditionally relied on states and local law enforcement agencies to address marijuana activity through enforcement of their own narcotics laws. For example, the Department of Justice has not historically devoted resources to prosecuting individuals whose conduct is limited to possession of small amounts of marijuana for personal use on private property. Instead, the Department has left such lower-level or localized activity to state and local authorities and has stepped in to enforce the CSA only when the use, possession, cultivation, or distribution of marijuana has threatened to cause one of the harms identified above.

The enactment of state laws that endeavor to authorize marijuana production, distribution, and possession by establishing a regulatory scheme for these purposes affects this traditional joint federal-state approach to narcotics enforcement. The Department's guidance in this memorandum rests on its expectation that states and local governments that have enacted laws authorizing marijuana-related conduct will implement strong and effective regulatory and enforcement systems that will address the threat those state laws could pose to public safety, public health, and other law enforcement interests. A system adequate to that task must not only contain robust controls and procedures on paper; it must also be effective in practice. Jurisdictions that have implemented systems that provide for regulation of marijuana activity must provide the necessary resources and demonstrate the willingness to enforce their laws and regulations in a manner that ensures they do not undermine federal enforcement priorities.

Source: Memorandum for All United States Attorneys. 2013. U.S. Department of Justice. https://www.justice.gov/iso/opa/resources/3052013829132756857467.pdf. Accessed on May 7, 2016.

Legitimacy of Industrial Hemp Research (2014)

An important breakthrough occurred in 2014 with regard to the legal status of hemp growing in the United States. After a very long period in which the cultivation of hemp was prohibited under any circumstances in the United States, the U.S. Congress decided to permit pilot programs for the growing of hemp in states that had approved such programs. As part of the 2014 Department of Agriculture funding act, it included the following brief section on the topic:

(a) IN GENERAL.—Notwithstanding the Controlled Substances Act of 1970 (21 U.S.C. 801 et seq.), the Safe and Drug-Free Schools and Communities Act (20 U.S.C. 7101 et seq.), chapter 81 of title 41, United States Code, or any other Federal law, an institution of higher education (as defined in section 101 of the Higher Education Act of 1965 (20 U.S.C. 1001)) or a State department of agriculture may grow or cultivate industrial hemp if—

   (1) the industrial hemp is grown or cultivated for purposes of research conducted under an agricultural pilot program or other agricultural or academic research; and

   (2) the growing or cultivating of industrial hemp is allowed under the laws of the State in which such institution of higher education or State department of agriculture is located and such research occurs.

(b) DEFINITIONS.—In this section:

   (1) AGRICULTURAL PILOT PROGRAM.—The term "agricultural pilot program" means a pilot program to study the growth, cultivation, or marketing of industrial hemp—

      (A) in States that permit the growth or cultivation of industrial hemp under the laws of the State; and

      (B) in a manner that—

         (i) ensures that only institutions of higher education and State departments of agriculture are used to grow or cultivate industrial hemp;

         (ii) requires that sites used for growing or cultivating industrial hemp in a State be certified by, and registered with, the State department of agriculture; and

(iii) authorizes State departments of agriculture to promulgate regulations to carry out the pilot program in the States in accordance with the purposes of this section.

(2) INDUSTRIAL HEMP.—The term "industrial hemp" means the plant Cannabis sativa L. and any part of such plant, whether growing or not, with a Δ^9-tetrahydrocannabinol concentration of not more than 0.3 percent on a dry weight basis.

Source: Agricultural Act of 2014. U.S. Congress. https://www .gpo.gov/fdsys/pkg/BILLS-113hr2642enr/pdf/BILLS-113hr 2642enr.pdf. Accessed on May 8, 2016.

Coats v. Dish Network (Colorado Supreme Court Case No. 13SC394) (2015)

Brandon Coats was a customer service representative for Dish Network. Coats is a quadriplegic who has been in a wheelchair since he was a teenager. He obtained a license in Colorado in 2009 for the use of marijuana for medical purposes. In 2010, Coats failed a test for THC conducted by Dish, the result of his having used marijuana during his off hours. He sued the company on the basis of Colorado law which prohibits a company from firing a person for carrying on legal activities while not on the job. Coats noted that medical marijuana was legal in Colorado at the time of his firing, so the company's action violated state law. The district court, appeals court, and Supreme Court all disagreed with Coats, as the following decision indicates. Ellipses indicate omitted text.

We review de novo the question of whether medical marijuana use prohibited by federal law is a "lawful activity" protected under section 24-34-402.5 *[the relevant state law on which Coats bases his claim].* . . .

We still must determine, however, whether medical marijuana use that is licensed by the State of Colorado but prohibited under federal law is "lawful" for purposes of section 24-34-402.5. Coats contends that the General Assembly intended the term "lawful" here to mean "lawful under Colorado state law," which, he asserts, recognizes medical marijuana use as "lawful." . . . We do not read the term "lawful" to be so restrictive. Nothing in the language of the statute limits the term "lawful" to state law. Instead, the term is used in its general, unrestricted sense, indicating that a "lawful" activity is that which complies with applicable "law," including state and federal law. We therefore decline Coats's invitation to engraft a state law limitation onto the statutory language. . . .

Echoing *[appeals court]* Judge Webb's dissent, Coats argues that because the General Assembly intended section 24-34-402.5 to broadly protect employees from discharge for outside-of-work activities, we must construe the term "lawful" to mean "lawful under Colorado law." . . . In this case, however, we find nothing to indicate that the General Assembly intended to extend section 24-34-402.5's protection for "lawful" activities to activities that are unlawful under federal law. In sum, because Coats's marijuana use was unlawful under federal law, it does not fall within section 24-34-402.5's protection for "lawful" activities.

Source: *Coats v. Dish Network.* Colorado Supreme Court. Case No. 13SC394. https://www.courts.state.co.us/userfiles/file/Court_Probation/Supreme_Court/Opinions/2013/13SC394.pdf. Accessed on May 5, 2016.

United States of America, Plaintiff, v. Marin Alliance for Medical Marijuana, and Lynette Shaw (2015)

The Rohrabacher-Farr Amendment adopted by the U.S. Congress in 2015 appeared to be fairly straightforward: It forbade the Drug Enforcement Administration from pursuing individuals for the use of medical marijuana in states where the practice was legal. The

DEA, however, had a different view of the amendment; it believed that the agency was prohibited from acting only against states in which medical marijuana was legal, not against individuals in those states. The question as to which interpretation was correct was first resolved later in 2015 when a case arose between a medical marijuana group in Marin County, California, and the DEA. The court concluded that "the Government's contrary reading so tortures the plain meaning of the statute" that it had to be rejected virtually out of hand. Specifically, it explained:

The plain reading of the text of Section 538 forbids the Department of Justice from enforcing this injunction against MAMM to the extent that MAMM operates in compliance with California law.

. . .

. . . this Court is not in a position to "override Congress' policy choice, articulated in a statute, as to what behavior should be prohibited." . . . On the contrary: This Court's only task is to interpret and apply Congress's policy choices, as articulated in its legislation. And in this instance, Congress dictated in Section 538 that it intended to prohibit the Department of Justice from expending any funds in connection with the enforcement of any law that interferes with California's ability to "implement [its] own State law that authorize[s] the use, distribution, possession, or cultivation of medical marijuana."

. . .

[The court then noted that the sponsors of the amendment had addressed this very issue in offering it to the House:]

In fact, the members of Congress who drafted Section 538 had the opportunity to respond to the very same argument that the DOJ advances here. In a letter to Attorney General Eric Holder on April 8, 2015, Congressmen Dana Rohrabacher and Sam Farr responded as follows to "recent statements indicating that the [DOJ] does not believe a spending restriction designed to protect [the medical marijuana laws of 35 states] applies to specific ongoing cases against individuals and businesses engaged in medical marijuana activity":

> As the authors of the provision in question, we write to inform you that this interpretation of our amendment is emphatically wrong. Rest assured, the purpose of our amendment was to prevent the Department from wasting its limited law enforcement resources on prosecutions and asset forfeiture actions against medical marijuana patients and providers, including businesses that operate legally under state law. In fact, a close look at the Congressional Record of the floor debate of the amendment clearly illustrates the intent of those who sponsored and supported this measure. Even those who argued against the amendment agreed with the proponents' interpretation of their amendment.

Conclusion

For the foregoing reasons, as long as Congress precludes the Department of Justice from expending funds in the manner proscribed by Section 538, the permanent injunction will only be enforced against MAMM insofar as that organization is in violation of California "State laws that authorize the use, distribution, possession, or cultivation of medical marijuana."

Source: *United States of America, Plaintiff, v. Marin Alliance for Medical Marijuana, and Lynette Shaw.* United States District Court for the Northern District of California. https://cases.justia.com/federal/district-courts/california/candce/3:19 98cv00086/116898/277/0.pdf?ts=1445324671. Accessed on May 6, 2016.

Marijuana is a very contentious issue about which volumes have been written in books, articles, reports, pamphlets, brochures, white papers, and other print documents, as well as on the Internet. Many of these resources provide relatively unbiased information on the history of cannabis, its physical and psychological effects, and efforts to establish legal controls (or to remove such controls) over the centuries. This chapter provides a sampling of that literature. The chapter is divided into four major sections, books, articles, reports, and Internet resources. Given the ubiquity of Internet references today, some items could be assigned to more than one category and where that is possible, it is so noted in the listing. The reader should be aware that a very large body of research is now available on the physical, mental, emotional, and moral effects of cannabis use that often produces ambiguous and contradictory results. The studies listed here must be regarded as no more than the tip of the iceberg of this research. An additional source of bibliographic references in this book can be found in the References section at the end of Chapters 1 and 2.

Competitors evaluate marijuana samples during the fifth annual Cannabis Cup, a competition for best marijuana, in Montevideo, Uruguay. The contest was held at a private building where bands played rock music while competitors smoked joints and vendors sold food and marijuana paraphernalia. Alcohol was banned. (AP Photo/Matilde Campodonico)

Books

Abel, Ernest L. 1980. *Marihuana, the First Twelve Thousand Years*. New York: Plenum Press.
> An older book that remains virtually without peer in its treatment of the history of the cannabis plant.

Anderson, Patrick. 1981. *High in America: The True Story Behind NORML and the Politics of Marijuana*. New York: Viking Press. Also available online at http://www.druglibrary.org/special/anderson/highinamerica1.htm. Accessed on May 24, 2016.
> Anderson presents a detailed and fascinating story about one of the major groups fighting for the decriminalization of marijuana use in the United States.

Armentano, Paul. 2016. *The Citizen's Guide to State-by-State Marijuana Laws*. Atlanta, GA: Whitman Publishing.
> This book, by the deputy director of NORML, provides detailed information about the legal status of marijuana in all states.

Barbour, Scott. 2011. *Should Marijuana Be Legalized?* San Diego, CA: ReferencePoint Press.
> This book for young adults presents all sides of the question of the legalization of marijuana.

Barcott, Bruce, 2015. *Weed the People: The Future of Legal Marijuana in America*. New York: Time Books.
> The author reviews the history of marijuana in the United States, discusses changes that have been occurring in the past decade with regard to legalization of the drug, and attempts to lay out the type of future that may develop if the current trade continues.

Bennett, William J., and Robert A. White. 2016. *Going to Pot: Why the Rush to Legalize Marijuana Is Harming America*. New York: Center Street.

Bennett is the former director of National Drug Control policy under President George H. W. Bush. He and White explain why the legalization of marijuana poses a serious threat to fundamental values of American society.

Bonnie, Richard J., and Charles H. Whitebread. 1999. *The Marijuana Conviction: A History of Marijuana Prohibition in the United States*. New York: Lindesmith Center.
This edition is a reprint of the original 1974 book, now widely considered to be one of the great classics in the literature of marijuana criminalization. The book describes in well-written detail the process by which marijuana went from a highly regarded medical substance to a banned drug in the United States.

Booth, Martin. 2005. *Cannabis: A History*. New York: Picador.
This book is the gold standard for an account of the history of marijuana.

Brown, Jeff. 2012. *Marijuana and the Bible*, 2nd ed. Clermont, FL: Createspace. Also available online at http://www.erowid.org/plants/cannabis/cannabis_spirit2.shtml. Accessed on May 29, 2016.
At the time this work was written, the author was a member of the Ethiopian Zion Coptic church, which used marijuana as part of its sacraments. The church no longer exists, but the work is of considerable interest in that it attempts to show references in the Bible that apparently refer to the use of marijuana as a psychotropic substance.

Casarett, David J. 2015. *Stoned: A Doctor's Case for Medical Marijuana*. New York: Current.
Casarett makes his case for the legalization of medical marijuana based on a number of specific cases in which the drug has been used to treat physical problems.

Castle, David J., Robin Murray, and Deepak Cyril D'Souza. 2012. *Marijuana and Madness*, 2nd ed. Cambridge, UK; New York: Cambridge University Press.

> This book provides a highly technical and detailed review of the existing scientific evidence about the relationship between marijuana use and mental illness. It includes chapters on the endocannabinoid system, recent changes in the potency of cannabis, cannabis and psychoses, and the effects of cannabis on the brain.

Caulkins, Jonathan P., et al. 2016. *Marijuana Legalization: What Everyone Needs to Know.* New York: Oxford University Press.

> This book provides information on virtually every conceivable aspect of marijuana, from methods by which the drug is produced and distributed, risks associated with its use, possible effects of legalizing the drug, possible medical benefits, and ways in which the legalization of marijuana differs from that of other drugs.

Chasteen, John Charles. 2016. *Getting High: Marijuana through the Ages.* Lanham, MD: Rowman & Littlefield.

> Chasteen focuses primarily on the history of marijuana in the United States, but also provides an interesting discussion of the drug's place in other parts of the world throughout history.

Clarke, Robert Connell, and Mark David Merlin, eds. 2013. *Cannabis: Evolution and Ethnobotany.* Berkeley: University of California Press.

> The essays in this book provide a fairly technical, yet quite readable, review of the history of the cannabis plant, including its many uses as hemp and recreational and medical marijuana.

Compton, Michael T., ed. 2016. *Marijuana and Mental Health.* Arlington, VA: American Psychiatric Association Publishing.

The papers in this collection deal with a variety of issues related to marijuana and its legalization, such as the effects of the drug on the body and mind, medical marijuana, legalization of the drug, synthetic cannabinoids, and treatment and prevention of marijuana misuse.

Dach, Jeffrey, Elaine A. Moore, and Justin Kander. 2015. *Cannabis Extracts in Medicine: The Promise of Benefits in Seizure Disorders, Cancer, and Other Conditions.* Jefferson, NC: McFarland & Company.
The authors focus on cannabidiol (CBD), a common component of *Cannabis sativa,* rather than THC in this book, exploring its method of production and its medical effects on the human body.

Derrickson, Jason, ed. 2014. *Marijuana Legalization: State Initiatives, Implications, and Issues.* New York: Nova Science Publishers.
The articles in this anthology examine federal policies on marijuana, trends in legalization of the drug at the state level, conflicts between the two, and issues that arise when marijuana use becomes a legitimate business.

Dijkstra, Valentin, ed. 2013. *Recreational and Medical Marijuana: Legalization Conflicts and Questions.* New York: Nova Science Publishers.
The four essays in this book discuss selected legal issues involved in the state legalization of marijuana use, conflicts between federal and state medical marijuana laws, the Controlled Substances Act, and fines and imprisonment conditions relating to marijuana convictions.

Duvall, Chris S. 2015. *Cannabis.* London: Reaktion Books.
Without ignoring marijuana, this book focuses its attention on hemp, its history in human culture, and its many potential applications in everyday life.

Fox, Steve, Paul Armentano, and Mason Tvert. 2013. *Marijuana Is Safer: So Why Are We Driving People to Drink?* White River Junction, VT: Chelsea Green Publishing.

The essence of this book is expressed in the title of one of its chapters: "Not Adding a Vice, but Providing an Alternative."

Geluardi, John. 2016. *Cannabiz: The Explosive Rise of the Medical Marijuana Industry.* Abingdon, UK; New York: Routledge.

The author focuses on the business aspects of dealing with marijuana that have arisen as the result of increased levels of legalization for recreational and medical purposes.

Gogek, Ed. 2015. *Marijuana Debunked: A Handbook for Parents, Pundits and Politicians Who Want to Know the Case against Legalization.* Asheville, NC: Chiron Publications.

The author makes the argument that the American public has been sold on the safety of marijuana, even for teenagers, by the press and the "marijuana lobby." He reviews the scientific and medical evidence for the drug's effects on the human body and explains why parents should become better informed and better organized to prevent further legalization of the drug.

Gold, Mark S. 2014. *Marijuana.* New York: Springer Verlag.

This book provides a somewhat more technical approach to the subject of marijuana, focusing on topics such as cannabinoid pharmacology, medical and psychiatric problems associated with marijuana use, diagnosis of marijuana dependency, and treatment and prevention of marijuana abuse.

Hageseth, Christian, and Joseph D'Agnese. 2015. *Big Weed: An Entrepreneur's High-Stakes Adventures in the Budding Legal Marijuana Business.* New York: Palgrave Macmillan.

This book provides a personalized view of the development of legalized marijuana as a major business endeavor, written by the founder of Green Man Cannabis, reputed to be the largest marijuana business operation in the United States.

Herer, Jack. 1994. *The Emperor Wears No Clothes*, 11th ed. Anaheim, CA: AH HA Publishing, 2001. Also available online at http://www.hampapartiet.se/25.pdf.
The publisher claims that this book is the "authoritative history of hemp's myriad uses and of the war on this plant." The book certainly contains a wealth of detailed information about the history of the plant, its many uses, and efforts to make its use for recreational purposes illegal.

Jacquette, Dale, ed. 2010. *Cannabis: Philosophy for Everyone: What Were We Just Talking About?* Malden, MA: Wiley-Blackwell.
This collection of essays deals with a variety of cannabis-related topics, including cannabis phenomenology, marijuana and spiritual enlightenment, effects of cannabis use on creativity, psycho-social dimensions of the cannabis culture, and ethics and politics of cannabis use.

Lee, Martin A. 2012. *Smoke Signals: A Social History of Marijuana: Medical, Recreational, and Scientific*. New York: Scribner.
The author provides a readable and comprehensive review of the use of cannabis products throughout history from the earliest ages to the present day.

Maguire, Mary, and Kim Schnurbush, ed. 2015. *Annual Editions: Drugs, Society, and Behavior*, 30th ed. Boston: McGraw-Hill Higher Education.
Annual Editions is regularly updated to provide expert views on the most important social topics of the day. Each book, written for the layperson, contains articles from newspapers, magazines, and journals written by experts in the field. The book comes with a resource guide and relevant testing materials.

[n.a.]. *Marijuana reform*. 2014. Ipswich, MA: H. W. Wilson.
This collection of articles focuses on the changes that have been taking place in Americans' attitudes about the use of marijuana. Articles cover topics such as decriminalization versus legalization, issues relating to the taxing of marijuana commerce, comparing the safety of marijuana and alcohol, shifting student attitudes about marijuana, the medicinal value of marijuana, and the reclassification "quagmire."

Marion, Nancy E., and Joshua B. Hill. 2016. *Legalizing Marijuana: A Shift in Policies across America*. Durham, NC: Carolina Academic Press.
The 12 papers in this anthology discuss a variety of topics related to the changing status of marijuana in the United States, including a brief history of the status of marijuana throughout history in the nation, the role of cannabis on campuses, the legal implications of legalizing marijuana, and legalization campaigns in Washington and Colorado.

Martin, Alyson, and Nushin Rashidian. 2014. *A New Leaf: The End of Cannabis Prohibition*. New York: The New Press.
The authors are journalists who write about the process by which marijuana legalization has started to become popular throughout the country.

Mills, James H. 2000. *Madness, Cannabis and Colonialism: The "'Native Only'" Lunatic Asylums of British India, 1857–1900*. London: Palgrave Macmillan.
The author tells the fascinating story of the creation of lunatic asylums by the British government following the Indian rebellion of 1857 as a way of keeping itinerant natives under control. The asylums were apparently occupied almost exclusively by individuals who had been users of cannabis products.

Nores, John, and James A. Swan. 2010. *War in the Woods: Combating Marijuana Cartels on America's Public Lands*. Guilford, CT: Lyons Press.

> The authors, a warden for the California Fish and Game Commission and a columnist for ESPN, describe episodes that have occurred during efforts to find and destroy marijuana crops on public lands. They discuss the threat to human life and the environmental damage caused by illegal marijuana farms.

Robinson, Rowan. 1996. *The Great Book of Hemp: The Complete Guide to the Environmental, Commercial, and Medicinal Uses of the World's Most Extraordinary Plant*. Rochester, VT: Park Street Press.

> This book provides an excellent history of the role of hemp in human civilization, with a good introduction to social and economic issues associated with its use in the past and present. The book itself has an interesting history, apparently having been written to a considerable extent by Robert A. Nelson. For the background of the book and a copy of the original manuscript, see Nelson, Robert A. 2016. "Hemp & History." http://rexresearch.com/hhist/hhicon.htm. Accessed on May 30, 2016.

Rubin, Vera D., ed. 1975. *Cannabis and Culture*. The Hague, The Netherlands: Mouton, 1975.

> This book includes papers presented at the IXth Ninth International Congress of the International Union of Anthropological and Ethnological Sciences held in Chicago in 1973. It contains articles on a whole range of cannabis-related topics, including "Early Diffusion and Folk Uses of Hemp," "The Origin and Use of Cannabis in Eastern Asia: Their Linguistic-Cultural Implications," "The Social Nexus of Ganja in Jamaica," "The Ritual Use of Cannabis in Mexico," "Traditional Patterns of Hashish

Use in Egypt," "Social and Medical Aspects of the Use of Cannabis in Brazil," "Sociocultural and Epidemiological Aspects of Hashish Use in Greece," "Memories, Reflections and Myths: The American Marihuana Commission," and "Sociocultural Factors in Marihuana Use in the United States."

Smith, Gregory L. 2016. *Medical Cannabis: Basic Science & Clinical Applications: What Clinicians Need to Know and Why.* Beverly Farms, MA: Aylesbury Press.

> The publishers of this book claim that it is "the first, single source for concise, up-to-date information about which conditions respond to cannabis, dosing guidance, and the safe use of cannabis by your patients." Although intended for medical professionals, it contains extensive information of interest to the lay person.

Tate, Katherine, James Lance Taylor, and Mark Q. Sawyer. 2014. *Something's in the Air: Race, Crime, and the Legalization of Marijuana.* New York: Routledge.

> In the first half of this book, the authors attempt to identify the factors that are driving current attempts to legalize marijuana in the United States, using the battle over California Proposition 19 as an example of this study. In the second half of the book, they turn to the special relationship of the war on drugs (especially marijuana) and the potentials for legalization on minority groups in the United States.

Tyson, Victor P., ed. 2015. *Marijuana: Emerging Legal Issues and Federal Tax Proposals.* New York: Nova Science Publishers.

> This short book deals with the two marijuana-related topics mentioned in its title.

Wilbur, Alicia K., Lori J. Glauser, and David M. Sipper. 2015. *Medical Marijuana Desk Reference.* Las Vegas, NV: Signal Bay Research.

This book is intended for medical providers. It includes the most recent scientific information on the use of marijuana for the treatment of more than 200 diseases and medical conditions.

Articles

Acworth, Alex, Nicolas de Roos, and Hajime Katayama. 2012. "Substance Use and Adolescent Sexual Activity." *Applied Economics.* 44(9): 1067–1079.
> The authors explore the relationship between early drug use and initiation of sexual activity among adolescents and find a strong correlation between the two for males, but no correlation for females.

Allen, Jadie, and Mark D. Holder. 2014. "Marijuana Use and Well-Being in University Students." *Journal of Happiness Studies.* 15(2): 301–321.
> This meta-analysis of studies on positive and negative well-being effects of smoking marijuana found complex and contradictory results that suggest additional research is needed to obtain definitive results on the article's hypotheses.

Anderson D. Mark, and Daniel I. Rees. 2014. "The Legalization of Recreational Marijuana: How Likely Is the Worst-Case Scenario?" *Journal of Policy Analysis and Management.* 33(1): 221–232.
> The authors attempt to predict the effects of marijuana legalization on alcohol use patterns, driving accidents, and patterns of marijuana use among youth. They conclude that the net results of marijuana legalization are likely to be positive.

Barry, Rachel Ann, Heikki Hiilamo, and Stanton A. Glantz. 2014. "Waiting for the Opportune Moment: the Tobacco

Industry and Marijuana Legalization." *The Milbank Quarterly*. 92(2): 207–242.

The tobacco industry has been interested in the commercial consequences of marijuana legalization for at least 50 years. Now that such an event is beginning to occur, it and large food corporations and other businesses are likely to become heavily involved in the production and distribution of marijuana products, a turn of events whose consequences the authors discuss.

Birdsall, Shauna M., Timothy C. Birdsall, and Lucas A. Tims. 2016. "The Use of Medical Marijuana in Cancer." *Current Oncology Reports*. 18(7): 1–9.

The authors review recent reports on the use of marijuana to treat cancer and summarize possible effects of such treatments as well as risks and benefits of using them.

Bonnie, Richard J., and Charles H. Whitebread, II. 1970. "The Forbidden Fruit and the Tree of Knowledge: An Inquiry into the Legal History of American Marijuana Prohibition." *Virginia Law Review*. 56(6): 971–1203. Also available online at http://www.druglibrary.org/schaffer/LIBRARY/studies/vlr/vlrtoc.htm.

This article is the basis for a book written by Bonnie and Whitebread on the history of the criminalization of cannabis in the United States (see "Books" earlier in this chapter). It is widely regarded as one of the most (if not *the* most) complete reports and analyses of this story.

Brunner, Theodore F. 1973. "Marijuana in Ancient Greece and Rome? The Literary Evidence." *Bulletin of the History of Medicine*. 47(4): 344–355.

The author uses a number of literary sources to make his case that the Greeks and Romans were familiar with the medical uses of cannabis and included it in their *materia medica*, but that there is no evidence that they knew of or took advantage of its psychoactive effects.

Caulkins, Jonathan P., Michael A. C. Lee, and Anna M. Kasunic. 2012. "Marijuana Legalization: Lessons from the 2012 State Proposals." *World Medical & Health Policy.* 4(3–4): 4–34.

The authors point out that the question of legalizing marijuana is not a "yes" or "no" proposition, but can be expressed in many different formats, each of which has a distinct set of possible outcomes for retail prices, tax income, availability, risk for arrest, and public and personal health. The paper discusses how these varieties of expression and their possible consequences differ from each other.

Cooper, Ziva D., Sandra D. Comer, and Margaret Haney. 2013. "Comparison of the Analgesic Effects of Dronabinol and Smoked Marijuana in Daily Marijuana Smokers." *Neuropsychopharmacology.* 38(10): 1984–1992.

The study was designed to compare the analgesic effects of smoked marijuana versus orally ingested dronabinol (Marinol). Researchers concluded that both products "decreased pain, with dronabinol producing longer-lasting decreases in pain sensitivity and lower ratings of abuse-related subjective effects than marijuana."

Fattore, Liana, and Walter Fratta. 2011. "Beyond THC: The New Generation of Cannabinoid Designer Drugs." *Frontiers of Behavioral Neuroscience.* 5: 60. doi: 10.3389/fnbeh.2011.00060. http://www.ncbi.nlm.nih.gov/pmc/articles/PMC3187647/. Accessed on June 2, 2016.

The authors provide an excellent general overview of the invention, development, distribution, and use of synthetic cannabinoids with psychoactive properties similar to those of THC.

Gerra, Gilberto, et al. 2010. "Pharmacology and Toxicology of Cannabis Derivatives and Endocannabinoid Agonists." *Recent Patents on CNS Drug Discovery.* 5(1): 46–52.

This paper provides an excellent introduction to the topic of marijuana derivatives with a discussion of their possible future applications as therapeutic agents.

Ghosh, Tista, et al. 2016. "The Public Health Framework of Legalized Marijuana in Colorado." *American Journal of Public Health*. 106(1): 21–27.

The authors report on an analysis that has been conducted on the potential effects of marijuana legalization on public health policy and activities in Colorado, at least partly as a possible guide to other states that may take similar actions in the future.

Hasin, Deborah S., et al. 2015. "Prevalence of Marijuana Use Disorders in the United States between 2001–2002 and 2012–2013." *JAMA Psychiatry*. 72(12): 1235–1242.

The authors compare data from the National Epidemiologic Survey on Alcohol and Related Conditions for 2001–2002 and 2012–2013 and find that the rate of marijuana users more than doubled, from 4.1% to 9.5%, while the rate of individuals who can be classified under the category of cannabis use disorder decreased from 35.6% to 30.6% over the same period. They discuss the implications of these findings for current trends in the legalization of marijuana use for recreational purposes.

Kamin, Sam. 2015. "The Battle of the Bulge: The Surprising Last Stand against State Marijuana Legalization." *Publius: The Journal of Federalism*. 45(3): 427–451. Also available online at http://publius.oxfordjournals.org/content/45/3/427.full.pdf+ html. Accessed on May 30, 2016.

The author notes that current trends toward the legalization of recreational marijuana use by the states are strong. He discusses some of the few remaining forces that can act against this trend, such as actions by the federal government and lawsuits by opposing states and professional organizations, such as police unions.

Kendell, Robert. 2003. "Cannabis Condemned: The Proscription of Indian Hemp." *Addiction.* 98(2): 143–151.

The author provides some very interesting history about the process by which marijuana became criminalized internationally, beginning with a 1925 League of Nations conference on opium, in which marijuana was declared by Egyptian representatives to represent a threat as serious as that posed by opium.

Kramer, Joan L. 2015. "Medical Marijuana for Cancer." *CA: A Cancer Journal for Clinicians.* 65(2): 109–122.

This article provides a review of studies on various aspects of the use of marijuana in the treatment of cancer and cancer-related conditions, such as pain management. It also reviews some of the best available data on hazards of smoking marijuana.

Mason, Brittany L., et al. 2016. "Novel Pharmacotherapeutic Interventions for Cannabis Use Disorder." *Current Addiction Reports.* 3(2): 214–220.

No medications have yet (as of 2017) been approved for the treatment of cannabis use disorder. However, a few promising candidates for treatment are being studied for possible therapeutic use.

Maxwell, Janet Carlisle, and Bruce Mendelson. 2016. "What Do We Know Now about the Impact of the Laws Related to Marijuana?" *Journal of Addiction Medicine.* 10(1): 3–12.

This article summarizes what is known about the effects of legalizing the use of recreational marijuana as of early 2016, based on surveys conducted among medical providers in Denver and Seattle.

McGuire, Jo. 2016. "Trends in Marijuana Legalization: A Wake-Up Call for Employers." *Occupational Health & Safety.* 85(2): 35–37.

The author points out that marijuana legalization poses issues for employers, about which they may not have thought thus far.

Merlin, M. D. 2003. "Archaeological Evidence for the Tradition of Psychoactive Plant Use in the Old World." *Economic Botany*. 57(3): 295–323.

The author provides an extensive and detailed review of the ways in which psychoactive drugs, including marijuana, were used for a variety of purposes perhaps as far back as 12,000 years ago.

Metts, Julius, et al. 2016. "Medical Marijuana: A Treatment Worth Trying?" *Journal of Family Practice*. 65(3): 178–185.

The authors outline conditions for which marijuana might be helpful as a form of treatment and cautions to observe for each condition listed.

Morningstar, Patricia J. 1985. "Thandai and Chilam: Traditional Hindu Beliefs about the Proper Uses of Cannabis." *Journal of Psychoactive Drugs*, 17(3): 141–165.

The author points out that cannabis has some diverse and contradictory effects on the human body, which may make it difficult for a society to know how to classify the use of the substance. She demonstrates how traditional Indian culture has resolved this problem over centuries of use of the drug for a variety of purposes, always taking advantage of its benefits while placing restrictions on its risks.

Myles, Nicholas, et al. 2012. "The Association between Cannabis Use and Earlier Age at Onset of Schizophrenia and Other Psychoses: Meta-Analysis of Possible Confounding Factors." *Current Pharmaceutical Design*. 18(32): 5055–5069.

This meta-study found that there is "robust evidence" for the possibility that, in some individuals, cannabis smoking may be a causative factor in the development of psychotic disorders such as schizophrenia.

Nahas, Gabriel G. 1982. "Hashish in Islam: 9th to 18th Century." *Bulletin of the New York Academy of Medicine.* 1982. 58(9): 814–831. Also available online at http://www.ncbi.nlm .nih.gov/pmc/articles/PMC1805385/pdf/bullnyacadmed 00095-0056.pdf.
   The author offers a superb review of the use of hashish in the Muslim Middle East during the time period mentioned in the article title.

Neavyn, Mark J., et al. 2014. "Medical Marijuana and Driving: A Review." *Journal of Medical Toxicology.* 10(3): 269–279.
   The authors review a number of studies on the effect of marijuana use on driving and find that results from laboratory studies differ from those of field studies. They suggest that individuals who consume marijuana should wait at least eight hours before driving.

Nickles, Dean M. 2016. "Federalism and State Marijuana Legislation." *Notre Dame Law Review.* 91(3): 1253–1285.
   This article provides an excellent general overview of the main legal issues created by the adoption of marijuana legislation in various states over the past decade.

Palamar, Joseph Jay, Lily Lee, and Michael Weitzman. 2015. "Prevalence and Correlates of Hashish Use in a National Sample of High School Seniors in the United States." *American Journal of Drug and Alcohol Abuse.* 41(3): 197–205.
   The authors note that most studies on the use of marijuana do not discriminate among the various forms in which the drug may be used. They claim that this demographic study of hashish use among high school seniors in the United States is the first such study to do so in the United States.

Pardini, Dustin, et al. 2015. "Unfazed or Dazed and Confused: Does Early Adolescent Marijuana Use Cause Sustained Impairments in Attention and Academic Functioning?" *Journal of Abnormal Child Psychology.* 43(7): 1203–1217.

> The authors explore the long-term effects of low or moderate marijuana use among adolescents on attention skills and academic performance. They conclude that such users experience "an increase in observable attention and academic problems, but these problems appear to be minimal and are eliminated following sustained abstinence."

Popovici, Ioana, et al. 2014. "Cannabis Use and Antisocial Behavior among Youth." *Sociological Inquiry.* 84(1): 131–162.

> The authors find, "[a]s expected," that antisocial behavior is strongly correlated with heavy users of marijuana, and the more frequent the use of the drug, the greater the antisocial behavior.

Rieder, M. J. 2016. "Is the Medical Use of Cannabis a Therapeutic Option for Children?" *Paediatrics & Child Health.* 21(1): 31–34. Also available online at http://www.cps.ca/en/documents/position/medical-use-of-cannabis. Accessed on May 31, 2016.

> This position statement from the Canadian Paediatric Society suggests that there is insufficient evidence to make strong statements about the use of medical marijuana among children, but the data that are available suggest that the drug be used in only very specific ways and as infrequently as possible.

Russo, Ethan. 2002. "Cannabis Treatments in Obstetrics and Gynecology: A Historical Review." *Journal of Cannabis Therapeutics.* 2(3/4): 5–34. Also available online at http://www.cannabis-med.org/membersonly/mo.php?aid=2002-03-04&fid=2002-03-04-1&mode=p&sid=.

The author points out that there is a long history associated with the use of cannabis for a variety of obstetrical and gynecological problems. He concludes from his own studies that cannabis may have applications in dealing with a variety of female disorders, including dysmenorrhea, dysuria, hyperemesis gravidarum, and menopausal symptoms.

Saper, Anthony. 1974. "The Making of Policy through Myth, Fantasy and Historical Accident: The Making of America's Narcotics Laws." *British Journal of Addiction to Alcohol and Other Drugs*. 69(2): 183–193.
The author argues that drug laws in the United States during the first three quarters of the 20th century were made on the basis of "myth, fantasy, historical accident; interwoven with occasional rationality."

Schrot, Richard J., and John R. Hubbard. 2016. "Cannabinoids: Medical Implications." *Annals of Medicine*. 48(3): 128–141.
The authors provide an excellent review of the current state of information about conditions for which cannabinoids may be an effective medical treatment, with a review of harmful side effects that should be considered.

Schwartz, David S. 2013. "High Federalism: Marijuana Legalization and the Limits of Federal Power to Regulate States." *Cardozo Law Review*. 35(2): 567–642.
This article provides a detailed and sophisticated legal analysis of the issues raised by state laws that permit the use of marijuana for medical and/or recreational purposes, in conflict with federal laws and regulations that restrict such use of psychoactive drugs.

Sherman, Brian J., and Aimee L. McRae-Clark. 2016. "Treatment of Cannabis Use Disorder: Current Science and Future

Outlook." *Pharmacotherapy: The Journal of Human Pharmacology and Drug Therapy.* 36(5): 511–535.

Cannabis use disorder (CUD) is a condition defined in the *Diagnostic and Statistical Manual of Mental Disorders* (DSM-5) as the continued use of marijuana despite clinically significant impairment, ranging from mild to severe. This article provides an excellent overview of current research on the condition and possible methods of treatment.

Small, Ernest. 2015. "Evolution and Classification of *Cannabis sativa* (Marijuana, Hemp) in Relation to Human Utilization." *Botanical Review.* 81(3): 189–294.

The author provides a very detailed review of the botanical characteristics of *C. sativa*, as well as a story of its use throughout human history.

Tashkin, Donald P. 2013. "Effects of Marijuana Smoking on the Lung." *Annals of the American Thoracic Society.* 10(3): 239–247.

The author reviews some of the acute and chronic effects of smoking marijuana on the lung and finds anatomical changes immediately after smoking, but relatively modest changes as a result of long-term use of marijuana. He concludes that "the accumulated weight of evidence implies far lower risks for pulmonary complications of even regular heavy use of marijuana compared with the grave pulmonary consequences of tobacco."

Temple, E. C., R. F. Brown, and D. W. Hine. 2011. "The 'Grass Ceiling': Limitations in the Literature Hinder Our Understanding of Cannabis Use and Its Consequences." *Addiction.* 106(2): 238–244.

The authors discuss methodological problems that limit the usefulness of the vast amount of research that has been done on cannabis use. Of special interest are two

responses to these articles: Earleywine, Mitch. "The El-
ephant in the Room with the 'Grass Ceiling.'" *Addiction*.
106(2): 245–246; and Copeland, Jan. "The Glass Ceiling
on Evidence of Cannabis Related Harms: Flawed or Just
False?" *Addiction*. 106(2): 249–251.

Van Gundy, Karen, and Cesar Rebellon. 2010. "A Life-Course
Perspective on the 'Gateway Hypothesis.'" *Journal of Health
and Social Behavior*. 51(3): 244–259.

> The researchers investigate the common belief among
> drug researchers and policymakers that marijuana is a
> "gateway" drug, that is, one that leads to increased risk
> for other forms of substance abuse later in life. They con-
> clude that, in the most general terms, the hypothesis may
> be correct, but confounding factors make the relation-
> ship much more complex. For example, they discover
> a low correlation between early marijuana use and later
> substance abuse among those who are employed early in
> life. They also find that the conversion from marijuana to
> other drugs is often quite short-lived, and that users often
> discontinue substance abuse quite early in life.

Wanlund, William. 2015. "Will Growth Continue Despite the
Challenges?" *CQ Researchers*. 25(37): whole.

> This issue of the journal explores expected trends in the
> marijuana business in light of recent legalization of the
> drug in four states and the District of Columbia.

Whiting, Penny F., et al. 2015. "Cannabinoids for Medical
Use: A Systematic Review and Meta-Analysis." *JAMA*. 313(24):
2456–2473. Also available online at http://jama.jamanetwork
.com/article.aspx?articleid=2338251.

> Researchers examined 79 studies attempting to determine
> the efficacy and safety of using marijuana to treat a vari-
> ety of medical conditions. They concluded that there was
> "moderate-quality evidence to support the use of canna-
> binoids for the treatment of chronic pain and spasticity.

There was low-quality evidence suggesting that cannabinoids were associated with improvements in nausea and vomiting due to chemotherapy, weight gain in HIV infection, sleep disorders, and Tourette syndrome." They also found that cannabinoids "were associated with an increased risk of short-term AEs" (adverse events).

Wilkinson, Samuel T., et al. 2015. "Marijuana Legalization: Impact on Physicians and Public Health." *Annual Review of Medicine*. 67: 453–466.

The authors review some of the issues that arise for physicians as more states begin to adopt legalization of marijuana. They point out that sound evidence for the drug's therapeutic effects is still fairly limited, and that further research on those effects is needed.

Zhang, Li Rita, et al. 2015. "Cannabis Smoking and Lung Cancer Risk: Pooled Analysis in the International Lung Cancer Consortium." *International Journal of Cancer*. 136(4): 894–903.

Reporting on a meta-analysis of 2,159 lung cancer cases and 2,985 controls, researchers found "little evidence for an increased risk of lung cancer among habitual or long-term cannabis smokers."

Reports

Caulkins, Jonathan P., et al. 2015. "Considering Marijuana Legalization: Insights for Vermont and Other Jurisdictions." Santa Monica, CA: RAND Corporation. Available online at file:///C:/Users/David/Downloads/RAND_RR864.pdf. Accessed on May 30, 2016.

This report was prepared for the Secretary of Administration for the state of Vermont in anticipation of the state's possible legalization of marijuana for recreational use. RAND researchers recommend the report for use by other states as well. It covers a range of topics, such as consequences of marijuana use; taxation and other sources of revenue; regulation; and possible effects on consumption rates, tax income, and public budgets.

"Conflicts between State and Federal Marijuana Laws." 2013. Hearing before the Committee on the Judiciary, United States Senate. One Hundred Thirteenth Congress, First Session. September 10, 2013. Available online at https://www.gpo .gov/fdsys/pkg/CHRG-113shrg93426/html/CHRG-113shrg 93426.htm. Accessed on May 26, 2016.

> This hearing was held to allow discussion of conflicts that have arisen as a result of certain states' having adopted laws that permit the use of marijuana for recreational purposes, a policy that stands in contrast to federal law with regard to use of the drug.

Dilley, Julia, et al. 2016. "Marijuana Report: Marijuana Use, Attitudes and Health Effects in Oregon." Oregon Health Authority. https://public.health.oregon.gov/PreventionWellness/ marijuana/Documents/oha-8509-marijuana-report.pdf. Accessed on May 31, 2016.

> This report summarizes information collected on the effects of the state's legalization of recreational marijuana in fields such as youth and adult use of the drug, attitudes toward marijuana, and public health and social consequence of legalization of marijuana.

Eddy, Mark. 2010. "Medical Marijuana: Review and Analysis of Federal and State Policies." Congressional Research Service. https://www.fas.org/sgp/crs/misc/RL33211.pdf. Accessed on June 3, 2016.

> This report was issued in response to the growth of legal medical marijuana in the states. The question before the author involved the consequences of the conflict between state laws and federal law about the use of marijuana for medical purposes. The report is especially useful because

of the detailed history of U.S. policies and legislation with regard to the use of marijuana.

Ekins, Gavin, and Joseph Henchman. 2016. "Marijuana Legalization and Taxes: Federal Revenue Impact." Tax Foundation. http://taxfoundation.org/sites/taxfoundation.org/files/docs/ TaxFoundation_SR231.pdf. Accessed on June 3, 2016.

This report attempts to estimate the effects of the legalization of marijuana for recreational and medical purposes on federal tax income.

Franco, Celinda. 2010. "Federal Domestic Illegal Drug Enforcement Efforts: Are They Working?" Washington, DC: Congressional Research Service.

Congress asked the Congressional Research Service (CRS) to assess the effectiveness of the nation's efforts to reduce illegal drug use in the United States. The CRS report points out that efforts to solve this problem have not changed since the mid-1980s, although the nature of the nation's "drug problem" has changed significantly over that period of time. The report concludes that there is not enough good research evidence on which to answer the original question, although overall, the nation's drug problem does not appear to have improved very much in spite of the time, money, personnel, and other efforts expended to reduce substance abuse.

"The Health and Social Effects of Nonmedical Cannabis Use." 2016. World Health Organization. http://www.who.int/sub stance_abuse/publications/msb_cannabis_report.pdf?ua=1. Accessed on June 3, 2016.

This extensive report attempts to summarize all that is currently known about the nonmedical use of cannabis with regard to its use, disorders, and treatments; neurobiological effects; short-term effects of cannabis use; mental health and psychosocial outcomes of long-term use;

long-term use and noncommunicable disease; and prevention and treatment protocols.

Hedden, Sarra L., et al. 2015. "Behavioral Health Trends in the United States: Results from the 2014 National Survey on Drug Use and Health." Rockville, MD: Center for Behavioral Health Statistics and Quality. Available online at http://www .samhsa.gov/data/sites/default/files/NSDUH-FRR1-2014/ NSDUH-FRR1-2014.pdf. Accessed on May 28, 2016.
This report is issued annually and provides complete statistical data on the use of legal and illegal drugs by individuals of all ages, both genders, and all ethnic backgrounds in the United States.

Joy, Janet E., Stanley J. Watson, and John A. Benson. 1999. *Marijuana and Medicine: Assessing the Science Base.* Washington, DC: National Academy Press.
Although now somewhat dated, this report is one of the most important studies ever conducted on the risks and benefits associated with the use of marijuana, especially for medical purposes.

Koppel, Barbara S., et al. 2014. "Systematic Review: Efficacy and Safety of Medical Marijuana in Selected Neurologic Disorders." *Neurology.* 82(17): 1556–1563. Available online at http://www.ncbi.nlm.nih.gov/pmc/articles/PMC4011465/. Accessed on June 2, 2016.
This report reviewed 34 studies conducted from 1948 to November 2013 on the effects of marijuana on a variety of neurological conditions. Researchers listed conditions for which THC and oral cannabis extract (OCE) were each effective. They recommended caution in using the product because of the relatively high rate (about 1%) of serious adverse psychopathological events.

"The Legalization of Marijuana in Colorado—The Impact." 2013/2014/2015. Rocky Mountain High Density Drug

Trafficking Area. http://www.yumacountysheriff.net/wp-con
tent/uploads/2016/03/3-Legalization-of-MJ-in-Colorado-
the-Impact-vol-1.pdf; http://www.yumacountysheriff.net/wp-
content/uploads/2016/03/4-Legalization-of-MJ-in-Colo
rado-the-Impact-vol-2.pdf; http://www.yumacountysheriff.net/
wp-content/uploads/2016/03/5-Legalization-of-MJ-in-Colo
rado-the-Impact-vol-3.pdf. Accessed on May 28, 2016.

The Rocky Mountain High Density Drug Trafficking
Area plans to produce regular reports on the effects of
marijuana legalization in Colorado, the first three of
which are listed here. The reports summarize information about topics such as impaired driving, youth marijuana use, adult marijuana use, emergency department
and hospital-related admissions, treatment, and diversion of Colorado marijuana.

"Lessons after Two Years of Marijuana Legislation: A Short
Report." 2015. Smart Approaches to Marijuana. https://learn
aboutsam.org/wp-content/uploads/2015/03/FINAL-REPORT-1
.pdf. Accessed on June 3, 2016.

This brief report highlights the major trends that appear
to have developed in the 2+ years since recreational marijuana use was first approved in Colorado and Washington.

"The Marihuana Problem in the City of New York." 1944.
Mayor's Committee on Marihuana. New York Academy of
Medicine. http://hempshare.org/pdfs/laguardia.pdf. Accessed
on June 3, 2006.

This report is the first formal study in the United States
on the effects of smoking marijuana. It was inspired by
reports reaching Mayor Fiorello LaGuardia of New York
City "of the smoking of marihuana by large segments of
our population and even by school children." Among
more than a dozen conclusions reached by the investigat-
ing committee was that "[t]he publicity concerning the
catastrophic effects of marihuana smoking in New York
City is unfounded."

National Commission on Marihuana and Drug Abuse. 1972. *Marihuana: A Signal of Misunderstanding.* Washington, DC: U.S. Government Printing Office.

> This so-called Shafer Report is one of the most famous reports on marijuana in U.S. history, producing results very much in conflict with view of the administration of President Richard M. Nixon who, in any case, decided to ignore the commission's recommendations for the legalization of recreational use of the drug in small amounts.

"National Drug Control Strategy." 2015. The White House. https://www.whitehouse.gov//sites/default/files/ondcp/pol icy-and-research/2015_national_drug_control_strategy_0.pdf. Accessed on May 28, 2016.

> The president of the United States annually sends to Congress a report on the current status of drug use in the United States and federal plans for dealing with that problem in the coming year. Among the 2015 goals were strengthening efforts to prevent drug use, seeking early intervention opportunities in health care, increasing access to treatment and supporting long-term recovery, and disrupting domestic drug trafficking and production.

"National Drug Threat Assessment." 2015. U.S. Department of Justice. National Drug Intelligence Center. Available online at http://www.dea.gov/docs/2015%20NDTA%20 Report.pdf.

> This annual publication is published for the purpose of providing policymakers and counterdrug executives with information about the potential threat from drugs as well as from gangs and violence associated with drug use. The 2015 report, for example, focused on the major drugs of abuse, such as cocaine, heroin, prescription drugs, and marijuana; transnational criminal organizations, and illicit financing of drug operations.

"Report of the Special Senate Committee on Marijuana."
2016. Massachusetts Senate. https://www.scribd.com/doc/
303174588/Report-of-the-Special-Senate-Committee-on-
Marijuana. Accessed on May 30, 2016.

This report was prepared for consideration by the Massachusetts Senate in light of the possibility that the state
would vote in November 2016 on legalizing the use of
small amounts of the drug for recreational purposes.

"The State of the Drugs Problem in Europe." 2012. European Monitoring Centre for Drugs and Drug Abuse. Luxembourg: Publications Office of the European Union. Available
online at http://www.emcdda.europa.eu/attachements.cfm/
att_190854_EN_TDAC12001ENC_.pdf.

This annual report provides a broad and detailed summary of the status of substance abuse within the 27 nations that make up the European Union. The publication
is an essential up-to-date guide of statistical data and analysis on the issue.

"Washington State Marijuana Impact Report." 2016. Northwest High Intensity Drug Trafficking Area. https://drive
.google.com/file/d/0Bxs3xMLjUamANHhRRkluWkRobXM/
view?usp=sharing. Accessed on June 4, 2016.

As part of the legalization of marijuana process approved by voters in 2012, the state is required to issue
regular reports on the impact of marijuana legalization
in Washington State. This report is the most recent available. It covers topics such as adult and youth impacts,
impaired driving, diversion data and patterns, marijuana-
related crimes, and current and future markets for the
drug.

Internet

"The Antique Cannabis Book." 2016. http://antiquecannabis
book.com/. Accessed on May 29, 2016.

This website provides one of the most complete and detailed descriptions of the history of cannabis and its uses in the medical field and everyday life. It is a treasure chest of interesting and valuable information.

Armentano, Paul. 2016. "Emerging Clinical Applications for Cannabis and Cannabinoids," 7th ed. NORML. http://norml .org/pdf_files/NORML_Clinical_Applications_for_Canna bis_and_Cannabinoids.pdf. Accessed on May 29, 2016.
This regularly updated publication reviews the most recent scientific evidence on potential applications of cannabis and cannabinoids in the treatment of medical conditions.

Aydin, Ani. 2015. "Cannabinoid Poisoning." Medscape. http:// emedicine.medscape.com/article/833828-overview. Accessed on May 29, 2016.
This website provides a technical review of the physical, psychological, and other effects of cannabinoids on the human body.

Berman, Douglas A. 2016. "US House Votes to Give Medical Marijuana to Veterans." Marijuana Law, Policy & Reform. http://lawprofessors.typepad.com/marijuana_law/medical-marijuana-commentary-and-debate/. Accessed on June 2, 2016.
This article reports and comments on the House of Representatives vote to prevent the Veterans Administration from using any funds to prevent its medical personnel from prescribing medical marijuana for veterans who would appear to benefit from use of the drug. The same blog carries a story reporting that Representative Dana Rohrabacher (R-CA) became the first member of Congress to report that he was currently using marijuana to treat his medical problems.

Bertoli, Andrea. 2016. "It's Time to Rethink Hemp Production in the US." Green Living Ideas. http://greenlivingideas .com/2016/04/21/hemp-production-in-the-us/. Accessed on May 31, 2016.

The author provides four reasons that the United States should once more begin growing industrial hemp.

Birkner, Christine. 2015. "How Marijuana Marketers Are Busting Stoner Stereotypes." American Marketing Association. https://www.ama.org/publications/MarketingNews/Pages/high-times.aspx. Accessed on May 31, 2016.
This article looks in depth at the business issues involved in the legalization of recreational marijuana. The title of the article suggests the basic problem of overcoming the long moral opprobrium associated with the drug's use.

Blanchard, Sean, and Matthew J. Atha. 2016. "Indian Hemp and the Dope Fiends of Old England." UKCIA.org. http://www.ukcia.org/culture/history/colonial.php. Accessed on May 29, 2016.
The authors provide an interesting sociopolitical history of cannabis in the British Empire between 1840 and 1928.

Buddy T. 2016. "The Health Effects of Marijuana." VeryWell. https://www.verywell.com/the-health-effects-of-marijuana-67788. Accessed on May 29, 2012.
The effects of marijuana on the brain, heart, and lungs are discussed along with other health issues related to the use of marijuana.

"Canna Law Blog." 2016. Canna Law Group. http://www.cannalawblog.com/. Accessed on May 31, 2016.
This website is maintained by a group of 10 attorneys that focuses on practical issues related to the growing of cannabis. It is an excellent source of the most recent information regarding the legalization of medical and recreational marijuana.

"Cannabis." 2016. The Vaults of Erowid. http://www.erowid.org/plants/cannabis/cannabis.shtml. Accessed on May 29, 2016.

The Vaults of Erowid are one of the most extensive and useful sources of information on all aspects of substance use and abuse issues. This website has a very large collection of essays on all aspects of cannabis, including botanical information, history of use, drug tests, medical marijuana, and hashish.

"Cannabis and Cannabinoids (PDQ®)." 2016. National Cancer Institute. http://www.cancer.gov/about-cancer/treatment/cam/patient/cannabis-pdq#section/all. Accessed on May 29, 2016.
The primary focus of this website is the medical applications of cannabis and cannabinoids. It provides information on current clinical trials, general questions and answers about the use of cannabis and cannabinoids for treating cancer, and general information on the topic.

"Cannabis and Mental Health." 2016. Royal College of Psychiatrists. http://www.rcpsych.ac.uk/mentalhealthinfo/problems/alcoholanddrugs/cannabis.aspx. Accessed on May 29, 2016.
This website contains a great deal of information on possible mental effects of using cannabis, along with a discussion of its current legal status in the United Kingdom. In general, the discussion is based on the assumption that the use of cannabis for recreational purposes is dangerous and generally a bad idea.

"Cannabis Drug Profile." 2015. European Monitoring Centre for Drugs and Drug Addiction. http://www.emcdda.europa.eu/publications/drug-profiles/cannabis. Accessed on May 29, 2016.
This website provides extensive detailed information about cannabis, including topics such as its chemistry, physical form, pharmacology, origin, mode of use, other names, analysis, typical purities, control status, prevalence, street price, and medical use.

"Cannabis sativa L." 2016. Natural Resources Conservation Service. http://plants.usda.gov/core/profile?symbol=casa3. Accessed on June 2, 2016.

This website provides extensive technical information about the cannabis plant, along with many useful links to other resources on the species.

Chemerinsky, Erwin. 2016. "Why Legalizing Marijuana Will Be Much Harder Than You Think." *The Washington Post.* https://www.washingtonpost.com/news/in-theory/wp/2016/04/27/why-legalizing-marijuana-is-much-harder-than-you-think/. Accessed on June 1, 2016.

This article reviews the legal problems involved in making marijuana legal nationwide.

Davison, Janet. 2016. "Marijuana Derivative 'Shatter' Poses Risks, Policy Challenges." CBC News. http://www.cbc.ca/news/canada/marijauna-shatter-1.3383095. Accessed on June 2, 2016.

This article describes a new derivative of marijuana, known as *shatter*, which may contain up to 80% cannabinoid content, with the attendant potent effect on users. The occurrence of the new derivative raises new issues for the monitoring of marijuana use in the country.

DiNicholas, Michelle. 2016. "How to Find the Best Marijuana Recovery Center." Recovery.org. http://www.recovery.org/topics/marijuana-recovery/. Accessed on June 2, 2016.

This website provides a good general overview of marijuana abuse treatment programs, including the types of programs that are available, the strengths and weakness of each kind of program, the cost of programs, their efficacies, and how to find various types of programs.

"Drug Facts: Synthetic Cannabinoids." 2015. National Institute on Drug Abuse. https://www.drugabuse.gov/publications/drugfacts/synthetic-cannabinoids. Accessed on May 30, 2016.

This website provides general information on a class of synthetic psychoactive substances with properties similar to those of natural cannabis.

Ehrensing, Daryl T. 1998. "Feasibility of Industrial Hemp Production in the United States Pacific Northwest." Oregon State University Extension Service. https://catalog.extension .oregonstate.edu/sites/catalog.extension.oregonstate.edu/files/ project/pdf/sb681.pdf. Accessed on May 29, 2016.
This brochure provides one of the best available descriptions on the Internet of the general botany, history, and potential applications of hemp in the United States.

"The Endocannabinoid System." 2016. Fundación CANNA. http://www.fundacion-canna.es/en/endocannabinoid-system. Accessed on June 5, 2016.
This website provides a good general introduction to the endocannabinoid system and its functions in the human body.

Featherstone, Steve. 2015. "Spike Nation." *The New York Times*. http://www.nytimes.com/2015/07/12/magazine/spike-nation .html?_r=0. Accessed on June 5, 2015.
This article discusses in detail the epidemic of synthetic marijuana (called "spike" in the city involved, Syracuse, New York) abuse in the city, with the attendant public health issues that have developed as a results of the epidemic.

Genen, Lawrence. 2014. "Cannabis-Related Disorders." Medscape. http://emedicine.medscape.com/article/286661-overview# showall. Accessed on May 29, 2016.
This website provides detailed information on the medical and psychiatric aspects of marijuana use with sections on pathophysiology, epidemiology, clinical presentation, physical signs and symptoms, causes, differential diagnosis, workup, treatment and management, consultation, medications, outpatient care, deterrence and prevention, complications, prognosis, and patient education.

[Gibson, Arthur C.] 2016. "The Weed of Controversy." http://
www.botgard.ucla.edu/html/botanytextbooks/economicbot
any/Cannabis/index.html. Accessed on May 29, 2016.

>   This essay is part of a series on economic botany produced
>   by Gibson, who taught a course on plants and civilization
>   at University of California-Los Angeles (UCLA) for many
>   years. It provides an excellent general introduction to the
>   history of cannabis in human civilization.

Griffing, George T. 2015. "Endocannabinoids." Medscape.
http://emedicine.medscape.com/article/1361971-overview.
Accessed on June 5, 2016.

>   This article provides a thorough review of endocannabi-
>   noids that includes a history of their discovery and re-
>   search, their chemistry and pharmacology, and their roles
>   in living organisms. The article includes an excellent list
>   of references.

Grinspoon, Lester. 205. "History of Cannabis as a Medicine."
http://www.maps.org/mmj/grinspoon_history_cannabis_
medicine.pdf. Accessed on May 29, 2016.

>   This statement was prepared for a legal case in which a
>   patient was suing the Drug Enforcement Administra-
>   tion (DEA) for not allowing him to use marijuana for the
>   treatment of a medical condition. It describes in detail the
>   long history of the use of marijuana for the treatment of
>   medical conditions.

Guither, Peter. 2016. "Why Is Marijuana Illegal?" DrugWarRant
.org. http://www.drugwarrant.com/articles/why-is-marijuana-
illegal/. Accessed on May 29, 2016.

>   The author provides a very interesting history of the
>   process by which the U.S. government (and other gov-
>   ernments) pushed for the criminalization of marijuana
>   during the early part of the 20th century.

"Hash Marijuana, & Hemp Museum." 2016. http://hashmu seum.com/en. Accessed on June 2, 2016.

This museum has two physical sites, one in Amsterdam and one in Barcelona. Both are good sources of the history and culture of these substances with special exhibits also available online on the history of marijuana smoking, the process of making hash, the history of hemp, medical marijuana, and opposition to the use of hemp and marijuana. Related topics, such as the place of cannabis in the arts, are also available.

Horvath, A. Tom, et al. 2016. "The Diagnostic Criteria For Substance Use Disorders (Addiction)." AMHC. http://www .amhc.org/1408-addictions/article/48502-the-diagnostic-criteria-for-substance-use-disorders-addiction. Accessed on May 31, 2016.

This article describes the condition known as marijuana (cannabis) use disorder (MUD/CUD) and the symptoms by which it can be recognized, as taken from the fifth edition of the *Diagnostic and Statistical Manual of Mental Disorders* (DSM-5) of the American Psychiatric Association.

"How Cannabis Was Criminalized." 2016. Independent Drug Monitoring Unit. http://www.idmu.co.uk/historical.htm. Accessed on May 29, 2016.

This website tells the story of the criminalization of marijuana in the United Kingdom in the middle years of the 20th century.

Jaeger, Kyle. 2016. "The Secret Enemy of the Marijuana Legalization Movement." http://www.attn.com/stories/8478/ marijuana-reform-and-the-drug-testing-industry. Accessed on June 1, 2016.

The author notes that the drug testing business is a large industry in the United States with a significant stake in keeping marijuana illegal to use. He discusses the impact of this fact on legalization efforts in the states.

Livingston, Ben. 2013. "Don't Call Him 'Pot Czar.'" *The Stranger.* http://www.thestranger.com/seattle/don't-call-him-the-pot-czar/Content?oid=16460452. Accessed on May 28, 2016.
In this interview, the new advisor on marijuana to the Washington State Liquor Control Board warned of the worst possible consequences of legalizing the drug, which would include "more 'heavy drinking,' 'a massive increase in use by minors,' or 'carnage on our highways.'"

"Marijuana." 2016. MedlinePlus. http://www.nlm.nih.gov/medlineplus/marijuana.html. Accessed on May 29, 2016.
This website, maintained by the U.S. National Library of Medicine, is a reliable source of information about every aspect of marijuana, including basic information, research, directories, organizations, and resources.

"Marijuana." 2016. National Institute on Drug Abuse. https://www.drugabuse.gov/drugs-abuse/marijuana. Accessed on May 29, 2016.
The National Institute on Drug Abuse is one of the most reliable sources of information on drug addiction and abuse available in the United States. This web page provides a general introduction to the topic of marijuana and to publications on the subject available from the institute.

"Marijuana Cannabis Research." 2016. Medical Marijuana Inc. http://medicalmarijuanainc.com/category/cannabis-research/. Accessed on June 4, 2016.
This website reviews recent and current research on all aspects of marijuana, related synthetic products, and derivatives. Some applications discussed include research on sleep disorders, tumors, hepatic encephalopahty, Ehlers-Danlos syndrome, schizophrenia, retinal damage, and neurological and liver disorders.

"The Marijuana Report.org." 2016. http://themarijuanareport .org/. Accessed on May 31, 2016.

This website is a project of National Families in Action. It contains daily updates of important national events relating to marijuana, including legalization, federal laws and other actions, treatment and prevention programs, use data and statistics, and court actions.

"Marinol." 2016. AbbVie, Inc. http://www.marinol.com/. Accessed on June 5, 2016.

This is the official website of Marinol (dronabinol), a synthetic form of THC approved by the U.S. government for the treatment of specific and limited medical conditions.

Martijn. 2015. "The Long and Rich History of Cannabis Sativa L." Sensi Seeds. https://sensiseeds.com/en/blog/the-long-and-rich-history-of-cannabis-sativa-l/. Accessed on June 2, 2016.

This website provides an unusually interesting and well-illustrated history of marijuana.

"Medical Marijuana." 2016. DrugWarFacts.org. http://drug warfacts.org/cms/?q=node/54. Accessed on May 29, 2016. 2012.

This is an enormously valuable website because of the extensive list of references it provides for all aspects related to the therapeutic use of marijuana.

Nelson, Robert A. "A History of Hemp." rexresearch.com http:// www.rexresearch.com/hhist/hhist1.htm. Accessed on December 12, 2011.

This website provides an excellent introduction to the history of hemp uses dating from the Neolithic period to the early Renaissance.

Noonan, David. 2016. "A New Era in Medical Marijuana Research?" *Scientific American.* http://www.scientificamerican

.com/article/a-new-era-in-medical-marijuana-research/. Accessed on June 4, 2016.

This article discusses the problems created for marijuana researchers by federal restrictions on the drug (listed as a Schedule 1 drug), and changes that might occur in research if the drug were to be reclassified.

Pannoni, Alexandra. 2014. "3 Ways High Schools Are Combating Marijuana Use." U.S. News High School. http://www .usnews.com/education/blogs/high-school-notes/2014/09/15/ 3-ways-high-schools-are-combating-marijuana-use. Accessed on June 3, 2016.

This article describes three approaches to the prevention of marijuana use by high school students: drug prevention programs, zero tolerance policies, and school-based marijuana treatment programs.

"Preventing Youth Marijuana Use: An Annotated Bibliography." 2014. Substance Abuse and Mental Health Administration. http://www.samhsa.gov/capt/sites/default/files/resources/ bibliography-youth-marijuana-use.pdf. Accessed on June 3, 2016.

This publication brings together some of the most highly regarded research dealing with ways of preventing young people from becoming involved in the use of marijuana.

"Prevention Programs That Address Youth Marijuana Use." 2014. Substance Abuse and Mental Health Services Administration. http://www.samhsa.gov/capt/sites/default/files/resources/ prevention-youth-marijuana-use.pdf. Accessed on June 3, 2016.

This publication brings together summaries of some of the programs that have been found to be most effective in the prevention of young adults' developing an unhealthy dependence on marijuana use.

"Public Health's Approach to Youth Marijuana Prevention."
2016. Oregon Health Authority. https://public.health.oregon
.gov/PreventionWellness/marijuana/Documents/HB3400-Leg
islative-Report-Youth-Prevention-2016.pdf. Accessed on June 5,
2016.

> In connection with legalization of recreational marijuana
> use in Oregon, the state legislature mandated actions by
> a variety of state agencies to monitor impacts of the new
> law on marijuana use in the state. This website reports
> on trends in marijuana use among youth in the state
> and outlines recommendations for programs that can be
> used to reduce the rate of marijuana use among young
> people.

"Recreational Marijuana." 2016. Oregon.gov. https://www
.oregon.gov/olcc/marijuana/Pages/Frequently-Asked-Ques
tions.aspx#top. Accessed on May 30, 2016.

> This website was prepared by the state of Oregon after the
> use of marijuana for recreational purposes was approved
> in 2014. It provides answers to a wide range of questions
> related to marijuana, such as licensing of dispensaries,
> personal use laws, tax regulations, research on the drug,
> and water rights.

"A Review of Potential Pharmacological Treatments for Cannabis Abuse." 2015. American Society of Addiction Medicine.
http://www.asam.org/magazine/read/article/2015/04/13/a-
review-of-potential-pharmacological-treatments-for-cannabis-
abuse. Accessed on June 5, 2016.

> As of early 2017, only psychosocial therapies, such as cog-
> nitive behavioral therapy and family-based therapies, are
> available for use in treating cannabis misuse, dependence,
> and addiction. This article reviews some possible chemi-
> cal treatments for those disorders, such as Marinol, Nabi-
> lone, and gabapentin.

"Risk and Protective Factors Associated with Youth Marijuana Use." 2014. Substance Abuse and Mental Health Services Administration. http://www.samhsa.gov/capt/sites/default/files/resources/risk-protective-factors-marijuana-use.pdf. Accessed on June 3, 2016.

> This publication summarizes an extended list of research studies on factors that may place youth at risk for, or that may help protect youth against, the abuse of, dependence on, and addiction to marijuana.

"The Science of the Endocannabinoid System: How THC Affects the Brain and Body." 2011. Scholastic. http://headsup .scholastic.com/students/endocannabinoid. Accessed on June 5, 2016.

> This presentation explains how the endocannabinoid system works in the human body, and how THC affects the functioning of that system.

"60 Peer-Reviewed Studies on Medical Marijuana." 2016. Pro Con.org. http://medicalmarijuana.procon.org/view.resource .php?resourceID=000884. Accessed on May 29, 2016.

> This excellent resource lists 60 scientific studies on marijuana conducted between 1990 and 2014, providing a description of each study, its journal reference, and whether the report produced results in favor of or opposed to the use of marijuana for medical purposes.

"Smart Approaches to Marijuana." 2016. https://learnabout sam.org/. Accessed on June 3, 2016.

> Smart Approaches to Marijuana (SAM) is a group of professionals from a variety of fields whose mission it is to "to educate citizens on the science of marijuana and to promote health-first, smart policies and attitudes that decrease marijuana use and its consequences." The organization has produced a number of helpful brochures, pamphlets, and other productions that are available at https://www .scribd.com/user/201501730/learnaboutsam.

Stebbins, Sam, Thomas C. Frohlich, and Michael B. Sauter. 2015. "The Next 11 States to Legalize Marijuana." *USA Today.* http://www.usatoday.com/story/money/business/2015/08/18/24-7-wall-st-marijuana/31834875/. Accessed on June 1, 2016.

The authors attempt to predict the next states most likely to legalize marijuana and the reasons that they have been selected to do so.

Sullum, Jacob. 2014. "How Is Marijuana Legalization Going? The Price of Pot Peace Looks Like a Bargain." *Forbes.* http://www.forbes.com/sites/jacobsullum/2014/07/10/how-is-marijuana-legalization-going-so-far-the-price-of-pot-peace-looks-like-a-bargain/#42327659167c. Accessed on June 1, 2016.

The writer reviews public opinion and studies on the effects of marijuana legalization in Colorado and finds that the results are less harmful than critics had predicted before the November 2012 referendum.

"10 Pharmaceutical Drugs Based on Cannabis." 2013. ProCon.org. http://medicalmarijuana.procon.org/view.resource.php?resourceID=000883. Accessed on June 2, 2016.

This web page provides information on 10 drugs that have been approved for one or more specific medical purposes in the United States and other countries.

"24 Legal Medical Marijuana States and DC." 2016. ProCon.org. http://medicalmarijuana.procon.org/view.resource.php?resourceID=000881. Accessed on April 25, 2016.

This website provides basic information on the status of medical marijuana in states where it is now legal, including the enabling legislation or vote, possession limits, and qualified users.

Varlet, Vincent, et al. 2016. "Drug Vaping Applied to Cannabis: Is 'Cannavaping' a Therapeutic Alternative to Marijuana?" *Scientific Reports.* 6: 25599. http://www.nature.com/articles/srep25599. Accessed on June 3, 2016.

The authors ask whether the administration of marijuana components by means of electronic cigarettes is an effective means of ingesting the material for therapeutic purposes. They raise a number of technical problems with such a form of delivery, but indicate that it is not without its possibilities.

Walton, Alice G. 2014. "Why Synthetic Marijuana Is More Toxic to the Brain Than Pot." *Forbes.* http://www.forbes.com/sites/alicegwalton/2014/08/28/6-reasons-synthetic-marijuana-spice-k2-is-so-toxic-to-the-brain/#2547471249eb. Accessed on June 5, 2016.

This article provides a general overview of synthetic marijuana, also known as spice and K2, with explanations of the ways in which the substance affects the brain's endocannabinoid system.

West, David P. 1998. "Hemp and Marijuana: Myths and Realities." North American Industrial Hemp Council. http://www.naihc.org/hemp_information/content/hemp.mj.html. Accessed on May 30, 2016.

This white paper was presented in 1998 on behalf of the North American Industrial Hemp Council to clarify the essential differences between hemp and marijuana and as well as to argue for the importance of hemp as an industrial product in the modern world.

"What Are the Differences between *Cannabis Indica* and *Cannabis Sativa,* and How Do They Vary in Their Potential Medical Utility?" 2012. ProCon.org. http://medicalmarijuana.procon.org/view.answers.php?questionID=000638. Accessed on June 2, 2016.

This website provides a variety of articles that explain the difference between two species of Cannabis.

"What Is Spice/K2? The Facts on Synthetic Marijuana." 2016. Spice Addiction Support. http://spiceaddictionsupport.org/what-is-spice/. Accessed on May 30, 2016.

This website provides extensive information on the form of synthetic marijuana known as spice or K2. It also provides access to a book called *Synthetic Marijuana: The Definitive Guide to the World's Worst Drug*, where it is for sale for $39 per copy.

Introduction

Marijuana and the cannabis plant from which it comes have been known to humans for thousands of years. During that time, the plant has had a variety of uses, for the production of fibers, in the form of hemp; for the manufacture of oil, from the plant's seeds; and as a recreational drug, produced from the dried leaves, seeds, and stems of the plant. The history of these three classes of products is long, complex, and often in dispute. The chronology provided here lists some of the most important of those dates, with points of dispute mentioned where they are appropriate.

ca. 6000 BCE Reports exist of cannabis seeds being used for food.

ca. 4000 BCE Reports are available of hemps being used for the production of textiles in China and Turkmenistan. Some authorities argue that hemp is the first plant material cultivated specifically for use in the production of textiles.

2737 BCE Claims are made that cannabis products are used for medicinal purposes. The Chinese emperor Shen Nung is reputed to have recommended the drug for treatment of beri-beri, gout, constipation, "female weakness," malaria, and

---

The buds on a marijuana plant, like the one shown here, contain the highest concentration of THC in the plant. (AP Photo/Rich Pedroncelli)

other medical conditions. Most evidence suggests that Shen Nung was a mythological character, and that what is reputed to be his most important work, *Shen-nung pen ts'ao ching* (*Divine Husbandman's Materia Medica*), dates instead to the fourth century BCE.

ca. 2000 BCE Egyptian healers reputedly recommend marijuana for the treatment of sore eyes.

ca. 1700 BCE Archaeological evidence suggests that smoked marijuana was used as an aid during childbirth in Judea, with the practice probably being widespread at the time throughout the Middle East.

ca. 1000 BCE The first recorded use of the drink known as bhang tells of the products being made from the leaves and flowers of the female cannabis plant, during Hindu religious ceremonies. The drink is still popular today for its mild intoxicant effects.

ca. 500 BCE The first certain identification of hemp, in any form, is recorded near Stuttgart, Germany. Cultivation and use of the fiber begins to spread throughout Europe shortly thereafter and eventually becomes an essential textile material.

446 BCE The Greek historian Herodotus writes of a Scythian ceremony in which participants throw hemp seed on a hot stone inside a tent and inhale the fumes produced, causing them such joy that "they would howl with pleasure."

ca. 200 BCE This period marks the first reported use of hemp for the production of paper during the Western Han dynasty in China. By this time in history, the plant was also being used widely for the manufacture of canvas sails, the name of which, "canvas," comes from the Latin word *cannabis*, the Greek word *kannabis*, and even earlier terms for "hemp."

70 CE Pedacius Dioscorides, a physician in the army of the Roman emperor Nero, compiles a pharmacopeia that lists marijuana as a useful herb for the treatment of a variety of disorders, including earache.

ca. 100 CE   Chinese scholar and government official Ts'ai Lun manufactures paper out of "rags, fish nets, bark of trees, and hemp well prepared," earning him the title of "the inventor of paper."

Second century CE   The famous Roman physician, Galen, writes about cannabis in his *De Alimentorum Facultatibus* (*On the Properties of Foodstuffs*), pointing out that when toasted and eaten with drinks, the substance is difficult to digest, but, upon absorption by the body, the drug "hits the head, if it is ingested in too much quantity in a short time, and sends hot, in the meantime pharmaceutical fumes to it."

ca. 400   Cannabis is cultivated for the first time in England at Old Buckeham Mare in Norfolk County.

1151   The first paper mill using hemp as a raw material is built by Moorish officials at Xatvia, Spain. Papermaking using hemp spreads throughout Europe with the first mills opening in France in 1189, Italy in 1268, Germany in 1390, Holland in 1428, Switzerland in 1433, and England in 1494.

1533   King Henry VIII decrees that all landowners who farm more than 60 acres of land are required to include at least a quarter of an acre for the growing of hemp.

1545   The Spaniards introduce cannabis growing to the world, establishing a hemp farm in Chile for the production of hemp for use in rope-making. By 1564, King Philip of Spain decrees that hemp is to be grown in Spanish possessions throughout the New World.

1606   French apothecary Louis Hébert plants the first commercial crop of *Cannabis sativa* in Nova Scotia.

1619   The first law in the United States mandating that farmers plant hemp is adopted in Jamestown Colony, Virginia. The law is imposed because of the huge demand for hemp in Great Britain. Similar laws are soon passed in Connecticut (1637) and Massachusetts (1639).

1753   *Cannabis sativa* is first classified by the Swedish taxonomist Linnaeus.

1758   French biologist Jean-Baptiste de Lamarck classifies a second species of cannabis, *Cannabis indica*. Most biologists now considered *C. indica* to be a subspecies of *C. sativa*.

1790s   Both George Washington and Thomas Jefferson promote the growth of hemp because of its many uses.

1839   Irish-born, Calcutta-based physician William Brooke O'Shaughnessy publishes the first scientific article on the medical uses of cannabis, based on his experiences with use of the drug among native Indians.

1860   The Ohio State Medical Society establishes a committee to study the medical effects of *C. indica*. The committee reports on the beneficial effects of the drug, including the cure of neuralgic pain, dysmenorrhea, uterine hemorrhage, hysteria, delirium tremens, mania, palsy, whooping cough, and infantile convulsions.

1870   For the first time, the *United States Pharmacopeia* lists cannabis as a medicine. The book is a collection of standards for chemical and biological drug substances, dosage forms, compounded preparations, excipients (inactive substances added to drugs), medical devices, and dietary supplements.

1895   The India Hemp Commission issues a report on the use of cannabis by native Indians and finds that it has some medical benefits and "no evil results at all."

1895   Historians attribute the first use of the word *marihuana* for the cannabis plant to supporters of Pancho Villa in Sonora, Mexico. Subsequently the word is spelled as *marihuana* or *marijuana*.

1906   The U.S. Congress passes the Pure Food and Drug Act, the first major piece of legislation designed to provide some monitoring of foods and drugs sold in the United States. The minimal requirement established for many drugs, including marijuana, was that products containing such drugs be labeled to indicate the drug's presence.

1911   South Africa bans the use of cannabis, largely because its use by mine workers resulted in a reduction in their productivity.

1911   Massachusetts becomes the first state in the United States to ban the use of cannabis.

1912   The First International Opium Conference is held in The Hague, Netherlands, at which the first international drug control treaty (The International Opium Convention, or "The Hague Convention") is adopted. A ban on cannabis is considered, but not included in the final treaty.

1913   California outlaws marijuana. The law was inspired at least to some extent by anti-Chinese immigrant feelings. It seems largely to have been ignored by the government and ordinary citizens.

1914   The U.S. Congress passes the Harrison Narcotics Tax Act, which regulates and sets taxes on the production and use of opiates. No mention of marijuana is made in the act. (But see **1934**.)

1915   The state of Utah passes an anti-marijuana law, apparently based on the tendency of young Mormon missionaries returning from their time in Mexico to bring back the custom of marijuana smoking with them.

1916   The U.S. Department of Agriculture (USDA) issues Bulletin 404, which calls for greater cultivation of hemp, pointing out that each acre planted to hemp produces as much pulp as would be obtained from more than four acres of trees.

1919   Texas outlaws marijuana.

1923   South African delegates to the United Nations ask that cannabis be added to the list of dangerous drugs included in the Hague Convention. Support for this position comes from Italy, Egypt, and Turkey.

1924   The Second International Opium Conference in Geneva agrees to list cannabis as a narcotic under terms of the Hague Convention.

1928   The UK Dangerous Drugs Acts make the use of marijuana illegal in the United Kingdom.

1931   Secretary of the Treasury Andrew Mellon appoints Harry J. Anslinger first commissioner of the new Federal Bureau of Narcotics. Over the next three decades, Anslinger becomes the foremost proponent for the criminalization of marijuana use.

1933   A report commissioned by the commanding general of the U.S. Panama Canal Department concludes that "[mari-ajuana] is not a 'habit forming' drug in the sense that the derivatives of opium and cocaine are such drugs, as there are no symptoms of deprivation following its withdrawal."

1934   Because marijuana was not mentioned in the Harrison Act of 1914, the National Conference of Commissioners on Uniform State Laws recommends a Uniform State Narcotic Drug Act, which they suggest that all states adopt so that there will be a common policy on marijuana prosecutions throughout the nation. At first, only nine states adopt the act, and it is soon superseded by the 1937 Marihuana Tax Act.

1936   An international conference in Geneva adopts the Convention for the Suppression of the Illicit Traffic in Dangerous Drugs (the "Trafficking Convention"). The United States declines to sign the treaty because it regards its conditions as too weak.

1936   The film *Tell Your Children*, describing the consequences of marijuana use, is released. The film eventually becomes famous under the title *Reefer Madness* and is re-created in a 2005 made-for-television film and a 2011 Broadway musical.

1937   The U.S. Congress passes the Marihuana Tax Act, imposing a tax on anyone who "imports, manufactures, produces, compounds, sells, deals in, dispenses, prescribes, administers, or gives away marihuana." Among other effects, the act essentially ends the growing of hemp in the United States.

1941 Cannabis is delisted from the *United States Pharmacopeia*, ending its designation in the United States as a legitimate medicine. The reason for this change has never been completely explained.

1941 President Franklin D. Roosevelt signs an order allowing production of hemp for industrial uses during World War II. The ban on hemp production is restored at the end of the war in 1945.

1943 The U.S. government produces a film and begins a campaign called "Hemp for Victory," urging farmers to increase their production of hemp for war uses.

1944 The LaGuardia Report, named after the mayor of New York City, concludes, among other findings, that "[t]he practice of smoking marihuana does not lead to addiction in the medical sense of the word . . . [m]arihuana is not the determining factor in the commission of major crimes . . . and [t]he publicity concerning the catastrophic effects of marihuana smoking in New York City is unfounded."

1951 The U.S. Congress passes the Boggs Amendment to the Harrison Act of 1914 (dealing with cocaine and opiates), providing for severe mandatory sentencing for the possession, sale, or use of narcotic drugs, including marijuana.

1956 The Narcotics Control Act increases mandatory fines and sentences beyond those set by the Boggs Amendment of 1951.

1957 The tax consequences of growing hemp become so onerous that the last hemp farm in the United States, located in Wisconsin, ceases cultivation of the product.

1968 A U.K. report on marijuana use chaired by the Baroness Wootton concludes that marijuana use does no more harm than tobacco or alcohol use and recommends that all penalties for possession and use of small amounts of the drug be repealed.

1969 In Mill Valley, California, the first organization in the United States to decriminalize marijuana is formed. The organization, originally called Le Mar (for "Legalize Marijuana"), later merges with another group with similar objectives, Amorphia, which, in turn, morphs into the California chapter of NORML.

1970 The U.S. Congress passes the Controlled Substances Act. The act is an effort to revise and update the complicated series of laws that deal with illegal drugs. One of its main provisions is the creation of drug "schedules" that specify the potential for abuse and medical value of various drugs. Marijuana is listed as a Schedule I drug, the highest and most dangerous category.

1970 Public interest attorney R. Keith Stroup founds the National Organization for the Reform of Marijuana Laws (NORML) in Washington, D.C.

1971 The English government ignores the recommendations of the Wootton Committee (see **1968**) and classifies marijuana as a Class B drug, banning its use for all medical purposes.

1972 The National Commission on Marijuana and Drug Abuse (the Shafer Commission), created by Public Law 91-513 to study marijuana abuse in the United States, issues its final report, entitled "Marijuana, A Signal of Misunderstanding." The commission recommends the decriminalization of marijuana.

1972 Amorphia sponsors state Proposition 19 in California, calling for the decriminalization of small amounts of marijuana for personal use. The proposition fails with a vote of 35.5 percent "yes" to 66.5 percent "no."

1972 Oregon becomes the first state in the United States to decriminalize the use of marijuana. Decriminalization differs from legalization in that it maintains the illegal status of the drug, but removes most of the penalties for using small amounts of the drug for recreational purposes.

1973 President Richard Nixon issues Reorganization Plan No. 2 of 1973, transferring most responsibility for the enforcement of federal drug laws from the Department of the Treasury to a new entity, the Drug Enforcement Administration (DEA) in the Department of Justice.

1974 Amorphia becomes the California chapter of NORML.

1976 President Gerald Ford bans all federal funding for research on the medical benefits of marijuana. The ban remains in effect today.

1976 The U.S. government establishes the Compassionate Investigational New Drug program that allows a select group of patients to use marijuana for medical purposes. President George W. Bush terminates the program in 1992 and, as of 2016, four patients remained in the program, which is administered by the University of Mississippi.

1976 The Dutch government adopts a "policy of expediency" with regard to the use of marijuana, which, while not legalizing the drug, instructs police and prosecutors to ignore retail sale to adults as long as the circumstances of the sale do not constitute a public nuisance.

1977 In a message to the U.S. Congress on August 2, 1977, President Jimmy Carter endorses the findings of the Shafer Commission and famously says that "penalties against possession of a drug should not be more damaging to an individual than the use of the drug itself."

1982 Newt Gingrich, later speaker of the House of Representatives, writes to the *Journal of the American Medical Association* (*JAMA*) to say that "patients have a right to obtain marijuana legally, under medical supervision, from a regulated source."

1983 According to marijuana researcher Jack Herer, the administration of President Ronald Reagan encourages all academic researchers to destroy all research on cannabis conducted between 1966 and 1976.

1988   U.S. Drug Enforcement Administration (DEA) law judge Francis Young finds that marijuana "in strict medical terms is far safer than many foods we consume" and, therefore, the drug should be transferred from Schedule I to Schedule II.

1991   The U.S. Court of Appeals for the District of Columbia upholds Judge Young's decision on marijuana, but DEA administrator Robert C. Bonner exercises his right to reject the recommended decision "with a vengeance."

1996   Voters in Arizona and California approve initiatives allowing the use of marijuana for the treatment of medical conditions. Officials of the Clinton administration announce that the actions in Arizona and California are in conflict with federal law, and any person acting under the provisions of either act will be subject to federal prosecution.

1997   The Arizona legislature passes legislation prohibiting any physician from acting under the recently passed medical marijuana bill until the use of marijuana had been approved by federal legislation, essentially invalidating voters' actions in the 1996 election.

1997   An editorial in the prestigious *New England Journal of Medicine* calls the prohibition on the use of marijuana for treating certain medical conditions "misguided, heavy-handed, and inhumane."

1998   Voters in Alaska, Oregon, and Washington approve ballot measures removing state penalties for the use of marijuana for medical purposes.

1999   The U.S. Institute of Medicine issues its report called *Marijuana and Medicine: Assessing the Science Base* on the medical uses of marijuana.

2001   Portugal decriminalizes the use of marijuana for personal use.

2001   Canada becomes the world's first country to regulate the use of marijuana, as legislation that allows people with serious illnesses to possess marijuana comes into force.

2004   The citizens of Montana vote about two-to-one to allow the use of marijuana for medical purposes. In 2011, both houses of the state legislature vote to repeal that vote, essentially eliminating the use of medical marijuana in the state.

2005   In the case of *Gonzales v. Raich*, the U.S. Supreme Court rules that the U.S. Congress may criminalize the production and use of home-grown marijuana, even in states where the use of the drug for medical purposes is legal.

2006   The U.S. Food and Drug Administration (FDA) issues a policy statement saying that there are "no sound scientific studies" that marijuana has any medical benefits and that, in fact, the drug has "high potential for abuse."

2009   Mexico decriminalizes the use of marijuana for personal use.

2010   The Czech cabinet approves decriminalization of drug possession for personal use.

2011   Representative Barney Frank (D-MA) introduces legislation (H.R. 2306) that would remove marijuana from the list of controlled substances (i.e., decriminalize marijuana in the United States).

2011   Representative Frank also introduces legislation (H.R. 1983) requiring the Secretary of Health and Human Services to recommend a relisting of marijuana under some category other than Schedule I or II and declares that federal regulations shall not be construed to conflict with the decisions of individual states to permit the medical use of marijuana.

2011   In response to a petition filed in 2002 requesting that marijuana be rescheduled as a drug of less than Schedule I, Michele M. Leonhart, administrator of the Drug Enforcement Administration, denies the request, indicating that marijuana has "a high potential for abuse. . . . no currently accepted medical use in treatment in the United States. . . . [and] lacks accepted safety for use under medical supervision," all of which are criteria for listing a drug under Schedule I of the Controlled Substances Act of 1970.

2012   Voters approve the Massachusetts Medical Marijuana Initiative by a vote of 63 percent to 37 percent, making it the 19th state to approve the use of marijuana for medical purposes. Connecticut approves the use of medical marijuana during the same election cycle.

2012   Voters in the state of Colorado approve Amendment 64, which permits the personal use of marijuana in the state. "Personal use" includes the cultivation of three immature and three mature cannabis plants and possession of one ounce of marijuana by individuals over the age of 21. Voters in Washington adopt a similar law that permits possession, but not growing, of marijuana.

2013   Illinois and New Hampshire approve the use of marijuana for medical purposes.

2013   The legislature of Uruguay approves the creation of a state-regulated marijuana industry, allowing citizens to grown, sell and buy, and consume cannabis products. It is the first country in the world to create such a comprehensive legal approach to the use of marijuana.

2014   The states of Nebraska and Oklahoma bring suit against the state of Colorado in the U.S. Supreme Court, arguing that the state's marijuana laws conflict with federal laws on the growing and consumption of marijuana. (Also see **2016**.)

2014   Maryland, Minnesota, and New York approve the use of medical marijuana. The use of recreational marijuana is approved in both Alaska and Oregon, with both laws taking effect over time at later dates (2015 and 2016).

2016   The state legislature of Pennsylvania approves the use of marijuana for medical purposes, bringing to 24 the number of states (and the District of Columbia) that have taken such actions by one action or another.

2016   The U.S. Supreme Court declines to hear the suit brought by the states of Nebraska and Oklahoma with regard to the legality of Colorado's marijuana laws. (See **2014.**)

2016   A review of the impact of new marijuana laws published in the *Journal of Addiction Medicine* finds an increase in the number of adults using marijuana over the past decade, no change in the number of adolescents using the substance, a decrease in marijuana-related arrests, and an increase in the number of treatment admissions for the drug.

2016   Voters in California, Maine, Massachusetts, and Nevada approve the legalization of marijuana for recreational use; Arizona voters defeat a similar proposal. Medical marijuana is approved for the first time in Arkansas, Florida, and North Dakota, while Montana voters expand the circumstances under which the drug can be used for medical purposes.

Introduction

Discussions of marijuana may involve terminology that is unfamiliar to the average person. In some cases, the terms used are scientific, technical, or medical expressions used most commonly by professionals in the field. In other cases, the terms may be part of the "street slang" that users themselves employ in talking about the drugs they consume, the paraphernalia associated with drugs, or the experiences that accompany marijuana use. This glossary lists and defines a few of the terms needed to understand explanations provided in this book.

accepted medical use   A term used in the Controlled Substances Act of 1970 not defined in the act, but later defined by the Drug Enforcement Agency to mean any drug (1) whose chemistry is known and is reproducible; (2) that has had adequate safety studies; (3) for which there are adequate and well-controlled studies proving efficacy; (4) that has been accepted by qualified experts; and (5) for which scientific evidence is widely available.

access point   A designated and approved physical location at which individuals can purchase marijuana for medical use. Also called a dispensary.

antiemtic   A substance with a tendency to reduce or inhibit vomiting.

blind trial   A research study in which a patient does not know whether he or she is receiving the experimental treatment or a placebo. Also see **double blind trial**.

cachexia   General physical wasting, usually associated with a chronic disease.

cannabinoid   Any one of a group of compounds that include cannabinol and the active constituents of cannabis.

cannabinol   A psychoactive substance found in plants in the genus *Cannabis*. Its systematic name is 6,6,9-trimethyl-3-pentyl-benzo[c]chromen-1-ol, and its chemical formula is $C_{21}H_{26}O_2$.

clinical trial   A research study conducted to determine the effect of some new experimental treatment, such as a new drug or a new vaccine.

concentrate   A physical form of a substance, such as marijuana, that contains an unusually high concentration of some desired component, such as a marijuana preparation with a high concentration of THC.

controlled substance   Any substance listed under Schedules I through V of the Controlled Substances Act of 1970, or a precursor of one of those substances.

decriminalization   Removal or reduction of penalties associated with some previously illegal act, such as reductions in penalties for possession or use of marijuana.

dispensary.   *See* **access point.**

double blind trial   A research study in which neither patients nor researchers know whether subjects of the study are receiving the experimental treatment or a placebo.

dronabinol   A synthetic cannabinoid used for anorexia with patients suffering from HIV/AIDS as well as nausea and vomiting associated with chemotherapy. Trade name: Marinol.

drug diversion   Providing a drug to an individual who is not authorized to use it.

efficacy   The degree to which a substance produces some effect expected of it.

endocannabinoid   A cannabinoid that occurs naturally in the brain.

gateway theory   The hypothesis that the use of one drug increases one's tendency to experiment with other drugs.

hashish   A product made from compressed trichomes (resin glands) of the cannabis plant, usually made available in the form of a sticky, often thick, paste that can be burned, smoked, or cooked in foods, with considerably more potent psychoactive effects than marijuana.

hemp   A tough, coarse fiber made from the cannabis plant; used to make textiles, canvas, paper, rope, and other items.

hydroponics   The process of growing plants in water solutions, without access to soil. Marijuana plants grown in hydroponic settings are said to have uniquely desirable qualities over those grown in soil.

incidence   The number of new cases of a disease or other events occurring within some given period of time, such as the number of first-time users of marijuana in the last year. (*Also see* **prevalence**.)

Investigational New Drug (IND) Program   A program sponsored by the U.S. Food and Drug Administration that allows researchers to test new drugs prior to approval.

marijuana   A greenish, brown, or gray mixture of the shredded leaves, flowers, and stems of the cannabis plant, smoked as a cigarette or in a special kind of pipe.

medical necessity   A legal doctrine that one may be permitted to carry out an act that is otherwise illegal if, in so doing, a greater harm is prevented.

narcotic   A drug that in moderate doses relieves pain and dulls the senses, but in greater doses may cause stupor, coma, convulsions, and/or death.

nostrum   A type of medication whose composition is secret and for which scientific evidence of its efficacy does not exist.

peer-reviewed study   A research study whose methodology and results have been examined by other experts in the same field to decide if the study is worthy of being published.

potency   The strength of a drug; in the case of marijuana, an indirect measure of the amount of Δ^9-tetrahydrocannabinol (THC) in a sample of the drug.

prevalence   The number of cases of a disease or other conditions currently in existence. (*Also see* **incidence**.)

psychoactive   Capable of producing mind-altering affects, such as changes in mood or perception.

psychotropic   *See* **psychoactive**.

purity   The amount of a desired component, such as pure cannabis, present in a mixture that also contains impurities.

sinsemilla   From the Spanish *sin* ("without") *semilla* ("seed"); a form of marijuana that has a very high percentage of THC and is, hence, much more potent than marijuana. It usually consists primarily of buds of the plant.

slippery slope   The argument that once an individual or society has taken the first step in some undesirable action (such as permitting the use of marijuana), it then becomes much more likely that worse eventualities will follow (such as permitting the use of other, more dangerous drugs).

Spice   The common name used for synthetic cannabis (q.v.); also known as Fire 'n' Ice, Genie, K2, PEP Spice, Solar Flare, Spice Diamond, Spice Gold, and Yucatan Fire.

strain   A type of organism that differs in relatively trivial ways from other organisms related to it (as to other members of the same species).

street slang   Some of the terms in the everyday vernacular used to describe marijuana, including Afghan, bhang, Buddha grass, dope, draw, gage, ganja, gangster, grass, herb, Jane, jive, joint, kiff, loco weed, Mary, Mary Jane, MJ, Mexican green, Panama red, pot, puff, reefer, roach, smoke, spliff, tea, Texas tea.

synthetic cannabis   A combination of natural herbs and synthetic chemicals that, when ingested, produce psychoactive effects similar to those of natural cannabis.

tetrahydrocannabinol   *See* **THC**.

THC   An abbreviation for tetrahydrocannabinol, the chemical compound responsible for the psychoactive effects produced by the ingestion of cannabis. The compound is commonly known as delta-9-tetrahydrocannabinol (Δ^9-tetrahydrocannabinol).

trichome   A fine hairy-like projection from the epidermal cells of a plant which, in the cannabis plant, contain the chemical substance, THC, responsible for the psychoactive effects of the drug.

AbbVie, Inc., 9
ABC News, 204
achene, 5
acquired immune deficiency
    syndrome (AIDS), 9,
    79, 106, 108, 149, 152,
    167
Act for the Advancement of
    Manufactures, 32
ADAMHA. *See* Alcohol,
    Drug Abuse, and
    Mental Health
    Administration
    (ADAMHA)
Addiction Research Center,
    216
Affordable Care Act, 220
Africa, 21–23
African Americans, 64
AIDS. *See* acquired immune
    deficiency syndrome
    (AIDS)
Alaska, 113, 142
Alaskan Natives, 221
alcohol, 103

Alcohol, Drug Abuse,
    and Mental Health
    Administration
    (ADAMHA), 216
Allegheny Undergraduate
    Council, 226
ALL-ONE-GOD-FAITH,
    Inc., 200
Ally, 190
Altoona Business College, 63,
    180
Alzheimer's disease, 108,
    154
AM-678, 9
AMA. *See* American Medical
    Association (AMA)
American Agriculture
    Movement, 230
American Alliance for
    Medical Cannabis, 196
American Coptics, 23
American Indians, 23
American Medical
    Association (AMA), 66,
    140–141